WHERE HAVE ALL THE BIRDS GONE?

Where Have All the Birds Gone?

Essays on the Biology and Conservation of Birds That Migrate to the American Tropics

BY JOHN TERBORGH

PRINCETON UNIVERSITY PRESS

Library of Congress Cataloging-in-Publication Data

Terborgh, John, 1936–
Where have all the birds gone? : essays on the biology and conservation of
birds that migrate to the American tropics / John Terborgh
p. cm.
Bibliography: p.
Includes index.
ISBN 0-691-08531-5 (cloth) — ISBN 0-691-02428-6 (pbk.)
1. Birds—Migration. 2. Birds—Tropics. 3. Birds—Ecology.
4. Birds, Protection of. I. Title
QL698.9.T44   1989
598.2'525—dc19   89-3733

This book has been composed in Linotron Times Roman

Clothbound editions of Princeton University Press books are
printed on acid-free paper, and binding materials are chosen for
strength and durability. Paperbacks, although satisfactory for
personal collections, are not usually suitable
for library rebinding

Printed in the United States of America by
Princeton University Press
Princeton, New Jersey

To my long-suffering parents
for their tolerance and understanding

Contents

List of Illustrations

List of Tables

Preface

This book is about the conservation of North American migratory birds, particularly those that migrate to winter homes south of the United States. It is intended for people who appreciate birds and care about them—birdwatchers, amateur naturalists, lovers of the outdoors, as well as my professional colleagues in the biological sciences. Readers attracted to bird books for their color illustrations will be disappointed, because I am much more a scientist than a photographer. Only a few birds are pictured here. Most of the illustrations are of the tropical habitats that serve as wintering grounds of migrants and accompany descriptions in the text. Some parts of the account have a personal flavor, others may seem dry and technical to the nonspecialist. Wherever technical subjects are discussed, as in Chapters 3, 8, 9, and 10, I have tried to present them in language an informed layperson could readily understand.

Migratory birds are under stress as never before, both on their North American breeding grounds and on their tropical and south temperate wintering grounds. My awareness of this harkens back to personal experiences in the 1950s as a young birdwatcher. The intervening years have provided the perspective. Over this period the bird communities of many places I know well in the Middle Atlantic region have changed dramatically, even though in some cases the places themselves have remained unaltered. The changes pertain to the composition of both forest and aquatic bird communities in the parts of the country most familiar to me. My experiences are by no means unique; my colleagues are keenly aware of these changes, but scientists are often reticent about communicating their findings and concerns to the public.

Recent changes in the bird life of the eastern states can be traced to a number of factors, many of them subtle and out of the public view. The nationwide outcry two decades ago over DDT focused attention on problems associated with the increasing use of pesticides. Today the United States uses more such chemicals than ever, and though they do not seem to be poisoning the reproduction of bald eagles and ospreys, their effects are widespread and insidious. Even less obvious in their impact on wildlife are a number of other correlates of our high-technology, high-efficiency age. The transition to mechanical harvesters, especially mechanical corn pickers, has had an explosive impact on the populations of birds that can exploit the wastage—Canada geese and mourning doves, as well as other species that are less desirable in great numbers, such as crows, starlings, grackles, and cowbirds.

With the very best of intentions, Americans annually stock home feeders with more than a billion pounds of birdseed, thereby unwittingly augmenting the populations of avian nest predators (bluejays) and parasites (cowbirds). Garbage from poorly covered waste cans subsidizes large numbers of raccoons, opossums, and feral house cats, which in turn are devastatingly effective in destroying the nests of ground-nesting birds, most of them migrants. Federal agricultural policies that encourage plowing every square inch of a farmer's land result in the eradication of bird-rich hedgerows, wooded stream margins, and prairie potholes, with a consequent loss of shrikes, ducks, and godwits, and increased soil erosion and stream siltation. Increasingly intensive forestry practices, employed in both federal and privately owned timberlands, result in replacing mixed forest with biologically sterile tree monocultures. All these changes are transpiring quietly and unobtrusively in a relatively stable landscape, where the proportions of land occupied by forest, pasture, and cultivation have changed little since World War II.

The relative stability of land-use patterns in the United States contrasts starkly with the current situation in the tropical countries to the south, where more than 250 migratory bird species spend the winter. With their human populations increasing at rates between 2 and 4 percent per year, the pace of change in these countries is truly startling. Some of the changes are parallel to concurrent trends in our own country—conversion from low intensity to high-intensity agriculture, increasing application of chemical agents to the environment, draining of marshes and estuaries, and reforestation with tree monocultures.

In many countries, however, the most pervasive changes are occurring in conjunction with a massive wave of abusive overexploitation of virgin lands, a wave propelled by a gold-rush mentality oblivious to the basic precepts of renewability, sustainability, and future need. The pattern is uncomfortably reminiscent of the excesses that occurred in our own country during the eighteenth, nineteenth and early twentieth centuries, before the federal government began to regulate the use of renewable resources such as fish, game, forests, soils, and water. The spasm of exploitation that is currently under way in the tropics is being pursued with the same total lack of government controls and official concern for posterity as occurred here between 1860 and 1920, when the American bison went from being the most abundant large mammal on the continent to the rarest, and when more than 400 million acres of virgin forest east of the Great Plains were felled in a mere sixty years. There is no excuse for allowing history to repeat such follies, because we in the United States should have learned from our own experience. Yet we are not imparting the wisdom gained from this lesson to our neighbors and aid beneficiaries with nearly enough conviction and urgency to stem the tide of destruction.

My principal message in this book is that if these excesses continue unchecked until they run their course, we shall wake up one day to a drastically altered spring—one lacking many familiar birds that we have heretofore taken for granted. If we are going to do something to prevent this, we shall have to do it soon. The year 2000 will be too late.

THE origin of this book goes back twenty years to my first winter trip to the tropics. Taking advantage of a week's break in my teaching schedule, I traveled to Puerto Rico with a companion for what was unabashedly a holiday. Since neither of us was attracted to the glitzy trappings of resort hotels, we spent most of the time roaming the island in a rented car, visiting some of its many unpublicized beaches, mountains, and forest reserves. Wherever we went, there were birds from home, especially warblers— black and white, black-throated blue, parula, Cape May, ovenbird, waterthrushes, and others. Somehow, seeing these familiar acquaintances in such unfamiliar surroundings was far more exciting to me than encountering the completely novel endemic birds of Puerto Rico, whose names I had learned from a field guide only the week before. Thus did I become hooked on the ecology of migratory birds in the tropics.

Since that first experience in 1967, I have made additional trips on nearly an annual basis, visiting overall more than eighty localities in fifteen countries. I have not found all the 250 North American species that winter principally south of our borders, but nearly all of them. The few I have missed are mostly western breeders that winter in a limited area in western Mexico.

Since 1972 my companions on these ventures have been students and other participants in Princeton University's "Biology 521—Tropical Ecology," as it is designated in the university's graduate catalog. Each year we have set out for a different destination, nearly always one that was as unfamiliar to me as to the undergraduates and graduates that accompanied me. To this day there is only one site we have visited twice—Costa Rica's Monteverde Cloud Forest Reserve. We traveled by plane, boat, car, bus, truck, even bicycle and horseback, and made numerous packing excursions into roadless areas no tourist ever visits. We surveyed migrants in deserts, rain forests, mangroves, and mountaintops. Nearly everywhere we slept out in tents and cooked our meals over campfires at an average cost per person of less than a hundred dollars per week, including everything except international airfare.

We were rained on countless times, even snowed on once in the mountains of Mexico, and on various occasions were temporarily stranded by stormy seas, raging floodwaters, or simply vehicles that refused to start. Through all this, we suffered no mishap worse than the occasional bout of diarrhea and a badly burned foot, the result of a pot of boiling water acci-

dentally tumbling off the fire. My student companions were always stimulating company and willing participants in the hard work of setting up mist
nets in dense tropical vegetation. By now there have been well over one
hundred of them, far too many to name, but not too many to thank for their
very considerable contribution to the thoughts and facts contained herein.

It is my pleasure to acknowledge the stalwart help of a number of colleagues who traveled with me to destinations other than those covered on
official Princeton University courses: Susan Bonn, Jane Brockmann,
David Duffy, John Faaborg, John Fitzpatrick, Mercedes Foster, Charles
Janson, Jeanne Panek, Kenneth Petren, Scott Robinson, Grace Russell,
John Weske, and David Willard. I am especially grateful for the many
years of banding expertise contributed by Hannah Suthers on university
field trips. Jeanne Panek and Kenneth Petren provided valuable assistance
with data analysis, bibliographic searches and computer processing of the
manuscript. I owe special gratitude to David Wilcove for his stimulating
discussions of conservation issues and for the portions of Chapters 2, 3,
and 5 that were drawn from his Ph.D. thesis. I am sorry that circumstances
prevented us from doing this book together as originally planned. Several
colleagues provided helpful comments on early drafts, for which I am most
grateful: Barbara D'Achille, Adrian Forsyth, Mercedes Foster, Scott Robinson, Anne Terborgh. I want to thank Russell Greenberg for perhaps the
most thorough, informed, and penetrating critique I ever received from a
reviewer. It is my hope that Judith May is content with the result of her
unfailing encouragement of this project through several conceptual trans-
formations. Two people who provided inspiration at critical stages of my
life and who, more than anyone else, showed me the path I eventually took
are my uncle John W. Murray, who first introduced me to the fascination
of birds in 1950, and Chandler Robbins, who served as a role model and
gave me unstinting encouragement for many years. Finally, I am pleased
to acknowledge financial support from the Chapman Memorial Fund,
Princeton University, and the National Science Foundation.

Cocha Cashu Biological Station
Manu National Park, Peru
November 6, 1987

WHERE HAVE ALL THE BIRDS GONE?

1 *Then and Now: Thirty-five Years in Suburbia*

Inspired by my uncle John, I became a birdwatcher in 1950 at age fourteen. At the time (and still today) my family lived on two acres of abandoned farmland in northern Virginia. The house fronted on a winding dirt lane that came to a dead end two doors down. Our mailbox was one of a cluster at the top of the hill where our lane met the paved road. From an upstairs window one could look across a sea of treetops to the distant spires of Georgetown University across the Potomac.

A narrow path led down behind the house to a quiet wooded stream and then continued for over a mile until ending on a high bluff overlooking the river. In all that distance, the path crossed but a single road and passed by only a single house.

These woods and the stream that ran through them were my childhood playground. As it happened, none of our few neighbors had any boys my age, so instead of playing football and baseball, as I otherwise might have done, I spent my days in the woods looking for snakes and salamanders or fishing in the river.

After Uncle John focused my attention on birds, I did what most birdwatchers do, I began to keep lists—a life list, a state of Virginia list, a list for the year, and of course a list for our own 2-acre homestead. We lived in the woods, and the birds that inhabited our domain reflected this. There was always a red-shouldered hawk in the estate across the lane, and yellow-billed cuckoos, scarlet tanagers, red-eyed vireos, peewees, hooded warblers, and other birds nested along the creek at the foot of the property. Although my list eventually grew to over 150 species, the house sparrow was not among them, and other denizens of suburbia, such as purple grackles, were mainly seen flying overhead. One of my fondest memories of the period was drifting off to sleep in the lingering twilight of early summer, being serenaded by a chorus of acadian flycatchers and whip-poor-wills.

Birds were not the only songsters to liven the evenings. There were frogs and toads along the stream, a succession of them that marked the passing of the season. Spring peepers and wood frogs heralded the approach of spring after the first warm rain of March. The next mild spell recruited toads and swamp cricket frogs to the cacophony. Shortly afterward the wood frogs fell silent, and the peepers began to sing with less ardor.

By now it was April, a time when the weather in Virginia can do almost anything.

Suddenly one day the temperature would soar into the eighties, and the tune would change. That evening for the first time there would be green frogs and gray tree frogs. The last to add their voices, usually not until May, were the bullfrogs, whose dronings imparted a special flavor to the summer nights.

Far less evident in their presence, but infinitely more exciting to discover, were the snakes. Though they were never easy to find, even though one knew how to look for them, there were many species, some familiar to the average country dweller, such as pilot and racer blacksnakes, garter snakes, green snakes, and water snakes, while others had names that rarely appear in print: mole snake, queen snake, worm snake, DeKay's snake.

Of all the reptiles, the most abundant and conspicuous were the box turtles. There were dozens of them, so many that one was forever having to stop the lawnmower to put one out of the way. They were a special nuisance in the garden, where they directed their attentions to our tomatoes, systematically biting a chunk out of each one as it approached the peak of ripeness. One day my father became so exasperated by these depredations that he ordered a roundup. In less than an hour, three of us gathered half a bushel of them. The unwelcome tomato thieves were then driven ten miles into the country and unceremoniously dumped in the woods. After that, the situation in the garden was better, but only slightly so. There were still plenty of turtles to be found.

A Few Years Later

It would be impossible for a boy growing up in Arlington, Virginia, today to relive these experiences. The population of the county has increased tenfold, from twenty to two hundred thousand. The woods and fields of 1950 have been converted to housing developments, roadways, and shopping plazas. Through this transition, which was essentially complete by 1960, the citizens who served on the county board were not mindless of environmental values. They zoned against high-rise apartments and large business and reserved a generous allotment of woodland to create a park system that needs no apology. But even in these protected lands, the state of nature is not the same as it was in 1950.

I know this very well, because one of the county's largest parks includes the valley behind our property. There is still a path along the stream to the river, but now one passes a number of houses and crosses three roads. Nevertheless, the park is extensive, and the woods it protects have matured over the years. A wall of trees rises behind the orchard where our land adjoins the park. On the other three sides of the property, the changes have been drastic, but not atypical. The erstwhile dirt lane is now a major commuter thoroughfare. The seventeen-acre estate across the road has become a housing development. On either side there are houses and lawns where before there had been woods and brush.

In spite of these changes, the woods along the stream are still there, little modified from their former condition except that the trees are now taller. What about the wildlife? I wish I could report that it too is very much the same, but it is not. To make a tennis court, our neighbors across the stream filled in the little marsh where the frogs bred. Spring evenings since then have been silent except for the rush of passing cars. I haven't heard a frog there in twenty years. The snakes too have vanished, though I am less certain of the reasons why. Strollers in the park are unlikely to tolerate the sight of a basking serpent. There are more cats and dogs and small boys than there used to be. But I suspect that the most important factor is the increased density of roads. Snakes, especially the larger, more conspicuous ones, do not long survive the incursion of roads into their ranges. The same can be said of box turtles. A few still survive, but finding one nowadays is a rare event.

The amphibians and reptiles of our little valley, a community that once numbered more than twenty species, have been decimated. Only the occasional box turtle affords a lingering reminder of former times. Casual observations in other parks in the county indicate that the disappearances are general; the proximity of suburbia, for one reason or another, is inimical to the survival of these humble forms of life.

The loss of lower vertebrates, about which most people care little, may not be regarded as a particular cause for concern, but birds have a following. Have they proven any more adaptable to urban encroachment? Sad to say, they have not. Granted, there are still lots of them. Robins, mockingbirds, catbirds, house wrens, song sparrows, woodpeckers, chickadees, titmice, and the like still abound, and with all these it may be easy for some, especially newcomers to the neighborhood, to assume this is the way it always was. But the birds that breed around our property now are a different lot from those we observed in 1950. My thirty-five year-old memory won't let me forget the thrushes, warblers, vireos, cuckoos, flycatchers, and tanagers that used to liven the woods along the stream. Now there are none of these, nor have there been for a long time.

Why not? What has happened? Draining the little marsh discouraged the green herons and kingfishers that used to visit from time to time, but the disappearance of warblers and tanagers must be attributed to something else. One is tempted to point to the encroachment of suburbia, with its roads, dogs, and small boys, but the causal linkage is obscure because the forest in the park remains very much as before. What has happened to our forest birds is something more subtle, something that does not meet the unaided eye, and that scientists are just beginning to debate in earnest.

All the answers are not yet in, and for that reason one might argue that my concern is premature. My reply is that things are going wrong with our environment, even the parts of it that are nominally protected. If we wait until all the answers are in, we may find ourselves in a much worse predicament than if we take notice of the problem earlier. By waiting, one risks being too late; on the other hand, there can be no such thing as being too early.

In the chapters that follow I shall look at what is happening to "our" birds. The species that are most affected are tropical migrants, ones that pass the winter in countries to the south of our borders. We shall see that they are being affected by conditions here in the United States, and in some instances by conditions abroad. In my efforts to identify the contributory causes, I shall try to distinguish fact from interpretation. Although the interpretations may sometimes be controversial, facts by themselves, in the absence of interpretation, are useless.

I shall begin, then, by considering what factors associated with the increasing fragmentation and urbanization of the eastern forest have contributed to the decline of forest bird populations. The focus will then shift to the tropics, where the wintering habitat of some 250 species of North American birds is being degraded at an alarming rate. Although the situation there is not yet desperate, it soon may be. Regardless of any lingering unanswered questions, there is no time to lose.

2 *The Importance of Controls in Ecology and Why We Don't Have Them*

As a naturalist, it is my idiosyncratic disposition to be preoccupied with the changing state of our environment. Having already been witness to more change than I ever cared to see, I am unabashedly nervous about our trajectory and where it is taking us.

Part of this uneasiness comes from our ignorance of the past. To predict how a trend will extrapolate into the future, one needs accurate information from the past. A single point does not suffice to establish a trend, and confidence in a particular trajectory increases with each additional point used in plotting it. From this perspective, it is clear that those of us who study the environment have been scientifically shortchanged.

Almost every other type of scientist takes controls for granted. A medical researcher, for example, maintains an untreated group of rats as a standard against which to measure the effect of a suspected cancer-causing substance on an experimental group. The use of controls lies at the very heart of the scientific method, and the notion of conducting experiments without them is ludicrous. Students are taught this in their first lesson. Environmental biologists receive the same training, but then find that they are the victims of circumstance. The controls they need to study environmental change have been preempted, often long before they were born. Because we have few records of how the environment was before humans disturbed it, we cannot say how much industrialization has increased the concentrations of certain chemicals in the atmosphere, what the pH of Adirondack lakes was before acid rain, or even which tree species were common in the virgin forests of the eastern lowlands.

Realizing this was perhaps my greatest disillusionment in growing up. It began gnawing at my consciousness at an early age. My mother used to read aloud to my sister and me when we were children. She read dozens of things, among them Evangeline and James Fenimore Cooper. At that impressionable age I was intrigued by the descriptions of America's primeval forests—majestic trees, deep shadows, hushed stillness—descriptions couched in poetic imagery that captivated my imagination. Eager to experience these aesthetic delights for myself, I found it impossible to accept my mother's patient explanation that there were no such forests anymore.

If our forests were as magnificent and inspiring as the books proclaimed, then why were there none left? It didn't make sense. Accepting what she said would have meant acquiescing to something so incongruous as to be unnerving. Would the civilization I belonged to systematically and maliciously destroy every last copy of Shakespeare's plays or of Beethoven's symphonies? That would have been unthinkable! Then why would that same society destroy every one of the giant trees that stood here when the Pilgrims landed? I just couldn't understand why there weren't other people who felt the way I did. This incredulity has lingered in my consciousness ever since, though today it takes the form of a simmering outrage.

While I was young, there wasn't very much I could do to prove my mother was wrong, but as soon as I was licensed to drive, I began to explore. At first, it was merely in the Washington suburbs, and then in ever-widening circles. I bought topographic maps from the U.S. Geological Survey and studied them in minute detail. While I was in college, every vacation was a camping trip in some portion of the East I had not visited before. With my birdwatching and botanical friends, I ranged over the entire tier of Atlantic seaboard states from Maine to Florida. We climbed the White Mountains, the Green Mountains, the Appalachians, and the Smokies. And we canoed the great rivers of the Southeast: the Potomac, Santee, Savannah, Suwannee, and St. John's.

I still haven't stopped exploring, but I no longer entertain hopes of discovering a forgotten wilderness. Basically, my mother was right. To a first approximation, there is no longer any virgin forest east of the Rockies. More than 99 percent of what the colonists found has been felled. The fraction of a percent that remains is scattered in inaccessible spots where logging was not an economic proposition: a basin in the New Hampshire mountains, some patches in the Adirondacks, Appalachians, and Smokies, a few remote swamps in the Deep South (Perry and Perry 1980). These are the only sizable blocks of 1,000 acres or more. There are a number of additional smaller remnants in New Jersey, Pennsylvania, West Virginia, Georgia, and elsewhere, but most of these are less than 100 acres and are located in steep ravines where the topography defeated efforts to extract heavy logs.

In sum, all we have left to represent the natural vegetation of the East are a few mountaintops, swamps, and ravines. What we so conspicuously lack are any surviving examples of what once must have been the dominant types of vegetation in the landscape: the upland forests of the coastal plain and piedmont. A few examples remained into the twenties and thirties, and a number of these were described in the classic book *Deciduous Forests of Eastern North America* by Lucy Braun (1950). Braun was a first-rank professional scientist in an era when women were expected to stay at home. A professor of botany and an intrepid explorer, her prescient efforts offer us the only quantitative record in existence of many forest types in the pre-chestnut-blight era. Her stunning photographs of virgin stands provide irre-placeable windows into the past. But her tireless efforts to forestall the future were to little avail. Nearly all the stands she studied have since fallen to the ax. Had she fully realized how bleak the future was to be, I wonder what it might have done to her zeal.

Lucy Braun was followed some years later by another eminent botanist, John T. Curtis, who devoted his life to studying the vegetation of Wisconsin. The year he died he published *The Vegetation of Wisconsin*, a book that, to this day, remains the most outstanding effort of its kind (Curtis 1959).

Wisconsin remained a wilderness for two hundred years after the Pilgrims arrived on the East Coast. The first settlers did not begin to plow its prairies until the 1830s and 1840s. Only a hundred years later Curtis began his researches on the vegetation of the state. It seems hardly credible, but in this brief period virtually all of the forests in the southern two-thirds of Wisconsin had been clear-cut or severely altered by logging (see Figure 2.1). Curtis was unable to find pristine examples of many common forest

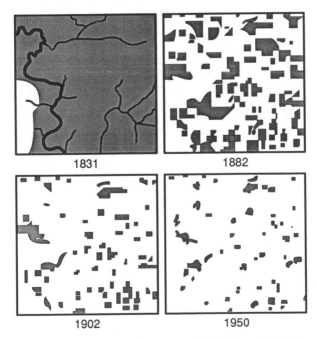

FIG. 2.1 Changes in wooded area of Cadiz Township, Green County, Wisconsin, during the period of European settlement. Within the span of one human lifetime, 70 years, the total area in forest was reduced by more than 90 percent and broken into over 60 fragments having an average area of 0.16 percent that of the original forest (Curtis 1956).

types. Secondary forests were in ample supply, but Curtis was a purist who wanted to have facts about about species compositions, tree dimensions, and basal areas in stands that had not been drastically modified by humans.

In some regions, his only recourse was to examine the yellowed records of the original land surveys still on file in county courthouses. Surveyors of the time followed the practice of using "witness trees" as landmarks to establish the position of property lines. By compiling lists of these witness trees, Curtis made a valiant attempt to reconstruct the original composition of forests in various parts of the state. He realized there were errors in this, since surveyors were likely to be biased in their choice of trees, but the compilations at least gave an indication of the original species composition, and that was better than nothing.

Via this circuitous digression I have tried to explain why environmental biologists find themselves with no satisfactory controls. As a nation, we simply lacked the foresight to preserve samples of the undisturbed environment. Had we done so, ecologists today could speak with authority on how greatly the rest of the environment has been altered. But in the absence of controls, we know we don't have a scientific leg to stand on, and so by and large we remain mute, even though we may be horrified by what we see.

Apart from the lonely efforts of Lucy Braun, the record from the past does nothing to fill the void. This is because the science of quantitative ecology itself did not arise until around the time of World War II, and by then it was too late. Several mammals widespread in the East at the time of settlement—wolf, elk, forest bison, and mountain lion—had been extirpated. The East's most important tree species, the American chestnut, was effectively extinct, and another, the American elm, was not far behind. Introduced weeds from Eurasia had invaded every field and pasture in the land, and the composition of all but a tiny handful of forests had been altered to an unknown degree by human activities. Competition for nest holes with the European starling had virtually eliminated the red-headed woodpecker from east of the Appalachians and had drastically reduced the eastern bluebird. And other species, such as the meadowlark, purple grackle, and cowbird, which would not have been able to make a home in the pristine eastern deciduous forest, were now abundant.

Even though we shall never have a quantitative record of the past, it is still important to take stock of where we are now, so that we can gauge further changes in the future. The key to this lies in having base-line data for as many ecosystems as possible. In spite of the obvious desirability of having such data, gathering them is a task we have hardly begun. Ironically, the leaders in ecological monitoring have not been scientists, but amateur ornithologists.

3 *The Beginnings of Ornithological Monitoring*

People like to count birds because it is a pleasant diversion from the workaday routine that combines aesthetic experience with intellectual challenge. These attractions draw thousands, some surveys say millions, to the pastime of birdwatching. Birdwatching is simply a sport or an excuse for outdoor recreation to some of its adherents, but to many others it is an acquired skill that leads to greater fulfillment when it can be put to the service of a worthy cause, especially one that carries the label of science. The urge to combine public service with recreation has so far this century attracted amateur birdwatchers in large numbers to three nationally coordinated efforts to gather data on bird populations. These are the "Christmas Counts" and "Breeding Bird Censuses," sponsored by the National Audubon Society, and the "Breeding Bird Survey," sponsored by the U.S. Fish and Wildlife Service.

THE CHRISTMAS COUNTS

The first systematic effort to maintain records on bird populations was the Audubon Society's annual Christmas Count. Launched in New York City's Central Park in 1900 by ornithologists Frank Chapman and Charles Rogers, the counts have since acquired the glamor and competitive appeal of a sporting event and annually engage thousands of participants. Christmas Counts are akin to a contest, in that participants go out with the objective of seeing how many birds they can discover in a large but defined area, with only minimal concessions made to precision. Although basically an organized competition and social event for birdwatchers, the ostensible purpose of the counts is to provide a record of winter bird populations. This purpose has generally been well served, although the data should always be interpreted with circumspection since environmental conditions within most of the censused areas have been continuously evolving. The data base accumulated since the turn of the century constitutes the longest continuous record of bird populations available in North America. In Chapter 4 we shall make use of some of these data to analyze long-term trends in the waterfowl populations of Chesapeake Bay.

BREEDING BIRD CENSUSES

There is a world of difference between a bird count, as practiced in the annual holiday competition, and a census. A breeding bird census is a far more serious proposition. Here the objective is to know exactly how many pairs of each species nested within a precisely defined plot of a particular type of vegetation. Every individual nesting pair must be detected and identified. Skill is an essential element, both in mapping the locations of birds from their calls and in carrying out the associated vegetation measurements. A need to distinguish resident breeders from transient nonbreeders calls for repeated coverage of each plot.

The methodology depends explicitly on the concept of territoriality, because one actually enumerates territories rather than individual birds. This concept is now so widely acknowledged that it is almost a part of our common cultural lore, but when it was first proposed in 1920 by the British ornithologist H. E. Howard, it was considered revolutionary. Howard's insight provided the fundamental breakthrough that opened the door to quantitative studies on bird populations. Like many other theoretical advances in the history of science, its full implications were not immediately appreciated. A standard technique for censusing breeding birds thus did not appear until many years later during World War II (Kendeigh 1944).

After the war ended, the Audubon Society lost no time in putting the method to work. In 1946 a society publication, *Audubon Field Notes* (a precursor of today's *American Birds*), began to devote one issue a year to reporting the results of breeding bird censuses taken by members. The prescribed procedure for gridding plots and counting the numbers of pairs of birds followed Kendeigh's methodology and was scientifically rigorous. What was not so scientifically rigorous was the matter of site selection.

Since the reports represent the voluntary efforts of mostly amateur birdwatchers, it was not practical to impose constraints on the siting of plots. Each individual was at liberty to select the area censused. Typically, this was the contributor's favorite birding spot. With no standardization of selection criteria, the plots consequently vary greatly in size, successional age, and degree of internal heterogeneity.

We now have a forty-year record of these censuses, which provides the best available source of information on the structure of North American bird communities. Although a forty-year perspective on the past is a far cry from having data to represent the presettlement virgin forest, it offers enough of a time frame to warn us that many bird populations have experienced major changes during the interim.

It is clear in retrospect that the effort invested to date could have produced results of far greater value had the censuses not been conducted in such a haphazard fashion. The major deficiencies in the laissez-faire system are: (1) the frequent inclusion of nonhomogeneous plots, (2) an imbalanced coverage of habitats, (3) generally inadequate plot sizes, and (4) a poor record of temporal continuity. To understand why these matters are important, I must first make clear the purposes that can be served by these censuses.

One purpose is simply that of documenting the structure and composition of the bird community of a particular type of vegetation. The important consideration here is that the vegetation within each plot be as homogeneous as possible. Habitat heterogeneity may raise the species total, but it greatly reduces the repeatability of the result, and thus defeats the purpose of doing the census. To account for all the species that might nest in, say, a county, it would be necessary to census a number of plots representing a range of successional stages (for example, abandoned pasture, shrubby old field, young forest), as well as the principal natural habitats.

Unfortunately, few workers have organized their efforts in so systematic a fashion. More typically, a contributor selects one or two plots without any prior consultation of other individuals who may be active in the same region. This lack of coordination leads to gross imbalances in the coverage of different habitats (for example, sixty-six censuses of "eastern deciduous forest" were reported in 1984, but none of many other habitat types).

Ideally, the plot size should be adequate to include one or more pairs of all regular members of the community. In practice, it may be difficult to achieve this ideal in the case of species that maintain low population densities. Examples of the latter are ruffed grouse, great horned owl, pileated woodpecker, and American crow. Actual densities of these are seldom reported. "As large as is practical" is a good rule in determining plot size. Year-to-year continuity is not important in censuses undertaken to document the composition of a particular community. Here one is asking "What is there?" not "Has anything changed since last year?"

The second question defines the other major purpose of conducting censuses, that of monitoring for population changes. Somewhat different design criteria are called for, if this is one's objective. Now vegetational stability and sample size become the paramount considerations.

Successional habitats are inappropriate because the vegetation changes over time (unless one is studying succession per se). This means that one is restricted to mature natural habitats, or perhaps certain man-made habitats that are managed in a consistent fashion, such as an orchard or regularly mown hayfield. But regardless of the type of habitat, the plot size should be large. How large? Here again one must rely on a rule of thumb, for there are no definite answers to this question, except that the larger the numbers one has, the more easily and reliably one is able to detect significant changes.

A sample size of, say, fifty pairs per species would be excellent for statistical purposes, but is wholly impractical. More realistically, one might strive to census a large enough area to include at least five pairs of the species of median abundance. This is to say that half the species would be represented by 5 or more pairs, the other half by fewer. Statistically, this constitutes a minimalist effort; as an exercise in fieldwork, it is not so minimal.

To make the argument more concrete, let us consider a typical census, one that approximates the median condition. One titled "Wild Cherry-Hickory Forest" taken in the summer of 1983 in Hancock County, West Virginia, nicely fits the bill (Van Velzen and Van Velzen 1984). Eight volunteers from the Brooks Bird Club visited the 6.1 hectare plot several times and documented the presence of thirty-two territorial males of twenty-three species. The most abundant species (red-eyed vireo) was represented by six pairs, the next most abundant (acadian flycatcher) by four pairs, and so on. Of the twenty-three species found, only five were represented by more than one pair and the species of median abundance was represented by only a single pair. One does not have to be much of a statistician to appreciate that a sample size of one does not offer a great deal of information.

Even the most strenuous efforts fall short of meeting the five-pairs-per-species criterion. The most extensive of the sixty-six censuses of "eastern deciduous forest" reported in the January–February 1984 issue of *American Birds* was one conducted in a 42 hectare plot in Ulster County, New York ("Mixed Upland Forest"). Even in an area as large as this (about 105 acres), there were only eleven and a half pairs of the most abundant species (ovenbird), and the median species was represented by one and a half pairs. (The number of pairs in a plot may not be an even integer if one or more of the territories overlaps the plot boundary.) It seems clear from this example that the coverage of even larger plots is desirable for the purpose of long-term monitoring. This takes us beyond the maximum possible scale of individual endeavor and into the range of team effort.

Suppose a team of volunteers conducted a recensus the following year and discovered that one of the species that was represented by a single pair in 1983 had doubled in abundance to two pairs, and that another species had disappeared from the plot. What statistically valid statement can be made about these changes? None. True, the global population of the first species might have doubled over the year, and the second might have gone extinct, but neither of these possibilities is likely. It is far more likely that there was some reshuffling of territories in the local populations of both species that resulted, by chance, in there being two pairs of the first and none of the second within the fixed boundaries of the plot.

The handicap of small numbers could be tempered somewhat if one could count on a high degree of year-to-year continuity. Time can, to a limited degree, substitute for sample size. For example, consider a species that had been present in a small plot for a long run of years at an average density of three pairs. If there then came a year in which none was present, one would notice the absence, but it would have no statistical significance. If the bird continued to be absent in subsequent years, at some point the absence would become significant, but by then much time would have been lost and the species could have suffered a serious decline.

Even if we were content to allow time to substitute for larger sample sizes, we would still not find the records published in *American Birds* very helpful. Looking again at the sixty-six censuses from deciduous forest reported in 1984, twenty-one represented new plots, twenty were from plots that had been censused only once previously, and a mere twelve had been censused five or more times. Thus, only a small fraction of each year's published censuses provide a perspective of more than a few years. As a long-term monitoring effort, this is not very impressive. Furthermore, as mentioned above, only a small proportion of the published censuses provides adequate documentation of particular communities, due to small plot sizes and a casual approach to site selection in which internal homogeneity is not a requirement.

One comes painfully to the conclusion that many of the censuses published in *American Birds* are of little more than passing interest. On the optimistic side, the same total effort, if directed in an organized fashion toward (1) documenting communities and (2) long-term monitoring, could produce results of real lasting value. The sooner the nation's amateurs can organize themselves with these explicit goals in mind, the better it will be for our future ability to gauge changes in the environment.

As a footnote to this discussion I must add that the publication of the annual Breeding Bird Census has been discontinued with the 1984 volume of *American Birds*. Would-be contributors are now requested to mail their results to the Laboratory of Ornithology in Ithaca, New York, where the data will be recorded on microfilm. One can earnestly wonder whether this change in policy will be the death knell of a forty-year effort and a step backward in progress toward the goal of establishing a countrywide program of monitoring bird populations. An indication that this is happening can be seen in the decline in the number of censuses reported annually, from 212 in 1984, when the results were published in full, to 78 in 1987, when each census received only a one-line acknowledgment (Van Velzen and Van Velzen 1988). We all have egos, and the anticipation of seeing one's results in print is a powerful incentive to action. The decision not to publish breeding bird censuses any longer is certain to dampen the enthusiasm of volunteers at a time when we should be redoubling our efforts.

In the hope that the publication of breeding bird censuses can be re-instituted, I offer the following suggestions: (1) continue to census the ten or twenty plots in the nation that boast a continuity of twenty-five years or more, for these are irreplaceable; (2) exhort the officers of state and local bird clubs to establish plots representing major vegetation formations in protected parks and reserves; (3) stress the important point that these per-manent plots should be as large as possible to meet or exceed the five-pairs-per-species criterion; (4) recommend that each club appoint an officer specifically to organize volunteers and to assure that each plot is adequately covered by skilled observers; (5) make every effort to assure the long-term continuity of each census; (6) coordinate these efforts through a national oversight committee that would be charged with promoting a more equita-ble distribution of censuses over habitats.

The Breeding Bird Survey

Organized in 1965 by Chandler S. Robbins and others of the U. S. Fish and Wildlife Service, the Breeding Bird Survey is a completely separate effort to marshal volunteers in the service of population monitoring. In scale it lies at the opposite end of the spectrum from the Breeding Bird Censuses, which focus on tiny plots. Instead, the Breeding Bird Survey is nationwide in scope and was designed to detect changes in the population levels of whole species. This is an ambitious and admirable goal that has only been partly achieved in the results as analyzed to date (Robbins et al. 1986).

The approach is extensive rather than intensive. Volunteers are assigned a route, usually consisting of a circuit along rural roads in their home states. The rules require that the observer stop his or her vehicle every half mile and listen for three minutes, recording all birds heard and seen during the stop. A route consists of fifty stops and is generally covered in two to three hours, starting a half hour before dawn. Each route is run once a year on a day in late May or June, when the vocal activity of territorial males is near its annual peak. This is a large-scale effort. In 1977, for example, volunteers ran 1,832 routes in 48 states and all the provinces of Canada (Robbins et al. 1986).

The concept behind these surveys is basically sound, though interpre-tation of the results is faced with two difficulties. The first of these arises from the fact that birds are counted along roads. Roads tend to pass over high ground rather than across swamps and marshes, and through agri-cultural and settled areas rather than through unbroken forest. The sampling of habitats is thus severely biased. For short-term monitoring purposes, this is not a serious problem if the distribution of routes across habitats does not change from year to year. This is likely to be a good assumption, provided large numbers of routes are covered in each geographical region. Given that this assumption is met, a statistically significant change from one year to the next in the numbers of individuals of a given species recorded per mile or route is likely to represent a real trend.

The second problem of interpretation arises when one attempts to monitor population changes over a longer time frame. Here changes in the distribution of habitats along routes can create artifacts. Since the end of World War II, the distribution of habitats in the East has changed significantly (see Chapter 13). Urbanization and suburbanization have claimed millions of acres. Large areas of marginal farmland in New England, Appalachia, and the southern Piedmont have been abandoned and allowed to grow in woody vegetation. Unless the survey is designed to control for such changes, they will inevitably register as apparent increases or decreases in particular bird populations.

This type of uncontrolled bias is evident at a glance in the recently published fifteen-year summary of the Breeding Bird Survey (Robbins et al. 1986). In the eastern section of the country, birds of suburbs and forest have shown statistically significant increases, while those of agricultural fields and pastures have tended to show significant decreases. These trends are undoubtedly real, but one can legitimately ask, "What do they mean?" In most cases the changes are probably related to a gradual maturation of habitats along the routes during the fifteen-year period of the study. Any secular changes in population sizes *independent of the distribution of habitats sampled by the routes* would be essentially undetectable by the methodology used.

This somewhat perplexing situation could be ameliorated by relating the results obtained to the changing patterns of land use in each section of the country. If the amount of forest over the East as a whole had increased, say, 10 percent over the past fifteen years, then one's "null hypothesis" in testing the results should be to expect a corresponding 10 percent increase in the counts of all forest-dwelling birds. By this measurement standard, a forest bird that showed no population increase over the interval has probably suffered a decline in density, if not in total numbers. The results published by Robbins et al. are valuable, but in the absence of reference to vegetation cover, they must be interpreted with caution.

As an effort complementary to the intensively analyzed plots of the Breeding Bird Census, the Breeding Bird Survey is extremely valuable, especially if the routes are calibrated with respect to habitat. By its production of vastly greater sample sizes, the method has the potential advantage of being statistically more sensitive to short-term population changes than plot counts. It thus offers the best available system for early warning in the event of precipitous population declines.

CODA

Although all three volunteer efforts to monitor bird populations—the Christmas Counts, the Breeding Bird Censuses, and the Breeding Bird Survey—have produced a wealth of irreplaceable data, the methodologies used in each case leave room for improvement. This is understandable largely as a consequence of history. The Christmas Counts and Breeding Bird Censuses both grew out of informal origins in which objectives were not clearly defined, and in which statistical criteria were not taken into account or were subordinated to the tastes and preferences of the participants. It is now clear that the results produced by all three methods contain biases and difficulties of interpretation. It is time that these efforts be overhauled to accord with the best available scientific methods. The monitoring of bird populations is too important a matter to be left to the accidents of history.

The vital importance of long-term monitoring will be brought out in Chapter 5 when we examine some of the very few available forty-year records from stable plots. Distributions and abundances of many populations have changed markedly over this relatively brief period of time, and it is to be expected that the future will bring continued changes that we cannot anticipate at present. Having proper base-line information is thus a matter of essential importance.

We may excuse our forerunners for not perceiving the value of creating a legacy of controls to pass on to the future. Until recently, the requisite scientific and statistical know-how was simply not available. But today we do have the required expertise, and so conservationists of the next generation will not look kindly on us if we fail to organize ourselves for the job.

4 *Wetlands in Trouble:*
The Chesapeake Bay

As a mobile teenage birdwatcher in northern Virginia, my attention naturally focused on the Chesapeake Bay. With its countless hidden coves and vast tidal marshes, the region seemed to hold endless possibilities for discovery. Nearly every outing produced surprises. This was especially true during migrations and in winter, when birding holds a high element of unpredictability.

To one accustomed to the winter bareness of the deciduous woods near Washington, the tall loblolly pines and dense evergreen thickets that line the shores of the lower bay provided an irresistibly exotic flavor, reminiscent of climes far to the south. The birds more than amply reinforced this impression. Even in midwinter, with sufficient diligence and skill one could find catbirds, brown thrashers, house wrens, yellowthroats, and pine warblers, none of which would have been anything but a fluke near Washington, less than 100 miles away.

Still greater satisfaction lay in discovering one of the species in the next echelon of difficulty: an orange-crowned warbler, perhaps, or a yellow-breasted chat. Not all the surprises were lingerers that failed to migrate farther south; there were overshoots from the north as well, such as the occasional glaucous gull, harlequin duck, or eider. The total list of species that could occur in the winter was over two hundred, yet on a given day one was doing well to find eighty or ninety. It was this large element of uncertainty that made birding in the Bay region so exciting.

Whereas stray and lingering land birds provided most of the surprises, water birds provided the spectacle. Renowned for its canvasbacks, black ducks, and wigeon, the Bay was and still is the waterfowl center of the entire East Coast. My memories of it in the 1950s, though perhaps somewhat exaggerated by the enthusiasm of youth, are of a vast abundance of ducks. Canvasbacks, scaup, redheads, and ruddy ducks dotted the coves and estuaries, and black ducks, teal, and wigeon sprang up by the dozens wherever one walked the marshes.

Returning to the same spots today, I do not find the same abundance. Houses have been built where once there were woods, the shores are lined with derelict plastic bottles, and the water is barren of birds. The Bay is sick.

This is no secret to these who have spent their lives there. It is a fact that has been officially acknowledged by a joint commission to "Save the Bay" established by the governors of Pennsylvania, Maryland, and Virginia. Their official concern was prompted by the plummeting revenues of a dying fishing industry, by the distress of bankrupt watermen, and by the bitter complaints of thousands of sports fishermen and waterfront home-owners who remember better days.

The purpose of this chapter is not to offer a comprehensive statement on the state of the Bay, but rather to show that the character of the waterfowl populations wintering in and around the Bay has, in the brief span of thirty years, changed drastically. The total number of birds may even have increased somewhat, but the composition of the community has been altered almost beyond recognition. Species that used to be common have since become rare, and vice versa, so that birders and hunters alike have had to adapt to a new reality.

We shall first examine evidence derived from the Audubon Society's annual Christmas Count. This evidence generally corroborates my more casual personal impressions and, in addition, points to some unsuspected trends. Once the facts are before us, I shall speculate on their possible causes. The potential causes are many and complexly intertwined, a consequence of our many-sided disregard of the environment.

WATERFOWL IN THE BAY: A THIRTY-YEAR PERSPECTIVE

In the Christmas Counts conducted every year by amateur birders around the country, we have a valuable source of data on winter bird populations. The institution dates to an unpretentious origin in 1900, as described in Chapter 3. Since then the counts have engaged a steadily growing number of enthusiastic volunteers. The latest published volume, covering counts made in the 1985–86 Christmas season, lists many thousands of participants in 1,503 separate counts taken in the United States, Canada, Mexico, Central America, the West Indies, Guam, and Saipan (*American Birds* 1986).

The ground rules for conducting Christmas Counts are established by the National Audubon Society. Although the rules are flexible as to the location of counts and the number of observers who may participate, they specify that every count must be completed within the twenty-four-hour span of a calendar day, that the day chosen must be within a two-week period surrounding Christmas, and that each area censused must be contained within a circle of 7.5 mile radius around a specific location. Different counts are thus comparable as to season, as well as to duration and area of coverage, but differ with respect to such factors as geographical location, types of habitat included, weather, and intensity of coverage (number of participants). Comparability can be enhanced by expressing results in terms of the number of birds seen per unit of coverage (for example, per hundred party-hours).

Normalizing results in terms of the number of party-hours of coverage is appropriate for comparing land bird numbers, because land birds tend to be dispersed; but such procedures are not appropriate for waterfowl, which tend to concentrate. Even when only a few observers attempt to cover the 177 square miles of a count circle, the participants will invariably check out all the known waterfowl concentration points. This is because waterfowl are colorful and impressive, tend to be highly visible, and are easily counted, even from a parked car. Most land birds, on the other hand, can be found only a few at a time by slogging through the habitat at a cost of forbearing the winter elements, barbwire fences, aggressive dogs, and unsympathetic landowners. For these reasons, waterfowl are preferentially censused, even in counts with small numbers of participants.

With a modest team of ten observers, coverage of waterfowl is likely to be nearly complete, whereas only a few percent of the individual land birds in the area will be registered. Thus, if one chooses reasonably well-attended counts, the numbers of waterfowl reported (except in years of inclement weather) will fairly accurately represent the numbers actually present within the count circles. By averaging several years' results, one can remove most of the short-term variability in the data due to vagaries in the weather, amount of icing of marshes and open water, and number of participants.

To investigate long-term trends in waterfowl numbers, I selected twelve Chesapeake Bay area counts from the reports contained in the annual Christmas Count volume of *American Birds*. Located in Maryland, Virginia, and the District of Columbia, these counts were all initiated in the late 1940s or early 1950s and provide a continuity of thirty years or more to the present. Five include portions of Chesapeake Bay itself (Annapolis, Saint Michael's, and Southern Dorchester County, Maryland; Little Creek and Newport News, Virginia), four are located on the estuaries of major Chesapeake Bay tributaries (Fort Belvoir, Virginia; Port Tobacco, Maryland; and Washington, D.C., on the Potomac; Hopewell, Virginia on the James), and three represent the nearby Atlantic coastline (Ocean City, Maryland; Chincoteague and Back Bay, Virginia). Eight of the circles represent unmanaged areas open to hunting, and four include managed federal wildlife refuges. Collectively, the set of twelve counts offers a balanced perspective on the principal waterfowl habitats of the region.

"Before" and "after" comparisons were made by averaging five years' results from the 1950s (1950–54 or the first five years of counts initiated after 1950 but before 1956) and five years' results from the 1980s (1980–84). A summary of the results is offered in Table 4.1.

TABLE 4.1 Counts of Waterfowl Wintering in the Chesapeake
Bay Region, 1950s versus 1980s

Species Group	1950s	1980s	% Change
Tundra swan	10,143	7,449	− 27
Geese	52,009	153,987	+ 196
Puddle ducks	61,547	34,180	− 44
Diving ducks	37,995	23,239	− 39
Saltwater ducks	7,788	9,095	+ 17
Ruddy duck	10,770	1,996	− 81
Meragansers	3,761	2,502	− 33
Total	184,013	232,448	+ 26

Source: Data taken from Christmas Counts.

Most of the major groups of waterfowl have undergone some degree of
population change during the three-decade interval. Contrary to the impressions I have recently gained in scanning miles of empty water in locations where ducks used to gather by the hundreds, the average total number
of waterfowl recorded on the twelve counts has actually increased by about
a quarter.

The apparent contradiction is explained by the fact that geese have increased by a factor of three, from about 50,000 to over 150,000, whereas
ducks have declined more than 40 percent from 120,000 to 70,000. The
empty water one currently sees in the Bay and its tributaries is entirely due
to the decline of ducks; geese feed mainly on land and are only a minor
element in my impressions of the 1950s.

The increase in geese and decrease in ducks are almost certainly independent events. Geese breed in the arctic, whereas the most common ducks
of the Bay area breed far to the south, mainly in the prairies. In the winter,
geese feed on land and ducks feed mostly in water. The possibilities for
competitive interactions therefore seem minimal.

The change in goose numbers is due to a spectacular ninefold increase in
greater snow geese along the coast, and to a tripling of the wintering population of Canada geese. Brant have meanwhile held their own at about
seventy-five hundred. Although the surge in snow goose numbers seems
impressive, it reflects only the recovery of a population that had previously
been reduced to very low levels by overhunting. The current population
level seems stable and can be taken as a base line against which to judge
future trends.

What has happened with the Canada goose, however, is a different
story. The center of gravity of the Atlantic Flyway population has shifted
northward from Florida and the Carolinas to the Chesapeake region in re-

sponse to the introduction of mechanical corn pickers. Prior to World War II, corn was harvested by hand, and generally every ear of a crop would find its way to the corn crib. Corn is now harvested by machine in a process that leaves up to 10 percent of the crop in the field. Given the magnitude of our annual harvest, 10 percent represents an enormous subsidy, enough to sustain millions of birds. Canada geese in the Bay area now feed almost entirely in harvested cornfields, seeking open water only for rest and as a safe haven from hunters. Due to mechanical harvesters, the winter carrying capacity of the Bay area for Canada geese has probably been raised many fold, and even further population increases may be in store.

This situation has been a boon to the area's hunters, who now shoot geese from camouflaged pits in cornfields rather than ducks from the traditional blinds that used to dot the Bay's marshes and coves. Since there are currently more geese in the region than there were ducks in the 1950s, and since geese are much larger, the annual take by hunters has undoubtedly grown. They have simply had to adapt to new targets and methods.

Whereas geese have increased, other types of waterfowl have mostly decreased, some drastically. Although the Chesapeake Bay continues to be the major wintering ground for the tundra swan, their numbers in the area have dropped by about a quarter since the 1950s. Puddle ducks and diving ducks have fared even worse, both having declined by about 40 percent, although some individual species have maintained their numbers, and two, the mallard and bufflehead, have even increased.

Puddle Ducks

The puddle ducks present a confusing picture. One species has shown a substantial gain (the mallard), two have maintained constant numbers (the gadwall and shoveller), two have declined slightly but perhaps not significantly (pintail and green-winged teal), and two have declined sharply (the black duck and American wigeon).

The wigeon was formerly the most abundant duck in the region. With an average census of 34,000, it made up 55 percent of the total count of puddle ducks. Lately the twelve counts have reported only 4,000, a drop of 88 percent. Why this species has suffered so much more than the others is not clear.

More can be said about the case of the black duck. Unlike most of the other puddle ducks, the black duck nests mainly in marshes along the northeast Atlantic seaboard and in eastern Canada. It also happens to be one of the shyest ducks, taking flight before other species at the approach of a human. These turn out to be particularly unfortunate traits. Wetlands in the Northeast have been in a steady decline due to filling, pollution, industrial contamination, and acid rain. Less than half of the original acreage of Connecticut's coastal marshes remain, for example, and other

FIG. 4.1 American wigeon

nearby states have been losing this habitat at rates of thousands of acres per year (Tiner 1984). Meanwhile, the human population of this part of the country has continued to increase, and as it has, proximity to man, inimical to the black duck, has resulted in the effective loss of even more habitat. We shall return to the situation of the other puddle ducks after reviewing the status of the remaining groups.

Diving Ducks

Open-water diving ducks, like the puddle ducks, have decreased about 40 percent. As was true of their marsh-dwelling relatives, different species have shown divergent trends. Buffleheads have more than doubled their numbers, golden-eyes and scaup have remained about the same, canvasbacks have declined moderately, and ringnecks and redheads have both suffered drastic losses of over 80 percent.

Although I am not able to offer a detailed explanation of these facts, one observation seems noteworthy. Canvasbacks in former times are known to have subsisted mainly on underwater plants, so-called "submerged aquatic vegetation." Birds collected more recently have been found to have invertebrates in their stomachs. Scaup also eat invertebrates. But redheads appear to be obligate vegetarians (Shelton 1981), a detail that assumes key significance in our inquiry.

Saltwater Ducks

A group of species I have called "saltwater ducks" includes the old-squaw and the three scoters. None of these has shown a noteworthy change. The recent counts suggest an aggregate increase of 17 percent, a figure that might simply reflect better boat coverage of some of the circles.

Ruddy Duck

Dense rafts of ruddy ducks used to be a common sight on the bays of the Potomac from Washington downstream. Now they are hardly to be seen. Indeed, the lack of ruddy ducks, perhaps more than any other single species, has been responsible for the contrasting impressions I have of the 1950s versus today. The Christmas Count data affirm this in indicating a regional decline of 81 percent.

Mergansers

As for mergansers, the two freshwater species (common and hooded) have increased slightly, though perhaps not significantly, whereas a sharp decline in the saltwater species (red-breasted) is entirely accounted for by Little Creek, Virginia, at which the average tally dropped from 2,500 to 200. Why this has happened is unclear, because it does not represent a general trend; many of the other counts have reported small increases over the same interval.

WHY HAVE SO MANY DUCK POPULATIONS DECLINED?

The answer to this question is unfortunately not a simple one. Chains of cause and effect in the environment are exceedingly difficult to prove. Multiple causes are more often the rule than the exception.

In the case of the declining duck populations of Chesapeake Bay there is no lack of incriminating evidence. There is so much that one is almost overwhelmed by it. Water quality has declined so obviously that the issue is not even controversial. But this does not prove our case. Instead, it compels us to distinguish between proximate and ultimate causes.

Ecological interactions often involve complex linkages and chain reactions. Consumer organisms, such as swans and ducks, are dependent, first, on their food supply. Alterations of the physical parameters of the environment—temperature, salinity, water chemistry, and so forth—may have no direct effects on the birds themselves, but if the changes adversely affect the organisms that provide their sustenance, then, naturally, the population may be affected. In this hypothetical example, changes in the physical properties of the water mass constitute ultimate causes, and a diminished food supply is the proximate cause. One can do nothing about the proximate cause until the correct ultimate cause(s) are identified and redressed. We shall next have a look at some of the proximal and ultimate factors that may have affected waterfowl populations in the Bay.

THE DETERIORATION OF CHESAPEAKE BAY

The deterioration of water quality in the Bay over the last thirty years is a first-class environmental horror story. Worse yet, what has happened here is a consequence of trends that are operating on a nationwide scale. There is no reason to think that the Bay is anything but typical. Indeed, a parallel, if not more extreme, complex of ills has affected San Francisco Bay, the Chesapeake's West Coast counterpart, as well as other California wetlands (Steinhart 1987). The list of complaints is a familiar one: eutrophication (excessive growth of bacteria and plankton due to nutrient overloads), siltation, nondegradable industrial wastes, and massive runoff of agricultural chemicals.

The scientific facts of the Bay's deteriorating water quality are well established. Because of its central role in the economy of the region, the Bay is the focus of several research organizations. For many decades Maryland and Virginia have maintained marine laboratories on the Bay for the purpose of studying and monitoring the populations of commercially important species, among these, crabs, oysters, and striped bass. In addition, Johns Hopkins University, the University of Maryland, and the Smithsonian Institution sponsor laboratories of their own where more basic studies are carried out.

One cannot claim that today's situation has snuck up on us because no one was looking. The essential facts have been available for some time. Conditions have continued to deteriorate because what is needed to reverse the trend is both costly and politically difficult.

The scientific ethic demands an open mind toward the evaluation of all possible causes of a problem as well as caution in arriving at interpretations. Scientists who objectively seek the truth independent of political considerations must freely admit to ambiguities in their results. Where their conclusions impinge on politically sensitive issues, they may find themselves torn between conscience and duty to an employer, especially if the employer is a political or bureaucratic agency.

Politicians loathe ambiguity because they loathe controversy. If scientists cannot confidently point an incriminating finger at a single identifiable cause, politicians typically will call for more study of the matter, even if delay will result in a worsening of the situation. When scientists obtain results that are contrary to the goals of a bureaucratic organization, their results may be suppressed, or buried deep in a report so thick and tedious that no one reads it. If they admit to uncertainty, their advice is likely to be rejected by politicians and ridiculed by advocates of special interest politics. These are familiar facts of life to scientists working toward a solution to the problems of the Bay (Horton 1984).

Proximate Factors

For an appreciation of how the Bay has deteriorated from the point of view of its waterfowl, we must look to changes in its aquatic life. The documented biological changes have been numerous and so fundamental as to have altered the entire ecosystem. The impact of these changes on the regional fishing industry has been mixed, but in balance strongly negative. Many traditional bayside communities have languished because the younger generation has eschewed the hardy and financially stressed life of their forebears. The sight of abandoned homes, overgrown with vines and trees, has become commonplace.

First, consider the fishery (see Figure 4.2). The annual takes of herring, shad, striped bass, and oysters have fallen to their lowest levels since record keeping began in 1880 (Shelton 1981). The plight of the American shad has become so serious that commercial fishing was banned in 1980. A similar ban on striped bass, the Bay's erstwhile premier gamefish, was instituted in 1985 (Horton 1984).

Not all the trends are negative. The annual catch of Atlantic menhaden has risen steadily since 1950. Formerly considered to have little commercial value, menhaden now have a market in the form of fishmeal. Most of this finds its way into chicken feed. When one's blessings are few, it is reassuring to count them. The blue crab is another. A delicacy that has contributed to the Bay's international culinary renown, it seems to have been holding its own against general adversity.

It is likely that many of these trends are consequences of the Bay's deteriorating water quality. Waste-water effluent and fertilizer runoff from agricultural land have greatly increased the amounts of nitrogen, phosphorus, and potassium in the Bay's surface waters. This, in turn, has resulted in enormously increased phytoplankton densities. Although some enrichment of plankton levels may have beneficial effects, too much of a good thing can often lead to disaster. So it is with phytoplankton.

Although these single-celled plants constitute the base of the food chain, and are hence the foundation of the Bay's productivity, excessive numbers of them carry adverse consequences. Light penetration into the water column is drastically curtailed, and the tremendous oxygen demand produced by their decomposing bodies creates a zone of anoxia on the bottom. In view of this, it is perhaps not surprising that of the two commercial species that are still prospering in the Bay, one, the menhaden, is a plankton feeder, and the other, the blue crab, is a general scavenger and detritus feeder. More important, neither depends on the quality of bottom waters

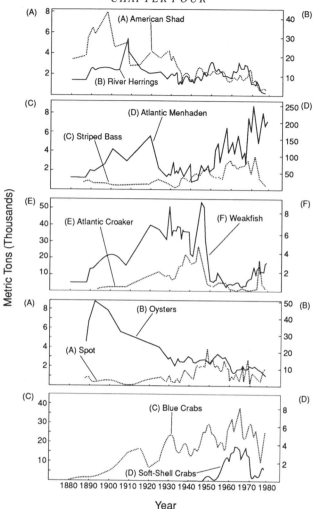

FIG. 4.2 Commercial landings of selected fish and shellfish in Chesapeake Bay and Atlantic Ocean waters of Maryland and Virginia from 1880 to 1979 (Shelton 1981).

for its reproduction. Menhaden larvae live in surface waters, and blue crabs breed in marshes and shallow tidal creeks. Species that depend on bottom conditions—oysters, clams, and striped bass—have not fared so well.

The gravity of the situation in the Bay's deeper waters was not fully appreciated by scientists until 1984, when an unusual combination of circumstances produced a catastrophic spread of anoxic water into normally well-aerated shallows. The deep water of the central Bay is normally anoxic in the summer, due to what is known as a stratified water column. This is brought about by the action of two complementary factors.

Fresh water derived from tributary rivers tends to flow out on top of denser saline water carried into the Bay by the tide. The density gradient is further enhanced when light absorption by plankton and particulate matter raises the temperature of water near the surface. Warm fresh water of low density thus overlies cooler saline water of higher density. The stratification will persist so long as cool weather or strong wind does not overturn the water column. Neither type of event is common in midsummer, so stratification normally persists for several months.

The summer of 1984, however, was atypical. It was preceded by the highest late-winter outflow on record from the Susquehanna River. Abnormally heavy rainfall then continued during June, July, and August. This unusual input of fresh water accumulated on the surface of the Bay, producing an exceptionally strong density gradient.

These already severe circumstances were further exacerbated by a summer that lacked any strong storms. The accompanying heavy winds would have churned the Bay and broken up or diminished the density gradient. Instead, throughout August, a stationary high pressure area off the Atlantic Coast generated mild but persistent southwest winds that nudged ocean water into the Bay under the surface cap of fresh water. This resulted in a further intensification of the density gradient and an accompanying expansion of the layer of anoxic bottom water.

The unusual combination of climatic circumstances that year led to the depletion of dissolved oxygen in the Bay's bottom waters two months earlier than usual. By August 23, scientists detected significant concentrations of toxic hydrogen sulfide in the anoxic layer, and by the end of the month the upper boundary of this layer had crept upward to the unprecedented depth of 5 meters. This allowed oxygen-depleted and hydrogen-sulfide-containing saline water to penetrate into several major tributaries (the Potomac, Patuxent, Choptank, and others) for the first time on record (Seliger et al. 1985).

The consequences of this were little less than catastrophic: "A survey of oyster bars in the Choptank River on 6 to 7 September 1984 along a transect with bathymetries [depths] from 3 to 10 m revealed the mortality of all shellfish as well as their fouling organisms on bars below 6 m. Seed-bed areas and bars above 5 m were unaffected. This has since been verified by two independent surveys, involving personnel of the University of Maryland Sea Grant program and the Maryland Department of Natural Resources" (Seliger et al. 1985).

What this means in nontechnical language is that nearly all bottom life in the Bay below a depth of 6 meters was killed. This would include major shellfish beds and the spawning grounds of commercially important fish, such as striped bass. The circumstances that brought on this calamity were admittedly unusual, but as long as eutrophication persists we can expect further such occurrences in the future. The outlook for many of the Bay's commercial fisheries thus appears bleak.

Duck food is another declining resource. Another symptom of catastrophe in the Bay's bottom waters has been the loss of "submerged aquatic vegetation," or SAV. The term is professional jargon that refers to rooted green plants, some of them grasses, that live underwater. Some aquatic plants, such as water lilies, are familiar to everyone, because their leaves float on the surface. But there are many others that live entirely below the surface and are invisible to anyone but divers. When they disappear, no one notices, at least not right away.

The Bay's submerged aquatic vegetation has disappeared. Underwater vegetation once covered the extensive flats and shoals of the northern and eastern portions of the Bay and of its major tributaries (see Figure 4.3).

> Areas densely vegetated in the Patuxent and lower Potomac rivers in the 1960's were devoid of vegetation by 1970. Upriver sections of many smaller subestuaries were devoid of vegetation by 1970. Major changes in all regions began in 1972, the year of Tropical Storm Agnes. This storm reduced salinities throughout the bay for periods of up to 4 weeks and transported large quantities of suspended sediment into the estuarine system. By 1974, the distribution and abundance of submerged grasses had been drastically altered throughout the bay. This alteration continued, and by 1980 the major tributaries of the bay and many of the smaller rivers contained only sparse beds or completely lacked vegetation. This condition has persisted through 1982. (Orth and Moore 1983, 51)

Although it is not known with certainty what has killed the aquatic grasses, scientists suspect that high plankton densities brought about by eutrophication are a major contributing factor. The plankton simply intercepts the light, leaving the rooted vegetation to languish in the dark. Heavy silt loads and bottom anoxia may serve as aggravating factors. That insufficient light is involved is supported by the observation that "one site in the lower bay showed a progressive shoreward shift of the bed's outer limits over a 10-year period" (Orth and Moore 1983, 51).

Ultimate Factors

In 1970 the Bay region held a population of 7.9 million people. By 2020 it is estimated that this number will more than double to 16.3 million (U.S. Army Corps of Engineers, in Shelton 1981). Water use is projected to grow by an even greater factor. Huge investments will therefore be required to finance the construction of adequate sewage treatment facilities. While there have recently been improvements in the level of waste-water treat-

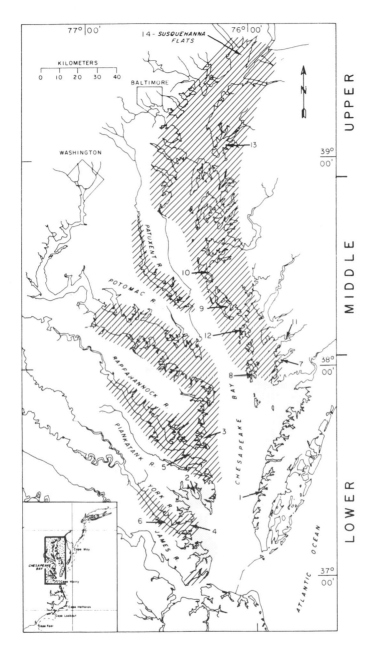

FIG. 4.3 Map of the Chesapeake Bay showing areas where submerged aquatic vegetation has experienced the greatest decline since 1960 (diagonal lines) and locations where vegetation is still found in large stands (stippled areas) (Orth and Moore 1983).

ment in the region, nothing but the most expensive tertiary treatment removes the excess nitrogen and phosphorus that are responsible for eutrophication (Smith et al. 1987). To prevent further backsliding, we must not only double the gross treatment capacity of the region, but upgrade its quality as well.

Nevertheless, one can be hopeful on this point. The need for proper disposal of human wastes is widely recognized, and programs exist at federal, state, and local levels to subsidize the improvement of substandard systems. Eutrophication resulting from inadequate waste-water treatment is thus a current but probably diminishing cause of the Bay's ills.

The same can be said for the uncontrolled release of industrial contaminants. The time when major rivers could legally be poisoned for miles downstream of mines or factories is now happily fading into the past. Here again progress has been achieved by broad public recognition of the problem, coupled in this case with the relative ease of dealing with point-source contamination (Smith et al. 1987).

A far more serious challenge awaits us in the need to reform agricultural practices. Given our gradual progress in reducing point-source contamination, we are left facing the far less tractable problem of non-point-source contamination. On this score, there can be no doubt that agriculture is the worst offender.

Take siltation, for example. The highest rates of erosion occur in the bare earth of construction projects, but the sources are local and temporary in nature. Severe dislocations may result, but given time, nature heals its wounds. But this is not true of cultivated land where the soil remains exposed more or less indefinitely (Clark et al. 1985).

Notwithstanding major gains in soil conservation made since the time of the dust bowl, we are sill losing our most precious resource at an alarming rate. In many areas soil is being eroded from agricultural land in amounts that exceed its rate of formation. An annual loss of 5 tons per acre is considered "tolerable," but at this rate an inch of soil that took natural processes hundreds of years to create is lost in a mere twenty-three years (Clark et al. 1985). Obviously, this situation cannot be allowed to continue, but relieving it requires a political will that we do not possess at the moment.

Recent trends toward the intensification of agricultural practices have resulted in increased rates of soil runoff. One study in Missouri showed that continuous corn cropping leads to an average annual loss of 19.7 tons per acre versus only 2.7 tons per acre under a more traditional rotation of corn, wheat, and clover (Miller, in Brown and Wolf 1984). Given that the watersheds of the Bay's major tributaries—the Susquehanna, Potomac, and James—are heavily agricultural, it is clear that the Bay will continue to be burdened with deleterious silt loads for the foreseeable future. No-tillage agriculture, introduced as an energy-saving measure following the

1973 hike in fuel prices, is no panacea, for its success relies on massive applications of herbicides. This brings us to another serious problem: agricultural chemicals in general.

The use of chemicals in agriculture has grown dramatically since the end of World War II. This is increasingly becoming true worldwide. Chemical fertilizers, pesticides, and herbicides constitute a troika of substances whose baneful environmental effects are only beginning to be understood. With anticipated further improvements in domestic waste-water treatment, runoff of agricultural chemicals will soon move into first place as the leading cause of water pollution. This is the unavoidable consequence of a 68 percent increase in the application of synthetic fertilizers to the nation's farmland between 1970 and 1981 (Smith et al. 1987). Telling the nation's farmers that they must not provide so generously for their crops will be far more difficult than convincing city dwellers to pay for better sewage treatment.

Since the celebrated victory in the battle against DDT, we have introduced an entirely new generation of pesticides. The long-term effects of these molecules on wildlife are not well known, and the victims have yet to be identified. This time around they may not have the same emotional appeal as did our national symbol.

Herbicides are synthetic analogs of plant hormones that, in low concentrations, can have stimulatory effects on plant growth. In high concentrations, they become lethal. The effectiveness of these substances in agriculture and weed control relies on the application of lethal overdoses. They are thus applied in amounts that, for some plants, may exceed the limits of physiological tolerance by several orders of magnitude. Some of the compounds used are environmentally stable and remain in the soil for months.

When I first began to notice fallow fields that were utterly brown and barren in May and June, when the growing season was well advanced, I was baffled. Such sights are now becoming commonplace and are the telltale sign of massive herbicide application in the previous growing season. How long do these effects linger, and what happens to aquatic vegetation when the runoff from such fields enters the water supply? These questions are being investigated, but all the answers are not yet in. Unless the effects are drastic indeed, the agrochemical lobby is likely to hold its ground in the legislative arena.

WHERE HAVE THE DUCKS GONE?

Now that we have some understanding of the biological and chemical factors that have so drastically altered the ecology of the Bay, perhaps we are ready to identify those most directly involved in the decline of its waterfowl populations. The huge flocks of swans, canvasbacks, redheads, and other species that once wintered on the Bay fed principally on submerged aquatic vegetation. Now almost none remains, and most of the birds are gone. One would have to possess the mentality of a tobacco industry spokesperson to doubt there was a connection.

Nevertheless, the strength of our conclusion would be bolstered if the results were to pass an internal test of consistency. Recall that the twelve Christmas Counts that are the source of our data include eight from non-refuge areas and four from circles that encompassed major federal water-fowl refuges. If the disappearance of submerged aquatic vegetation has been a major cause of the decline in Bay-area waterfowl populations, one would expect to see much sharper drops in the waterfowl totals for the nonrefuge counts.

The reasons for presuming this seem sound. Several nonrefuge counts are in areas known to have lost their submerged aquatic vegetation—Anna-polis, Newport News, Port Tobacco, Saint Michael's—whereas the main waterfowl feeding grounds on federal refuges consist of carefully managed impoundments. Rainfall provides the main water supply for these im-poundments, so deteriorating water quality cannot be implicated in changes in refuge waterfowl populations. If loss of submerged aquatic vegetation in the Bay since 1960 has contributed to the decline in water-fowl, one could thus expect that the declines would have occurred princi-pally in nonrefuge areas.

To my great surprise when I added up the figures, what has occurred has been exactly contrary to the prediction. There have been major declines in refuge populations of puddle and diving ducks, but no significant changes in the eight nonrefuge counts (see Table 4.2). Only swans show the ex-pected trend. The contribution of the four refuge counts to the total tally of puddle and diving ducks for the twelve areas has fallen from 68 percent to 46 percent. It is not clear how this development should be interpreted, but one cannot so confidently point a finger at the loss of submerged aquatic vegetation in the Bay. What else could be the problem?

TABLE 4.2 Dabbling and Diving Ducks in Refuge versus Nonrefuge Counts, 1950s and 1980s

	Nonrefuge	*Refuge*	*Total*
Dabbling ducks			
1950s	12,778	48,769	61,547
1980s	11,171	23,009	34,180
Diving ducks			
1950s	19,363	18,632	37,995
1980s	20,056	3,183	23,239

A different approach to the question would be to look at the species showing the most pronounced declines and ask whether there is any common thread that could unite them. At first sight it is an unlikely collection—black duck, American wigeon, green-winged teal, redhead, canvasback, ringneck, and ruddy duck—three dabblers and four divers.

What they might have in common is trouble on the breeding grounds. We have already seen that this seems to be the case for the black duck, which breeds in the Northeast. The rest breed in prairie potholes (see Figure 4.4).

BREEDING GROUNDS OR WINTERING GROUNDS: A CRISIS ON THE PRAIRIES

The most critical habitat on the continent for waterfowl is situated in a broad belt across the northern plains known as the prairie pothole region. Encompassing about 300,000 square miles, the flat, poorly drained land-

FIG. 4.4 Aerial infrared U-2 photograph of North Dakota showing the vast numbers of prairie potholes that characterize much of the state's topography (Wallace 1985).

scape is dotted with countless water-filled depressions, ranging in size from mere puddles to major lakes. Although constituting "only about 10 percent of the wetland acreage in the United States and Canada, [the pothole region] produces half of North America's game ducks in an average year—and, in some years, up to two-thirds. A lesser known fact is that the pothole country provides critical nesting or staging habitat for dozens of species of nongame migratory birds" (Louma 1985, 9).

"In pre-settlement days, there were perhaps 20 to 25 million shallow ponds and marshes here. Before the pioneer sodbusters reached the northern prairies, the U.S. share of these wetlands covered some 115,000 square miles. By the mid-1950's, more than half of the wetlands had been drained for agriculture: only 56,000 square miles of prairie potholes remained in the Dakotas and Minnesota, with a few scattered holdouts in Iowa" (Louma 1985, 9).

Since the 1950s the situation has grown steadily worse. "Mid-America's wetlands have been almost totally converted to croplands: Iowa has lost 99 percent of its natural marshes and potholes; 80 percent of Minnesota's prairie wetlands are gone; Missouri and Nebraska have lost 90 percent each of their original wetlands; Illinois has lost 89 percent; Michigan has lost 71 percent; and Oklahoma, 70 percent" (Reffalt 1985, 37).

The only substantial area of prairie potholes remaining is in the Dakotas, a mere 3 million acres out of an original 7 million acres (Tiner 1984). The ducks literally have nowhere left to breed.

Rather than encouraging farmers to retain their potholes and marshes, federal policies have had the opposite effect. In spite of chronic surpluses, price supports for corn, wheat, and other commodities have provided the stimulus for conversion of rangeland to cropland on a large scale. "Between 1965 and 1975, approximately one half of the rangeland in the Coteau du Missouri counties of North Dakota was converted to cropland" (Tiner 1984, 43). Land bank programs, designed to reduce surpluses by paying farmers to retire erstwhile cropland, have often had perverse consequences. In order to maximize profits under the program, farmers have first drained marshes and felled woodlots so that every possible acre of their holdings would qualify. The drained marshland is then quickly consigned to the land bank, where it languishes in a condition no longer suitable for waterfowl.

The federal government has further aggravated the situation by subsidizing the construction of ditches and canals to aid farmers in draining their land. Even highway ditches are called into service.

"In western Minnesota alone, nearly 100,000 acres of wetland have been lost in this way. In addition, stream channelization sponsored by Federal flood control projects, such as the Small Watershed Protection and Flood Prevention Program (P.L. 83-566), has led to accelerated wetland drainage in the Pothole Region as they have elsewhere in the U.S. (Erickson, et al. 1979). Drainage data for the Dakotas and Minnesota obtained from the U.S. Department of Agriculture's Production and Marketing Administration show that 188,000 acres were drained with Federal assistance in 1949 and 1950 alone. Countless other acres were privately drained at the same time'' (Tiner 1984, 42).

As so often happens in politics, expediency prompts different arms of the government to proceed in opposite directions. While subsidizing farmers to drain and plow potholes through various programs administered principally through the Department of Agriculture, the Fish and Wildlife Service under the Department of the Interior actively sponsored the acquisition of pothole lands for refuges and paid for conservation easements to forestall further drainage.

From subsequent developments, it is clear that the Department of Agriculture held by far the stronger hand. The situation we must live with now is essentially irreversible. Even if we could hold the line and retain all remaining wetlands, the net loss of waterfowl breeding habitat from presettlement times probably amounts to 80–90 percent. The prairie duck situation has not quite reached the extremity of that of the American bison, but it is not far behind.

ASSESSMENT

Our quest to understand the puzzling disappearance of ducks from Chesapeake Bay has unexpectedly led us far afield to the northern plains. What we have found there is a situation that, if anything, is worse than the one existing in the Bay. Having to face such adversities at both ends of their migratory route, it is little wonder that waterfowl populations have suffered. It would appear that environmental deterioration on both the breeding and wintering grounds, and perhaps at stopover points along the migratory route, have all contributed to the unhappy situation that exists today. Detailed explanations of what has happened to particular populations probably vary.

An obligate plant eater, such as the redhead, may be hardest hit by the loss of submerged aquatic vegetation in its traditional points of concentration in Chesapeake Bay. The response to this might simply be to shift to a new wintering ground. The nation's largest concentration of wintering redheads is now along the Texas coast (Monroe 1986).

Another species, such as the American wigeon, whose winter requirements do not seem particularly specialized, may be down for other reasons. Without more information than is available to me, it is impossible to offer a definitive explanation, because so many different explanations are possible.

Fɪɢ. 4.5 Redhead

In addressing questions such as these, it is important that one's conclusions not go beyond the data in hand. One could easily assume, for example, that redheads and American wigeon have declined throughout the country because they are now so scarce around Chesapeake Bay. This, however, would be a mistake, because nationwide data of the Fish and Wildlife Service indicate that redheads have actually increased since the late 1950s, whereas the wigeon has indeed decreased, but only by about 20 percent (U.S. Fish and Wildlife Service and Canadian Wildlife Service 1986). Nevertheless, the status of waterfowl nationwide is in general accord with the impression one gets from looking at the Bay.

In 1985 the total duck breeding population estimate from the combined survey areas was 30,883,000 and represents the lowest ever recorded. Declines in 1985 from 1984 and the 1955–1984 average were observed for nine of ten major species for which population information is presented annually in this status report. Breeding populations of mallards and northern pintails reached all-time low levels and several other species were near record low levels. Production indexes in 1985 of total ducks and mallards resulted in fall flight forecasts that were the lowest on record. Habitat conditions in recent years, prior to the low duck flights observed in 1985, were generally not favorable. Lack of sufficient wetland numbers due to dry conditions and adverse impacts on nesting cover by agricultural activities, combined to reduce the production capability of many key areas. (U.S. Fish and Wildlife Service and Canadian Wildlife Service 1986)

It is clear that ducks are under pressures of one kind or another nearly everywhere. Any recovery program will have to address the problem on a national level if it is to be successful. Local tinkering, such as improving the water quality of Chesapeake Bay, won't bring back the birds if the ponds and marshes they breed in no longer exist.

Migratory birds have evolved complex annual cycles that depend explicitly on encountering suitable conditions at all points along their routes. Wherever conditions deteriorate, a bottleneck can develop that may begin to limit the population. When conditions are deteriorating everywhere at once, it becomes very hard to pinpoint the bottleneck except in the most obvious cases. Scientists face this dilemma not only with waterfowl, but with migratory songbirds, as we shall see in Chapter 5.

5 *The Mystery of the Missing Songbirds, Part I*

My recollections in the first chapter of times past at our family home in northern Virginia left hanging the question of what had happened to the tanagers, vireos, and other birds that used to breed in the wooded park at the foot of the hill. Although covering several hundred acres, and carrying timber big enough to support a healthy population of pileated woodpeckers, this park, like many others in the region, no longer harbors the wood thrushes, acadian flycatchers, and hooded warblers that it did in days I remember well. There is a sickness in the woods, one that has worked to eliminate the birds that migrate north each spring from winter homes in the tropics.

In attempting to analyze the causes of this sickness, by pulling together bits and pieces of evidence, we shall find that no single explanation can account for all the facts. The quest for decisive answers is, as one has come to expect in ecology, hampered by a lack of controls, for the environment is changing in several ways at once. More than one type of pathology is identified by the evidence, but in the end we are left wondering which of several evils is the worst, and what can be done about any of them.

To begin, I shall present records from two of the very few sites reported in the Breeding Bird Census of *American Birds* to boast a forty-year continuity. I have chosen these two because they are ones with which I am personally familiar, although the declines of migratory songbirds found in them are similar to those documented at a number of other sites in several northeastern states. The two are at Cabin John Island, Maryland, and Rock Creek Park in the District of Columbia. Both are located in federal parkland and represent, respectively, mature floodplain forest and upland deciduous forest. The census plots were established in the late 1940s and have been censused regularly by members of the local Audubon Naturalist Society until at least the mid-1980s, when *American Birds* discontinued publication of the Breeding Bird Censuses.

Several species have undergone "terminal extinctions," in that they disappeared from the plots many years ago and have not returned. These include the yellow-throated vireo, black-and-white warbler, Kentucky warbler, and hooded warbler. Others, such as the scarlet tanager at Cabin John, have decreased in abundance to the point of disappearing, only to reappear sporadically in later years. Still others, such as the great crested and acadian flycatchers, wood thrush, and red-eyed vireo, have decreased to a fraction of their former abundances in both localities but are still present in small numbers. Altogether, the breeding densities of tropical migrants have declined by about 45 percent in both plots (Robbins 1979). Meanwhile, residents (for example, woodpeckers, chickadees, titmice, and cardinals) and short-distance migrants (those wintering in the southern United States, for example, catbirds, house wrens, and purple grackles) have roughly held their own in both localities. The overall trend has thus been a strong decline in birds that migrate to the tropics, with a loss of several common species in both plots, accompanied by no clear trend in the populations of species that winter in North America (Johnston and Winings 1987). The total numbers of breeding birds have dropped by half and the composition of the communities has been drastically altered (see Table 5.1).

In the late 1940s, 60–80 percent of the breeding pairs of both plots were tropical migrants; today the proportion has fallen below 40 percent, and it is possible that even further declines lie in store for the future. The changes are quantitatively and qualitatively similar to those documented at several other forested sites in the Washington metropolitan area (Robbins 1979; Johnston and Winings 1987). The effects on the bird community are only slightly less extreme than those accompanying the conversion of a large tract of forest into a suburban housing development (Aldrich 1980). What has happened?

This is a very difficult question to answer. A number of investigators have turned their attention to the problem, and some have obtained results that seem to offer partial solutions, but we still lack a fully satisfying explanation. More than likely, multiple factors are involved.

The first cries of alarm at the decline of tropical migrants were raised in the late 1970s by a mixed chorus of amateur and professional ornithologists (Forman et al. 1976; Galli et al. 1976; Whitcomb et al. 1977; Briggs and Criswell 1979; Robbins 1979, 1980). Most of these authors perceived the problem as a ''forest fragmentation effect,'' implying that the declines were somehow a consequence of subdividing the initially continuous forest into discontinuous urban and rural woodlots.

Their publications emphasized the fact that certain species (the worm-eating warbler being a prime example) could be found only in large tracts of forest and were invariably absent in small woodlots (Robbins 1980: Figure 5.1). These findings then led investigators to a closer examination of ''area effects,'' in which bird populations were compared in otherwise similar forest fragments of different sizes (Robbins 1980; Ambuel and Temple 1983; Lynch and Whigham 1984; Askins et al. 1987). Lists were then compiled of ''area-sensitive'' species (for example, acadian fly-

TABLE 5.1 Changes in the Abundance of Breeding Birds in Two Middle Atlantic Forests, 1940s–1980s

Cabin John Island: Mature floodplain forest (numbers represent mean number of pairs recorded per census during the 10-year interval).[a]

Species (number of censuses)	1940s (N=3)	1950s (N=6)	1960s (N=8)	1970s (N=10)	1980s (N=4)	Change in no. of pairs (1940s–1980s) (E=extinct)	Status[b]
American redstart	13.3	12.6	5.8	4.3	0.9	−12.4	M
Northern parula warbler	14.0	12.3	11.8	6.5	2.3	−11.7	M
Red-eyed vireo	15.3	16.0	14.1	9.7	4.8	−10.5	M
Kentucky warbler	4.5	4.5	2.5	0.0	0.0	−4.5 (E)	M
Wood thrush	4.0	4.3	2.5	0.1	0.0	−4.0 (E)	M
Acadian flycatcher	7.3	9.9	11.0	8.4	3.4	−3.9	M
Scarlet tanager	2.2	1.4	0.3	0.2	0.0	−2.2 (E)	M
Eastern wood peewee	4.5	3.2	2.8	1.7	1.3	−3.2	M
Starling	11.2	12.3	18.6	18.4	8.5	−2.7	R
Yellow-throated vireo	2.0	1.1	0.4	0.3	0.0	−2.0 (E)	M
Hooded warbler	1.7	0.4	0.0	0.0	0.0	−1.7 (E)	M
Louisiana waterthrush	1.3	0.9	0.0	0.0	0.0	−1.3 (E)	M
Yellow-billed cuckoo	1.0	1.1	0.2	0.2	0.0	−1.0 (E)	M
White-breasted nuthatch	2.5	1.5	1.0	0.6	0.6	−1.9	R
Carolina wren	3.3	5.8	3.6	5.1	2.0	−1.3	R
Tufted titmouse	4.8	5.0	5.6	4.5	3.5	−1.3	R
Northern cardinal	5.0	5.2	4.5	4.7	4.4	−0.6	R
Song sparrow	1.2	2.2	2.4	1.4	0.9	−0.3	R
Blue jay	0.0	0.0	0.6	0.1	0.0	0.0	R
Brown-headed cowbird	0.8	1.3	4.1	1.7	1.0	+0.2	S
Veery	0.0	0.0	2.1	0.9	0.3	+0.3	M
American crow	0.2	0.0	0.3	0.6	0.5	+0.3	R
Blue-gray gnatcatcher	1.8	3.2	2.9	2.3	3.0	+1.2	S
Prothonotary warbler	0.2	0.4	2.4	1.5	1.3	+1.1	M
Carolina chickadee	3.3	3.7	3.6	3.7	4.3	+1.3	R
Downy woodpecker	2.5	2.6	3.8	3.2	3.3	+1.8	R
Total species	31.0	26.8	25.6	23.8	27.3	−3.7	
Density (pairs/100ha.)	261.1	263.0	255.2	194.9	130.1	−131.0	

Rock Creek Park: Upland deciduous forest (numbers represent mean number of pairs recorded per census during the 10-year interval).[c]

Species (number of censuses)	1940s (N = 3)	1950s (N = 6)	1960s (N = 8)	1970s (N = 10)	1980s (N = 4)	Change in no. of pairs (1940s–1980s) (E = extinct)	Status[b]
Red-eyed vireo	41.5	39.2	28.1	10.6	5.8	− 35.7	M
Ovenbird	38.8	39.2	24.5	6.0	3.3	− 35.5	M
Acadian flycatcher	21.5	22.5	16.4	1.0	0.1	− 21.4	M
Wood thrush	16.3	13.1	5.2	4.5	3.9	− 12.4	M
Yellow-throated vireo	6.0	1.0	1.6	0.0	0.0	− 6.0 (E)	M
Hooded warbler	5.0	3.5	0.7	0.0	0.0	− 5.0 (E)	M
Scarlet tanager	7.3	4.3	2.4	4.1	3.5	− 3.8	M
Black-and-white warbler	3.0	0.2	0.0	0.0	0.0	− 3.0 (E)	M
Eastern wood peewee	5.5	6.9	5.2	1.0	2.8	− 2.7	M
American crow	2.0	0.7	2.0	0.9	0.6	− 1.4	R
Kentucky warbler	1.0	2.5	0.4	0.0	0.0	− 1.0 (E)	M
Yellow-billed cuckoo	0.8	0.0	0.0	0.0	0.0	− 0.8 (E)	M
Carolina chickadee	5.0	3.4	5.4	4.9	4.3	− 0.7	R
Tufted titmouse	5.0	6.7	8.7	6.4	4.5	− 0.5	R
Downy woodpecker	3.5	4.5	4.8	3.4	3.0	− 0.5	R
White-breasted nuthatch	3.5	2.7	3.3	2.8	3.1	− 0.4	R
Northern parula warbler	0.3	0.9	1.0	0.0	0.0	− 0.3 (E)	M
Eastern phoebe	1.0	0.0	0.0	0.3	1.0	0.0	S
Blue-gray gnatcatcher	0.0	1.3	1.1	0.0	0.0	0.0	S
American redstart	0.0	0.2	0.9	1.0	0.0	0.0	M
Brown-headed cowbird	0.5	2.1	4.4	0.5	0.8	+ 0.3	S
Louisiana waterthrush	0.0	1.1	0.3	0.3	0.5	+ 0.5	M
Purple grackle	0.0	0.0	0.3	0.3	0.5	+ 0.5	S
European starling	0.0	0.2	2.1	0.8	0.8	+ 0.8	R
Northern cardinal	1.3	2.2	3.4	3.5	2.1	+ 0.8	R
Veery	0.0	3.8	6.4	2.4	1.3	+ 1.3	M
Carolina wren	0.0	1.4	0.1	2.0	1.4	+ 1.4	R
Blue jay	0.0	0.3	2.7	3.9	3.6	+ 3.6	R
Total species	26.5	24.0	24.0	20.5	24.5	− 2.0	
Density (pairs/100ha.)	90.1	82.4	87.1	43.2	34.9	− 55.2	

Source: Yearly breeding bird censuses published in Audubon Field Notes (American Birds) vols. 1–37 (1947–84). Not all birds censused are included in the table.

[a] Cabin John Island: 7.6 hectares; located on the Potomac River, Glen Echo, Maryland. (For a detailed description, see Audubon Field Notes, vol. 1.)

[b] Status: M = long-distance migrant; S = short-distance migrant; R = resident.

[c] Rock Creek Park: 32.2 hectares before 1961; 26.3 hectares after 1961; located in Rock Creek Park, Washington, D.C. (For a detailed description, see Audubon Field Notes, vol. 2.)

catcher, veery, and worm-eating warbler) that appeared mainly or exclusively in large tracts of contiguous forest versus "area-insensitive" species that could be found in small woodlots (Galli et al. 1976; Robbins 1980; Lynch and Whigham 1984; McLellan et al. 1986). Following what seemed like sound logic, many of these authors then took the position, given limited resources for land acquisition, that it would be better to maintain forest reserves in a few large blocks than in a greater number of small ones. We shall later review several additional lines of evidence that affirm the basic wisdom of this policy.

The notion that scientific evidence favored the creation of large parks at the expense of small ones was based on the assumption that the abnormal composition of the bird communities of forest fragments was a consequence per se of their small areas. But this assumption had not yet been adequately tested in the field. Certainly the presence of area-sensitive species in large blocks of forest indicated that conditions were somehow more natural there. But it was not yet proven that limited *area* was the cause of the problems in forest fragments.

The argument about area failed to stand up under test. Recall that drastic compositional changes had been observed on Cabin John Island and in Rock Creek Park. Both census plots are embedded in extensive corridors of intact forest. Rock Creek Park, for example, although located within the District of Columbia, is about 10 kilometers long and variously from about 100 meters to more than 2 kilometers wide, including in total over 400 hectares of respectably mature forest. Large numbers of tropical migrants had been present in Rock Creek Park when censuses were initiated in 1948, but as we noted above, most of them subsequently disappeared. Yet the surrounding areas were fully urban long before 1948, and there have been no major disturbances to the park in the subsequent period. Here was a clear counterexample in which a reduction in area could not be implicated in the decline of migrants.

Additional counterexamples began to appear in accounts from other parts of the East in which observers reported supposedly area-sensitive species breeding in isolated 10–20 acre woodlots (Lynch and Whigham 1984). Either the same species were responding differently to small patches of habitat in different parts of the country, or the cause of the population declines of tropical migrants in the middle Atlantic states was not fragmentation per se but something associated with it.

Since the first of these possibilities seemed inherently unlikely, and would be a difficult proposition to study in any case, investigators turned their attention to other possible correlates of fragmentation.

Avoidance of edges? One inevitable consequence of fragmentation is increased amounts of "edge" habitat. Some authors thus seized on possible inimical qualities of edge as an explanation of the fragmentation effect

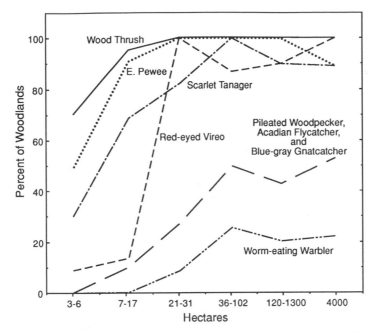

FIG. 5.1 Proportion of woodlots of each size class in which the species indicated were found (Robbins 1980).

FIG. 5.2 Worm-eating warbler.

(Whitcomb et al. 1977, 1981). The finding that certain species (for example, ovenbirds) seemed to cluster their territories near the center of forest tracts, avoiding areas near the boundaries, seemed to support this conclusion (Whitcomb et al. 1981).

Nevertheless, exactly what the deleterious properties of edge might be remained unclear. Moreover, the notion that edges were somehow detrimental in their effects was at odds with the long-held opinion of wildlife managers and birdwatchers that edges possess inherent virtue. White-tailed deer, turkeys, quail, rabbits, and other game species, for example, are known to prefer the vicinity of edges, and birdwatchers gravitate to them because more species can be encountered along them than in homogeneous habitat. Yet the virtues of edge might not be unalloyed.

Resolution of the argument is clouded by multiple interpretations. Were forest birds avoiding edges per se, or were the truly deleterious factors merely associated with edges? This question was answered by a very simple set of observations that required only the right situation.

Edge habitat occurs at the boundary between different types of vegetation, such as where a field or pasture adjoins a forest. Birds of open environments will predominate on one side, and forest birds on the other. There may even be a few "edge specialists" such as brown thrashers and towhees to enrich the mixture. This is why birdwatchers so assiduously stick to edges in their searchings. But if some forest species were really avoiding edges, it is unclear in this context whether they were avoiding edges as such or other species that are associated with edges (Ambuel and Temple 1983).

This question can be resolved in a straightforward fashion by examining bird territories along an edge that is merely a void on one side, such as the rim of a cliff or shore of a lake. To David Wilcove, then a graduate student at Princeton, a large reservoir in Maryland surrounded by an extensive forested watershed provided just the right conditions. The forest ended abruptly at the water's edge; there was no habitat beyond to confuse the issue. When Wilcove mapped the territories of birds in this forest, he found generally that they extended right up to the open water (Wilcove 1985a). There was no suggestion that birds were avoiding the edge.

At the same time, another ornithologist, Donald Kroodsma, undertook an examination of the edge question under more varied circumstances and obtained similar results. Most forest-dwelling species occupied territories that extended right up to various sorts of habitat boundaries (Kroodsma 1984). Contrary to the report of Whitcomb et al. (1981), when people began to look systematically for evidence of "edge avoidance" they failed to find it.

Now that area and edge had both failed to account for the disappearance of migratory songbirds in small urban and suburban woodlots, the problem became a lot more difficult. This is because edge and area are easily quantifiable features of small habitat fragments and, as such, are amenable to critical analysis. Once the two most obvious variables had been discounted, speculation turned to other possible factors. Perhaps other species had played a role in the declines. But what kinds of species might these be? Competitors? Predators? Parasites? It is easy to suggest the categories, but that is all. It would not be a simple matter to identify the culprits.

The Roles of Competitors, Predators, and Parasites in the Declines of Migratory Songbirds

Competitors

Let us begin by considering the possibility that competitors could be involved. On the face of it, this might seem a reasonable proposition. Even under the best of circumstances, however, it is not readily shown that birds are strongly influenced by interspecific competition, and thus the whole subject is highly contentious. To study competition rigorously, one has to remove one species and then show that another species subsequently increases in abundance. Correlational analyses seldom yield persuasive results (James and Boecklen 1984), probably because conditions vary significantly from year to year, and because bird populations may be limited by overwinter survival rather than by events on the breeding grounds (Fretwell 1972; Morse 1980).

Given that no methodology yet devised has been able to remove these ambiguities in the study of competitive relationships, one is probably stymied from the outset. Nevertheless, in considering the decline of migratory songbirds in forest fragments, even the prima facie case for competition lacks any convincing elements. The birds that have declined—for example, warblers, vireos, flycatchers—bear little resemblance, either taxonomically or ecologically, to those that seem to have increased, such as mourning doves, titmice, catbirds, grackles, and blue jays. And unlikely as it may seem, even if there were competitive links between the two sets of species, it would remain unclear whether the latter group increased at the expense of the first or merely in its absence. It can thus be said, without ruling out the possibility, that at this point the evidence for a role of competition in the decline of tropical migrants is nil.

Predators

In considering predators, the prospects for positive findings seemed somewhat brighter, though the preliminary evidence, if one could call it that, lay more in the realm of folklore than of science. Eastern suburbanites are reminded almost daily of the presence in their neighborhoods of a host of commensal species—squirrels, raccoons, opossums, blue jays, feral housecats, among others. All of these maintain higher densities in the vicinity of human settlement than in wild nature, presumably because of the absence of higher predators (for example, bobcats) and the availability of ample food subsidies at garbage cans and feeding stations.

One study of raccoons on Long Island, for example, found that individuals living in suburban areas had smaller ranges, much higher population densities, and grew to nearly twice the size of their country cousins (Hoffman and Gottschang 1977). Like most of the other species listed above, raccoons are omnivores and highly opportunistic, switching from one set of food resources to another as dictated by the season and situation. Eggs and nestlings are welcome fare whenever encountered. It thus seemed to David Wilcove that nest predation rates might be higher in suburban than in rural areas due to the artificially elevated abundances of raccoons and other opportunist predators.

To test this possibility, Wilcove took advantage of a method first developed by Betty Anne Loiselle of the University of Wisconsin (Loiselle and Hoppes 1983). He obtained fresh *Coturnix* quail eggs from a commercial supplier and set them out in artificial wicker nests of a type sold in pet stores for canaries. The nests were lined with fine grass and stocked with clutches of three eggs.

Wilcove employed 50 or 100 nests in each of 11 tracts of forest, placing them at 20–meter intervals, alternately on the ground and at heights of 1–2 meters in shrubs and saplings. After one week he checked the nests and scored any that had lost one or more eggs as having been preyed upon. The 11 sites, 10 of which were ₁n Maryland, included 3 large tracts (greater than 250 hectares; recall that 1 hectare equals 2.5 acres), 4 rural woodlots (3.8–11.7 hectares), and 4 suburban woodlots (3.8–13.3 hectares; Wilcove 1985b).

The tests produced unexpectedly dramatic results. Nest predation rates in the smaller suburban woodlots approached 100 percent (see Figure 5.3). In contrast, only 2 of 100 nests set out in the Great Smoky Mountains National Park were raided. This park served appropriately as the control because it represents the least disturbed environment remaining in the East. Intermediate predation rates prevailed in less remote large tracts and in rural woodlots.

Judging the results from the perspective of the Great Smoky Mountain National Park, nest predation rates elsewhere seem to have increased from 10 to 50 *times* over the levels experienced in a nearly pristine environment. Such a large increase in predation rates could hardly be without effect on bird populations.

We should be cautious, however, in accepting Wilcove's results at face value. They leave little doubt that nest predation rates have increased sub-

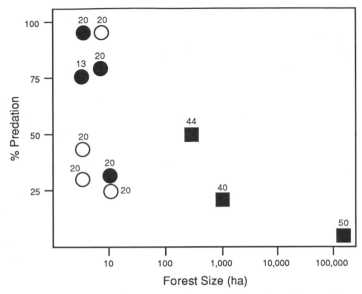

F<small>IG</small>. 5.3 Percentage of nests preyed upon as a function of forest size. Closed squares are large forest tracts, open circles are rural fragments, and closed circles are suburban fragments. The number above each point is the number of artificial nests placed in that forest (Wilcove 1985b).

stantially outside of the largest remaining tracts of forest, but it is fair to argue about the amount of the increase. First, it has to be realized that the nests put out in the experiments were not hidden as cleverly as a bird might have done it. Second, the exposed eggs were certainly more conspicuous than a clutch that was being incubated by a dull-colored female warbler or vireo. And third, the nests were close enough together that a predator that began to search intensively after finding one might have been able to discover others. For all these reasons, Wilcove's results are likely to convey an inflated impression of the actual nest predation rates in the woodlots he studied. Nevertheless, the differences between the rates obtained in the Great Smoky Mountains and all the other sites are so pronounced that one can marvel that any birds at all survive in our suburban parks and woodlands. The conclusion is inescapable-nest predators have become abnormally abundant almost everywhere outside of the very largest remaining areas of forest.

Half of the artificial nests set out by Wilcove were placed on the ground and the other half were fastened to low branches. The intent of this design was to discriminate between terrestrial predators (principally mammals) and arboreal predators (principally birds). Terrestrial nests proved to be more vulnerable than arboreal nests, though the difference was statistically significant at only two sites.

In another experiment, performed at a site that gave a high predation rate in a preliminary set of trials, he compared the survival of eggs in cup nests, placed as usual half on the ground and half in trees, with that of eggs placed in artificial tree cavities. The latter were intended to simulate the kind of nest used by many common hole-nesting species—woodpeckers, nuthatches, titmice, house wrens. They were prepared by drilling a hole in a log, splitting it, hollowing out the center, wiring it back together, and hanging it on a tree. None of the nests prepared in this fashion suffered egg loss, whereas 95 percent of those in open cups did.

At this stage, Wilcove had demonstrated the presence of abnormal numbers of both terrestrial and arboreal nest predators in forest fragments, but the identity of the culprits remained unknown. Both mammals and birds had been implicated by indirect evidence, but it was important to go beyond this and determine which species were to blame.

This required the techniques of a detective. Wilcove covered the rims of cup nests with a coating of plasticene modeling material to capture the toe and claw marks of avian predators that perched on them, and placed cardboard squares that had been dusted with dry masonry black next to ground nests in order to preserve the footprints of marauding mammals. He also coated branches leading to arboreal nests with a sticky substance, "tanglefoot," to record the tracks of climbing mammals, such as squirrels.

The success of these methods was less than total, though enough results were obtained to permit a qualitative assessment. Raiding ground predators typically overturned or tore apart the nests, but frequently left blurred tracks so that identification was impossible. Nevertheless, with the help of experts at the Smithsonian Institution, Wilcove determined that at least six different predator species were raiding the nests (see Table 5.2). Raccoons were implicated at all four sites he examined, blue jays at two, and four additional species at one site each.

TABLE 5.2 Predators Identified as Raiding Artificial Nests in Two Rural and Two Suburban Woodlots in Maryland

Predator	Rural		Suburban	
	8.8 ha.	3.8 ha.	7.4 ha.	4.2 ha.
Oppossum				X
Raccoon	X	X	X	X
Striped skunk				X
Dog	X			
Cat			X	
Blue jay		X		

Source: Wilcove 1985a.

The list is discouragingly long, although it is surely incomplete, since most predators did not leave identifiable tracks. Nests set on the ground were nearly always overturned or dragged away from their original positions, suggesting the work of mammals, while arboreal nests and the tanglefoot on approachways were seldom disturbed, suggesting that birds (or possibly snakes) had visited.

To confirm the identity of the arboreal nest thieves, Wilcove one day set up a blind near eight artificial nests and conducted a vigil. Within half an hour a blue jay discovered one of the nests, and later in the day a second was raided, also by a jay. In both instances, the predator flew in to a perch next to the nest, speared an egg with its bill, and flew off without disturbing the nest or leaving any sign of its visit.

It is clear from Wilcove's experiments that nest predation rates are exceedingly high in suburban parks and rural woodlots, possibly high enough to eliminate species that might otherwise be able to nest successfully. Can we then confidently associate the decline of tropical migrants in fragmented forests with the presence of excessive numbers of predators? The conclusion is certainly a tempting one, but we have to bear in mind that it is based on prima facie evidence. What is needed now is direct evidence that migrants are failing to nest successfully in suburban habitats. This will require discovering and following the fates of numerous nests, a task that is beyond the capacity of a single unassisted graduate student.

In lieu of evidence of the most ideal sort, a strong circumstantial case can nevertheless be made that the nesting habits of many tropical migrants are such as to render them particularly vulnerable to unusual rates of nest predation (Wilcove and Whitcomb 1983). With few exceptions, the tropical migrants that breed in the eastern United States construct open nests, either on the ground or in trees. Such nests are accessible to mammals and blue jays. A number of species nest on the ground, a location Wilcove found especially hazardous. Several of these are showing signs of trouble: whip-poor-will, black-and-white warbler, worm-eating-warbler, ovenbird, Louisiana water-thrush. In turn, *none* of the residents or short-distance migrants that commonly breed in suburban settings places its nest on the ground. Ground nesters thus appear to be on the way out in these habitats.

Long-distance migrants as a group are vulnerable in another way. They are frequently single-brooded (Whitcomb et al. 1981). Once a pair successfully fledges young, even if only a single chick, it may not attempt to renest. If success is achieved early in the season, the parents may make a second attempt, but two broods are the maximum. The adults then escort their offspring for much of the time remaining before the southward migration begins.

In contrast, many resident species and short-distance migrants routinely attempt second and even third broods. This is true of mourning doves, mockingbirds, house wrens, robins, cardinals, and song sparrows. Most of these arrive earlier and stay later than tropical migrants and hence have time for more attempts in a season. It may be sheer persistence that is keeping them in the running.

Yet another factor that may prejudice tropical migrants is that most of them are small and unable to drive off squirrels, blue jays, or house cats. Larger residents such as mourning doves, mockingbirds, robins, cardinals, and grackles are more likely to be able to defend their nests, particularly against jays. Wilcove observed that jays raided nests singly rather than in groups. A lone thief might not care to tangle with a highly agitated pair of cardinals or catbirds, while a pair of warblers or vireos would be much less intimidating.

In sum, tropical migrants seem to have three strikes against them in relation to nest predators: (1) most build cup nests that are placed in the open, frequently on the ground; (2) many are single brooded, and (3) most are poorly equipped to defend their nests against blue jays and other marauding species. When all these points of vulnerability are considered, the selective disappearance of long-distance migrants no longer seems so mysterious.

Parasites

We come to the last of our troika of potential culprits: parasites. Here there is an obvious suspect: the brown-headed cowbird, termed a parasite because of its habit of laying eggs in other species' nests. Cowbirds are becoming a serious problem throughout the United States due to the historical increase in open habitats where they feed.

Already cowbirds have effectively eliminated one species, the Kirtland's warbler. Successful reproduction by the 200-odd remaining pairs is assured only through a concerted annual campaign to remove cowbirds from the breeding habitat (Mayfield 1977). During the 1960s before the removal program had begun, cowbirds were parasitizing 70 percent of the nests, and few young warblers were being fledged, fewer than needed to compensate for adult mortality (Mayfield 1983; Walkinshaw 1983). If the cowbird removal program was relaxed for just five years, the species would probably be extinct. As it is, to keep the Kirtland's warbler with us, we must be psychologically prepared to do annual battle with cowbirds for the indefinite future.

Other species are not far behind. The least Bell's vireo has been eliminated by cowbirds from all but a tiny remnant of its erstwhile range in California (Goldwasser et al. 1980), and the endemic black-capped vireo of Oklahoma and Texas seems to be following in its footsteps. Still other species may be in worse jeopardy than we currently realize because threshold effects are involved. A host species will appear to be holding its own

FIG. 5.4 Kirtland's warbler

until parasitism reduces its breeding success to below the replacement rate. Beyond that point a crash is unavoidable and can occur precipitously (May and Robinson 1985).

Whereas brown-headed cowbirds are believed to have used roughly 50 host species in precolonial times, they now parasitize some 200 (Mayfield 1965). Many of these new hosts may be especially vulnerable because they have no innate defenses, such as recognition and "dumping" of cowbird eggs.

Still another insidious trait of cowbirds is their tendency to prefer certain hosts. A particularly dramatic example of this is the case of the shiny cowbird, a South American species that has recently invaded Puerto Rico. Here it encountered the endemic yellow-shouldered blackbird, a species that so far as is known had never experienced cowbird parasitism in its evolutionary history. Shiny cowbirds have shown such a marked preference for yellow-shouldered blackbirds that the latter species has become as gravely endangered as the Kirtland's warbler (Post and Wiley 1977). Since its invasion of Puerto Rico, the shiny cowbird has continued to expand its range in the Caribbean region, and in 1985 reached southern Florida where it now co-occurs with the brown-headed cowbird (Smith and Sprunt 1987). What this double-barreled scourge will do to Florida's avifauna remains to be seen.

Given that cowbirds accept many hosts, a preferred host may not account for more than a small fraction of the cowbirds fledged each year. Cowbird numbers can thus continue to build up while the population of a preferred host decreases, forcing an accelerating decline in its numbers. There is no latitude for complacence when dealing with cowbirds.

I have already mentioned why some of the factors that kept cowbirds in equilibrium with their hosts prior to settlement have been relaxed. The creation of huge expanses of agricultural land in the previously forested East has greatly increased the amount of foraging habitat. Grain, especially rice, left in fields after mechanical harvesting, along with the widespread availability of feeding stations, has vastly expanded the species' winter food supply (Meanley 1971). Forest fragmentation has multiplied the amount of exposed edge along which cowbirds have access to species nesting in the forest interior. This, in turn, has been partly responsible for the fourfold increase in the number of host species being parasitized.

The explosion in cowbird numbers has impelled a major expansion of the geographical distribution of the species. Prior to settlement, it was essentially a bird of the Great Plains, but today it occupies the entire continent north to the boreal forest (Mayfield 1977). Meanwhile, range expansion has brought it into contact with still more new hosts. We see here the effects of positive feedback loops driving a system toward a state that is far removed from the natural equilibrium.

The increase in cowbird numbers that has taken place in the current century is truly fantastic. This can be judged from Christmas Count records that go back to 1900 (see Figure 5.5). Some of the population increase is dispersed over a larger geographical area, as explained above, but much of it contributes to higher local densities of cowbirds during the breeding season. This translates to greater numbers of cowbirds per available host, hence higher levels of parasitism than our native birds have ever previously experienced.

These levels of parasitism can be alarming. The Smithsonian Institution's Russell Greenberg, who has been studying worm-eating warblers at Sugarloaf Mountain near Frederick, Maryland, reports that every one of the 20-plus nests he has found in the past two years has been parasitized. His colleague, Eugene Morton, is finding that the situation of hooded warblers is similar. In a third study in Illinois, Scott Robinson found a total of 37 cowbird eggs in 11 wood thrush nests, versus only 12 eggs of the host species. In a total of 30 wood thrush clutches or broods examined by Robinson, 29 had been parasitized. Robinson's assessment of the situation is that "wood thrushes are doing nothing but raising cowbirds." None of the

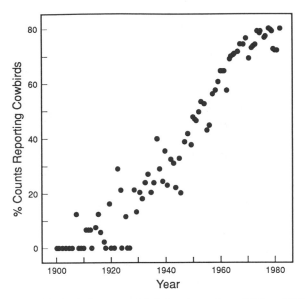

FIG. 5.5 An index to cowbird abundance from 1900 to 1980 taken from Audubon Christmas bird count records (Brittingham and Temple 1983).

FIG. 5.6 Brown-headed cowbird

victims mentioned above is a historical host of cowbirds, and worm-eating and hooded warblers have declined precipitously in recent years in middle Atlantic woodlands (Powell and Rappole 1986). Reports from elsewhere in the country are hardly more encouraging: 65 percent of all nests found along the edge of woodlands in Wisconsin, for example, were parasitized (Brittingham and Temple 1983). These are not numbers one can pass off lightly, especially in view of the thresholds involved in species' declines.

Might cowbirds be playing a part in the decline of migratory forest songbirds? Again, as with predation, there is only circumstantial evidence, but it is persuasive circumstantial evidence. Wilcove (1985a) found that cowbirds were more abundant along edges than several hundred meters into the forest interior. Nevertheless, spot censuses conducted in Maryland showed them to be present in the interior of woodlots of all sizes up to 1,000 acres (Wilcove 1985a). Much the same result has been obtained in Wisconsin (Brittingham and Temple 1983).

The latter authors carried the analysis one step further to show that parasitism rates decreased from an average of 1.1 cowbird egg per nest near forest edges to 0.23 egg per nest in locations more than 300 meters from the nearest edge. I have personally found cowbirds more than 2 kilometers into the Monangahela National Forest in West Virginia, but such occurrences are rare. Wilcove (1985a) detected none in several weeks' fieldwork in the interior of the Great Smoky Mountains National Park. Apart from the few remaining large tracts of unbroken forest, most of which are in the Appalachians, songbirds have few refuges from cowbirds. What can be concluded from this?

A great deal of research has been invested in cowbirds, to the point that the species is coming to be one of the best studied North American birds. We know that its numbers have increased explosively in this century, that its geographical distribution has greatly expanded in postsettlement times, and that its host range has perhaps quadrupled. We also know that cowbirds feed predominantly in agricultural land, and that egg-laying females concentrate their nest hunting activities along habitat edges (Rothstein et al. 1984). And we know that rates of parasitism are extremely high in many parts of the country, especially on certain preferred hosts. But in the absence of carefully conducted demographic studies, all this does not *prove* in a scientifically rigorous fashion that cowbirds are causing their hosts to decline. The only irrefutable case that has been made so far is that of the Kirtland's warbler.

The population of this highly endangered species has been under intensive investigation. Banding and nesting studies have produced data on overwinter survival, and the reproductive success of nesting pairs has been determined in the presence and absence of parasitism. When cowbirds have unrestricted access to Kirtland's warbler nests, the pairs simply do not produce enough young to offset normal mortality in the population. One cannot argue with such facts as these (Walkinshaw 1983).

Kirtland's warblers can be studied in such detail because the global population consists of only a few hundred individuals that nest in a small portion of one state. The logistical obstacles to studying more widespread species in similar depth are practically insurmountable.

The most valiant attempt to do something like this is contained in Nolan's (1978) monumental study of the prairie warbler in Indiana. Nolan found that 24 percent of prairie warbler nests suffered parasitism by cowbirds, and that parasitized nests produced only 0.9 fledglings versus 3.4 for unparasitized nests. Similarly drastic effects of parasitism have been documented for a number of other species (May and Robinson 1985). The relatively low parasitism rate of 24 percent in the prairie warbler might be comfortably sustained by the population, were it not for the fact that nearly 80 percent of all nesting attempts fail due to predation. Many pairs thus did not produce any young in a season, and those that did sometimes expended their efforts in rearing cowbirds.

Using computer simulation models, Nolan estimated that the effect of cowbirds was to reduce the annual production of young that could be expected to survive until the next breeding season from 79 to 69 per 100 females. At first glance, this may not seem like a serious decrement, but to know its effect on the population, the net production of young has to be balanced against mortality. Returns of banded adults suggested that annual survival was 65 percent, implying a mortality of 35 percent. Thus, of 100 females breeding in one season, 35 would not return to breed again the next year. But in the presence of cowbirds, 100 females produce only 70 young, of which approximately 35 will be females. Indiana prairie warblers thus seem to be balanced right on the demographic threshold: were there no cowbirds, the population would be producing a comfortable annual surplus of young; if parasitism were to increase slightly, the population would go into steady decline. On top of high rates of nest predation, the burden of parasitism can push a population over the demographic edge.

In view of the extreme pressure being applied to many songbird populations by the double-barreled effects of nest predators and cowbirds, one can marvel that things are not worse than they are. Why aren't many populations disappearing altogether? In the absence of detailed demographic studies, such as those on the Kirtland's and prairie warblers, one cannot make any definitive statement. What is clear is that the densities of nest predators and cowbirds are highest in suburban and agricultural areas, and that these are the environments that have seen the greatest changes in their bird communities.

The largest remaining expanses of unbroken forest retain what appear to be healthy communities, in which two-thirds or more of the breeding pairs are tropical migrants. From this arises a suggestion that has been offered by a number of my colleagues. The remaining large tracts of forest may be producing a surplus of young each year, and these young may then be replenishing the stocks of breeders in outlying areas where the annual production of fledglings is insufficient to offset mortality (Askins et al. 1987). If this is true, bird populations in major portions of the East would be receiving hidden subsidies, permitting them to live, as it were, beyond their means.

Such a mechanism as this seems necessary, for example, to account for the persistence of worm-eating warblers on Sugarloaf Mountain, Maryland, where literally every nest is parasitized by cowbirds. Much more research will have to be done before we know how many species are receiving hidden subsidies, and over what areas, but in the meantime we can appreciate, perhaps more than before, the value of our great national forests and parks as songbird reservoirs.

6 *The Mystery of the Missing Songbirds, Part II: Where Is the Problem?*

In recent years when I have gone into the woods near Washington in late May or June, they have seemed strangely silent. The accustomed sounds of black-and-white warblers, redstarts, hooded and Kentucky warblers have been missing. There are woodpeckers, chickadees, Carolina wrens, and others, but the species that are so conspicuously absent, without exception, are tropical migrants.

In Chapter 5 we reviewed some of the reasons these long-distance migrants, rather than year-round residents or short-distance migrants, might be particularly hard hit by the ecological correlates of urbanization—abnormal numbers of nest predators and parasites. Still, the uncanny consistency with which the missing or diminished species are tropical migrants has raised the possibility of another explanation—loss of wintering habitat through tropical deforestation. Just as most of the affected species nest in forests while they are at the northern end of their migratory circuits, so do they tend to winter in forests at the southern end of these circuits. The cause for concern is that the tropical forests that provide winter habitat for many species—just like the prairie potholes of our northern plains—are being lost to agricultural expansion. When winter habitat is severely altered or, more commonly, eliminated altogether, the birds that live in it have nowhere to go and presumably perish.

Tropical forests are being felled worldwide at a rate estimated at 2–4 percent a year (Myers 1980; Melillo et al. 1985). Satellite images show that deforestation is particularly advanced in areas where large numbers of North American migrants spend the winter—in southern Mexico, Central America, and the West Indies. One can fly across Cuba, for example, and see nothing from coast to coast but an endless sea of sugarcane. It seems reasonable to suppose, then, that such major modifications of the natural landscape will have had a measurable effect in reducing migrant numbers.

This is an easy suggestion to make, but a difficult one to test. Far more accurate statistics are available on the numbers of prairie potholes remaining in the Dakotas than on the condition of habitats in the countries south of our border. Accurate information is potentially obtainable through the analysis of satellite images, but this entails great expense, both in computer time and in personnel. Mainly for these reasons, none of the major conservation organizations has yet initiated a large-scale program to monitor land-use trends in the tropics. The information that is available is of spotty quality and rapidly becomes outdated. It is clear that a major project is called for, and it is to be hoped that one will be launched in the near future.

THE FIRST VICTIM?

There is at least one plausible case of a species whose numbers have declined from the wholesale destruction of its wintering grounds. This is the elusive Bachman's warbler, now so rare that it teeters on the brink of extinction. A century ago the species was widespread, if uncommon, across the South. Breeding records exist for a block of states from Virginia through Kentucky to Missouri and south to the Gulf Coast. By the early decades of this century, its numbers had dwindled and it gained a reputation for extreme rarity. By the 1950s it could reliably be seen only in a few spots in coastal South Carolina, although scattered birds occasionally turned up elsewhere (Hamel 1986).

I was once lucky enough to see one of these. One evening in May 1954, an acquaintance from the local Audubon Naturalist Society called me to pass the word that one had been discovered that day on Pohick Creek, a minor tributary of the Potomac south of Washington. I doubt that news of any other bird on earth would have been so exciting to me at the time.

The next morning I was on the road by four-thirty, driving through the darkness with fears that my quarry might vanish with first light. The spot on Pohick Creek where the bird had been sighted was on the estate of Paul Bartsch, a renowned Smithsonian scientist, one of whose many accomplishments was to introduce bird banding to the United States. I had been to his estate many times before and knew the way well. He was always hospitable to birdwatchers, so I didn't hesitate to drive up the long entrance lane and park beside his colonial manor.

By the time I had reached the banks of Pohick Creek, the sun was shining brightly, and birds were singing everywhere. I was familiar with the sounds of all the local species and was mentally sorting through them for something unusual. The song of the Bachman's had been described to me as resembling that of a black-throated green warbler with a redstart-like downward sweep at the end: "zee-zee-zee-zee-tsew."

To my astonishment, I walked up to the place that had been described to me and heard it! I had no trouble seeing the bird. A full-plumaged male, it sat on an open branch about 20 feet up and gave me a perfect view while it sang. It hardly stopped singing during the two hours I spent there. Reluctantly, I pulled myself away, wondering whether this was an experience I would ever repeat. It was not.

FIG. 6.1 Bachman's warbler

I later learned that a Bachman's warbler, presumably the same bird, reappeared on the banks of Pohick Creek during the next two springs. There was never a hint of a female, and indeed, the extraordinary vocal exertions of the male suggested that he was in search of a mate. Since that time, Bachman's warblers have been seen barely a handful of times anywhere in the country. It is quite possible that the species is already extinct.

Although no one knows with certainty what has happened to the Bachman's warbler, my guess is that it lost out on the wintering grounds. All known winter specimens and sight records are from Cuba (Hamel 1986). Large parts of the island were once covered with dense evergreen forest similar to the southern bottomland hardwood forests in which it was known to nest. Although 80 percent of its U.S. habitat has now been cleared for soybeans and rice cultivation, this does not seem enough to account for the complete disappearance of the species (Tiner 1984). There are other southern bottomland warblers, such as the Swainson's and prothonotary whose breeding habitat has been similarly reduced, but these remain plentiful where suitable conditions still occur. Something else has happened to the Bachman's warbler.

That something else may well have been the rise of the sugar industry in Cuba. By the mid-1950s the island's forest cover had been reduced to 15 percent of its original extent, and clearing continued, even in mountainous country unsuitable for cultivation (Smith 1954). But this fact alone does not account for the extinction of the species. There would still have been survivors in the remaining pockets of forest vegetation, even if their numbers were small. What is more likely to have delivered the coup de grace was the consequent dilution of the breeding population.

Small migratory songbirds are not known to winter as pairs. Males tend to arrive first on the breeding grounds to establish territories and are later joined by females seeking mates. Males and females may often return to the same general area to breed in successive years, but banding studies indicate that it is unusual for the same individuals to pair more than once. The separate arrival of males and females thus requires that potential mates find each other. This is the problem.

By the 1950s most of Cuba's evergreen forest had already been converted to sugarcane fields, whereas large areas of bottomland hardwoods remained in the United States. There thus developed a gross imbalance between the area available for wintering and the area available for breeding.

I imagine that each spring a tiny remnant of birds crossed the Gulf of Mexico and fanned out into a huge area in the Southeast, where they became, so to speak, needles in a haystack. Toward the end, it is likely that most of the males in the population, like the one at Pohick Creek, were never discovered by females. Once this situation developed, there could have been no possible salvation for the species in the wild. The threat of continuing tropical deforestation is that this scenario will be repeated.

TROUBLE ON THE WINTERING GROUND?

How would it be possible to discover that tropical deforestation, or indeed any form of inimical environmental destruction along the migration route, was decimating a species that bred in North America? Here again we are faced with the less than ideal task of drawing inferences from circumstantial evidence. Moreover, we must be careful not to confuse the finding of local extinctions brought about by excesses of nest predators and parasites with evidence of a general population decline (Wilcove and Terborgh 1984).

One way these complicating factors can be avoided is by examining bird populations in the largest remaining blocks of mature vegetation. In such habitats, one can more or less safely presume that there has been no local alteration of conditions that would have affected the density of breeding species. In this situation, the expectation ("null hypothesis") is that of stasis, that is, no change over time in the density of each species. Testing the null hypothesis, as explained in Chapter 3, requires long-term records for designated census plots.

Unfortunately, there are very few data sets that meet the required qualifications. I shall present the two that seem most appropriate, one from West Virginia, the other from the Great Smoky Mountains. The first of these was obtained by George Hall and his energetic associates in the Brooks Bird Club (Hall 1984). Since 1947 they have been conducting breeding bird censuses in a virgin tract of red spruce–northern hardwoods forest in West Virginia. Their results indicate a steady decline in the numbers of several tropical migrants (see Table 6.1).

TABLE 6.1 Density and Diversity of Birds Nesting in a
Virgin Spruce-Hardwood Forest in West Virginia, 1947–83

Date	Total no. species	Density (pairs/100 ha.)	Total Neotropical species	Density of Neotropical species
1947	25	325	14	238
1948	27	376	14	243
1953	28	369	16	238
1958	18	233	9	119
1964	13	288	8	175
1968	17	373	9	181
1973	15	273	8	105
1978	15	253	8	164
1983	15	273	8	150

Source: Hall 1984.

Since no other cause was apparent, Hall concluded that the declines were possibly due to tropical deforestation. But as we saw above in the case of the redhead in Chesapeake Bay, one is taking a risk in attributing a local development to a global cause. Here the data derive from a single 6 hectare (15 acre) plot where the average number of breeding pairs is only one to two per species. Moreover, the results refer to only one forest type that could possibly be anomalous in some way. If the trends observed by Hall and his associates are truly general, they should be paralleled in other similar studies.

Unfortunately, comparable studies from large tracts of old-growth forest were not to be found in the literature, or at least not prior to 1981, when an astonishing paper appeared in the *Wilson Bulletin* describing the results of breeding bird censuses made in the Great Smoky Mountains National Park some 33 years before (Kendeigh and Fawver 1981). Some scientists are notoriously slow to publish their results, but never had I encountered so extreme a case as this. Nevertheless, it could not have appeared at a more propitious time.

David Wilcove was just then planning his doctoral research on the disappearance of tropical migrants in fragmented eastern forests. When the Kendeigh and Fawver paper came to our attention, everything else was put on hold. It was already March or April and Dave was preparing to depart for the field in Maryland only a few weeks hence. Through some quick telephoning, he obtained the use of a small cabin in the the Smokies that belonged to the Biology Department of the University of Tennessee. From there he could reach most of the sites he wanted to census by or before dawn.

The Smokies lie at the heart of one of the largest forested areas in the East and retain some of the last remaining virgin tracts of several forest types. A number of the plots censused by Fawver in the 1940s had been in these virgin tracts.

The most difficult challenge faced by Wilcove lay in relocating the exact plots that Fawver had censused 33 years before. This required some detective work. Fawver himself was extremely helpful in several protracted telephone conversations. His Ph.D. thesis provided detailed botanical descriptions of the plots and instructions on how to reach them (Fawver 1950). The trouble was that many trails in the park had been relocated in the intervening years. Outdated maps on file in the park library and recollections of long-time residents helped fill in the missing information.

In the end, Wilcove recensused ten of Fawver's original plots, rejecting those that had been disturbed by road construction or modified naturally by vegetational succession. The ten plots represented mixed hardwood (cove) forest (three sites), hemlock-deciduous forest (three sites), chestnut oak forest (two sites), red oak forest (one site) and beech gap forest (one site).

Nine of the ten plots were located in virgin forest. The tenth was a low-elevation cove forest that had been logged sometime in the nineteenth century and was approaching maturity by 1947. Another site, although unlogged, had formerly been dominated by American chestnut. Nearly 30 percent of the standing trunks in 1947 had been dead chestnuts. By 1982 the canopy had filled in with oaks whose shade had reduced the density of the understory compared with 1947. With these two minor exceptions, Wilcove found the plots to be otherwise botanically identical to their conditions in 1947. It would be nearly impossible to locate another set of plots in the eastern United States that had experienced so little change in the last 30 years.

TABLE 6.2 Neotropical Migrants and Other Birds Nesting in Ten Virgin Forest Plots in the Great Smoky Mountains National Park, 1947–48 and 1982–83

	Tropical migrants (pairs/10 ha.)			Other species (pairs/10 ha.)		
Locality	*1947–48*	*1982*	*1983*	*1947–48*	*1982*	*1983*
Cove forests						
Lower Ramsey Creek	53.0	54.5	—	10.0	14.0	—
Middle Ramsey Creek	19.0	25.0	15.0	5.0	13.0	10.0
Lower Porter Creek	36.5	34.5	—	13.5	16.0	—
Hemlock-deciduous forest						
Spruce Flats	35.0	34.0	25.0	10.5	7.5	12.0
Roaring Fork	58.0	67.0	42.0	22.0	25.0	24.0
Brushy Mountain	48.5	57.5	—	25.0	32.0	—
Chestnut oak forest						
Bullhead Trail	24.0	33.0	—	6.5	13.0	—
Greenbriar Pinnacle	41.0	30.5	29.5	15.0	7.5	11.0
Red oak forest						
Greenbriar Pinnacle	35.0	18.0	—	5.0	27.5	—
Beech gap forest						
Double Spring Gap	13.5	7.0	—	16.5	20.5	
Total	363.5	361.0		129.0	176.0	

Source: Fawver 1950 and Wilcove 1985.

Wilcove's results bore this out. In contrast with what Hall had found in West Virginia, the number of tropical migrants breeding in the ten Smoky Mountain plots had not changed at all (see Table 6.2). In fact, there were larger differences in the results for the four plots Wilcove censused in 1982 and 1983 than there were between 1947–48 and 1982 (Wilcove 1988).

Although the grand totals for all ten plots indicate no overall change in the number of tropical migrants, there were several individual species that seemed to have increased or decreased. The rose-breasted grosbeak was present in five of the plots in 1982 versus two in the 1940s. Neither the northern parula warbler nor indigo bunting was recorded by Fawver, but Wilcove found the warbler at four sites in 1982 and at a fifth in 1983, while the bunting appeared in two localities and was represented by a surprising ten pairs in one. Because of the small numbers involved, only the increase in indigo buntings was statistically significant. We shall see later that all three of these birds commonly winter in tropical second growth.

Four species declined sufficiently to warrant special mention. These were the wood thrush, chestnut-sided warbler, blackburnian warbler, and hooded warbler. Only one of these declines was statistically significant,

however (the chestnut-sided warbler at Double Spring Gap). We shall see
later that all four of these species winter predominantly in primary tropical
forest.

Surprisingly, the most striking population changes documented by Wilcove were in the set of species that are resident in the park or migrate only
within the United States. Birds in this category increased by 36 percent in
the 31-year interval, an amount that is highly significant statistically. This
increase resulted in a 9 percent rise in the total number of birds recorded in
the ten plots, and a consequent decline, from 74 percent to 67 percent, in
the proportion of tropical migrants.

The increase in short-distance migrants and residents was primarily contributed by three species: blue jay, American crow, and dark-eyed junco.
Fawver recorded jays as breeding at only one site and casually present at
two others. By 1982 jays were breeding in seven of the ten plots. Fawver
did not find crows at any of the sites; Wilcove found them at three. Juncos
increased even more dramatically. Fawver had them at six sites, but commonly only at the three that were highest in elevation. Wilcove had them
at all ten sites and documented overall more than twice the number recorded by Fawver (81 vs 36).

At first glance, jays, crows, and juncos represent an odd trio. What they
have in common is that they are short-distance migrants that profit oppor-
tunistically from winter food supplies provided by humans. Jays and juncos are commonplace visitors to feeding stations, whereas crows, like Canada geese, feed on the wastage in cornfields.

The total amount of food available from both sources is staggering. U.S.
citizens buy over $500 million worth of birdseed every year (Klinger
1982). This is enough to provide a pound of seed to each of more than 1
billion birds. Given that our most abundant species, such as robins, grackles, red-wings, and song sparrows, have world populations that number
in the tens or, at most, hundreds of millions, the dietary supplement we
provide at feeders is enough to sustain the entire populations of several
species.

What are the effects of this massive intervention at a time of year when
energetic stress can lead to high mortality? It would be a simple matter to
compare the winter densities of jays, juncos, and song sparrows in suburban areas that were well provided with feeders with those in rural areas that
were not, but I have not run across such a study.

Corroborative support for an increase in blue jays has been obtained
from Christmas Count results. According to Bock and Lepthien (1976), the
North American blue jay population grew 30 percent between 1962 and
1972, presumably in response to the abundant resources available at feeders. Small but significant increases in eastern crow populations have been

documented by the Breeding Bird Survey, but junco numbers have shown no change on a continentwide scale.

It is noteworthy that two of the species that have increased in the Smokies, blue jay and common crow, are leading nest predators. Now that their populations have been enhanced by both intentional and unintentional supplements to their winter food supplies, they seem to be penetrating the East's ultimate forest stronghold. Nest predation rates in the Smokies are still very low, as we saw in Chapter 5, but any increase in predator density must be considered an adverse trend.

Fortunately, cowbirds have not yet arrived on the scene. In two seasons of censusing, Wilcove found none in the virgin forest plots. This should not be cause for complacency. If their numbers continue to increase according to the trend seen in the recent past, it can be expected that they will become ever more insistent in pursuit of their victims. The best protection for songbirds is retaining the largest possible blocks of intact forest.

We can feel relieved, even if only temporarily, that Wilcove's findings upheld the null hypothesis. The results as a whole are reassuring, since nothing drastic has yet happened to the populations of tropical migrants breeding in one of the East's most pristine sanctuaries. Although we should keep a watchful eye on hooded and blackburnian warblers, and perhaps a few others, in general they seem to be holding their own where local pressures are not depressing their nesting success. Nevertheless, Hall's results from West Virginia and the few nonsignificant suggestions of declines in the Smokies could represent the first signs of trouble. Only time will tell.

Regardless of the current situation, the threat of tropical deforestation remains a potentially severe future threat. What happened to the Bachman's warbler can easily happen again. With our woefully inadequate data base, we may not discover that something is amiss until it is too late to act. This is why it is worth taking a closer look at the tropics now. By understanding what is happening there, we can prepare ourselves better for what is to come.

POSTSCRIPT

As this goes to press I have just learned of a unique study that provides a tropical counterpart to the results of Hall and Fawver/Wilcove. The authors have systematically netted birds each year in January in the Guanica Forest of Puerto Rico between 1973 and 1988 (Faaborg and Arendt ms). The Guanica Forest is protected, and over this period has not experienced discernible change, either in its vegetation or resident avifauna. Nevertheless, the numbers of wintering migrants captured there have declined steadily (see Figure 6.2). Some species that were common at the begining of the period, such as parula, Cape May, and prairie warblers, have not been captured since 1985, whereas others—black-and-white warbler and redstart—seem to be holding their own. How these results are to be interpreted in terms of possible global trends is not clear, although the signs are obviously not propitious.

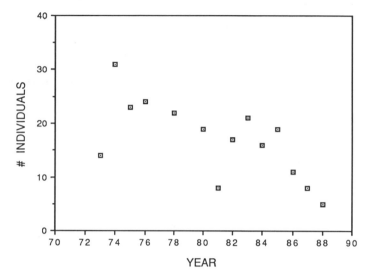

FIG. 6.2 North American migrants captured in mist nets in the Guanica Forest, Puerto Rico, 1973–88 (J. Faaborg unpublished data).

7 Summer North, Winter South: Where Migrants Spend Their Lives

The arrivals and departures of migratory species adhere to an orderly sequence whose schedule any seasoned birder knows by heart. February brings woodcock, redwings, and grackles; with March come wood ducks, phoebes, and tree swallows; in April we expect pectoral sandpipers, barn swallows, and palm warblers; and scores of others in May.

Our common lore about these birds is curiously one-sided. Ask any accomplished birder, and he or she will tell you just which mountaintops in New England have breeding populations of blackpoll warblers, and just where in Maryland one might see a Swainson's warbler, but ask the same people where these birds spend the winter, and the chances are you will draw a blank. The birds come north in the spring and fly south in the fall, but most of us give little thought as to where they go. It's about time we did, because where the birds spend the winter is every bit as important to their lives as where they spend the summer.

To this end I shall present a brief overview of the distribution of North American long-distance migrants at both ends of their migratory routes. By long-distance (or Neotropical) migrants, I mean species that breed mainly in the temperate region of North America and winter mainly to the south of the Tropic of Cancer. There are approximately 250 species that conform to this definition. We shall see that the distributions of these species are aggregated, that is, that there are habitats and regions that harbor large numbers of them and other areas where there are relatively few. An appreciation of these distributional patterns will be important for assigning priorities in any future conservation plan.

MIGRANTS ON THE BREEDING GROUNDS: WHERE ARE THEY?

The Breeding Bird Census, published annually in *American Birds* through 1984, presented information on the breeding communities of plots representing a wide range of habitat types over all of North America. The data contained in these censuses is not without its limitations, as we saw in Chapter 3, but they nevertheless constitute a vast storehouse of information that has been underutilized for scientific purposes.

Here we shall make use of the censuses reported in the January–February 1984 issue of *American Birds*, to demonstrate the continentwide pattern of distribution of Neotropical migrants. Our task would be easier if the volunteers had been encouraged to spread their coverage of habitats more evenly. The 212 reported censuses include 66, for example, from "eastern deciduous forest," but only 5 from "eastern coniferous forest," and none from the great boreal forest that extends across the continent from the Canadian maritime to Alaska.

The disparities in geographical coverage are equally pronounced. There are only two censuses reported from Florida, and only one to represent the entire Gulf Coast region west of Florida, and that one is described as "Suburban Cemetery." The vast expanse of the Southwest, with its plains, deserts, canyons, and mountains, is represented by only three censuses, one each from Texas, New Mexico, and Arizona, and one of these is described as "Shaded Ranch House on High Plains," a site that was obviously close to the contributor's heart, but of dubious value to any broader conservation need. Clearly there is a lot of room for improvement in the organization of these volunteer efforts.

Notwithstanding the omission of many important habitats from the published censuses, the information available is sufficient for resolving broad geographical patterns. If we are interested in the overall numbers of Neotropical migrants, then we must look at both the density of breeding birds in different types of vegetation and the proportion of all breeding pairs in these habitats that are long-distance migrants. By multiplying these two values together and taking means, one obtains estimates for the average number of pairs of migrants per unit area of each type of habitat (see Table 7.1).

Long-distance migrants play a larger role in the bird communities of the North and East than of the South and West. Mature eastern deciduous forest supports high densities of breeding birds, of which nearly 70 percent migrate to the tropics. Each square kilometer of this habitat supports approximately 600 pairs of long-distance migrants. No other habitat comes close to matching this number. Given the immense size of the eastern deciduous forest, which extends from southern Canada to the Gulf Coast and from the Atlantic seaboard to the Great Plains, one easily estimates that in presettlement times the region accommodated nearly 2 billion migrants. With the complex transformation of the landscape that has occurred following settlement, this number has surely diminished, probably to far less than half of its original value. The estimation of current numbers of migrants is an important conservation issue, one to which we shall return later.

The pattern of occurrence of migrants in the central and western portions

TABLE 7.1 Densities of Neotropical Migrants in Some North American Habitats

Vegetation type	No. of censuses	Pairs km²	% migrants	Pairs migrants/ km²
Eastern deciduous forest	10	863	68	587
Eastern coniferous forest	6	644	64	412
Central oak-hickory forest	7	417	45	188
Prairie grassland, tall	10	214	47	101
Prairie grassland, short	3	174	3	5
Cultivated field, Iowa	2	24	0	0
Rocky Mountains, deciduous forest	6	449	70	315
Rocky Mountains, coniferous forest	7	382	18	69
Riparian, California	7	1596	25	399
Chaparral, California	6	608	10	61
Tundra, Alaska	7	79	36	28

Source: *American Birds*, 1983 and 1984.

of the continent is more complex than in the East, though the reasons for this complexity are only dimly understood by ornithologists.

Take the prairies for example. Nearly half the birds in tall-grass prairie are long-distance migrants, whereas only 3 percent of those in short-grass prairie are. The superficial reason for this is that the tall-grass bird community is dominated by insectivores, including such migrants as bobolinks, yellowthroats, yellow warblers, and dickcissels. The short-grass prairie, for some reason, has few obligate insectivores, and instead is dominated by facultative seed eaters such as horned larks, lark buntings, and grasshopper sparrows, or in another case, by savannah sparrows, western meadowlarks, Sprague's pipits, and Baird's sparrows. Although the two types of prairie seem similar to the undiscerning human eye, the birds don't see them that way, and the respective communities are consequently quite different.

Our perspective on the bird communities of the Great Plains would be severely biased if we failed to include at least a token plot or two of cultivated land. The tall-grass prairie is largely a thing of the past, and the contemporary landscape of states such as Illinois and Iowa is completely dominated by cornfields. In two Iowa plots, the bird density was a mere 24 pairs per square kilometer, by far the lowest value recorded for any habitat. One hundred and fifty years ago the same land would have been tall-grass prairie or central oak-hickory forest, and as such would have accommodated 100-200 pairs of migrants per square kilometer. As cornfield, the same land supports very few birds of any kind, and no long-distance migrants at all. It is essential to note such changes as this in the carrying capacity of our own landscape before we attempt to evaluate the effects of habitat alteration in the tropical wintering grounds.

In the Rocky Mountain region, long-distance migrants abound in deciduous woodlands but curiously seem to avoid coniferous forest. This is unfortunate, for deciduous forest in the western states is confined mainly to the bottoms of canyons and narrow riparian strips in the desert. These are among the most threatened habitats on the entire continent, since canyons are favored for residential development, and more than 90 percent of the original extent of desert riparian woodland has been eliminated for flood control or irrigation projects (Hendrickson and Kubly 1984). It thus seems probable that the populations of such typical riparian species as black-chinned hummingbird, Virginia's warbler, and lazuli bunting may already have been reduced to mere remnants of their former numbers. And now, just as this goes to press, comes the news that olive-sided flycatchers have disappeared from a plot of virgin sequoia forest in California (Marshall 1988). Let us hope that this report does not represent the beginning of a trend for the western states.

In the benign climate of Southern California, it is no surprise to find that the birds of chaparral are loath to migrate. The few that do are mostly hummingbirds and flycatchers. If the degree of seasonal change were the only predictor of migratory behavior, one could expect to find the strongest tendencies in the high Arctic. Yet the proportion of long-distance migrants nesting on the treeless tundra in Alaska is a modest 36 percent. The reason for this is that the most abundant bird on every plot was either lapland longspur or snow bunting, neither of which qualifies as a tropical migrant. Among the latter, pectoral sandpiper was the most numerous, followed by Baird's sandpiper, red phalarope, golden plover, and others. These are the champion long-distance migrants, for they all winter in southern South America, more than 10,000 kilometers from their summer homes.

This quick overview of the distribution of Neotropical migrants on the North American breeding grounds is less comprehensive than one might wish, although adequate to portray the broad geographical pattern (see Figure 7.1). Tropical migrants are concentrated in the eastern deciduous forest. Boreal forest also harbors large numbers of them, although this important habitat was missing from our survey due to a lack of any reported censuses in *American Birds*. Other habitats harbor lower densities and are far less extensive in area. A few species are abundant in the tall-grass prairies of the Great Plains, but west of the hundredth meridian, the proportion of long-distance migrants drops off drastically, except in riparian woodlands. Most of the West, as is evident to anyone who has driven

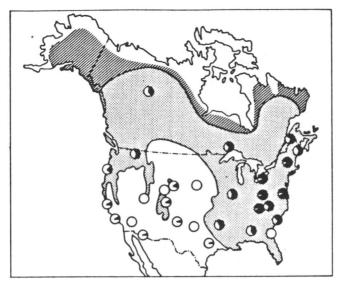

FIG. 7.1 The black portions of the circles represent the proportions of
Neotropical migrants in the breeding bird communities of mature
vegetation at the locations indicated. The forested region is stippled
(MacArthur 1972).

across it, is occupied by short-grass prairie, sagebrush, and desert scrub,
habitats that support few tropical migrants. The Neotropical migrants that
do breed in the West mostly frequent canyons and forests in the mountains.
Their total populations are consequently much smaller than those of their
eastern or boreal counterparts, a fact that makes western species particularly vulnerable.

The world populations of many shorebirds that breed along the Arctic
coasts are also relatively small and concentrated, and hence vulnerable to
localized environmental deterioration that might have only a slight effect
on a more widespread species. Thus, while the eastern deciduous and boreal forests are quantitatively the major sources of tropical migrants, the
West and Arctic may hold a larger number of potentially threatened species
(Hutto 1986).

MIGRANTS IN THE TROPICS: WHERE DO THEY GO?

Our knowledge of the winter ecology of Neotropical migrants is in a
nascent state. Far more is known about the routes and destinations of so-
called Palearctic migrants (species nesting in the temperate regions of the
Old World and migrating to the tropics). This is because the tropical regions of Africa and Asia were long held under the power of European

nations. The museums, universities, and learned societies of the colonial
states sent out countless expeditions to explore the far corners of their em-
pires, while administrative officers and other expatriates frequently contributed to the accumulation of knowledge.

One can point to many explanations for why we are so far behind in this
hemisphere—a lack of former colonial dependencies, unfamiliar languages
and cultures, difficulties of travel—but perhaps most important of all is a
lack, until recently, of field guides to Neotropical birds in general. The first
guide to tropical American birds was Blake's *Birds of Mexico* (1953).
Guides to other Neotropical areas subsequently began to appear in rapid
succession—the West Indies (Bond 1961), Guyana (Snyder 1966), Surinam (Haverschmidt 1968), Guatemala (Land 1970), South America
(Meyer de Schauensee 1970), Trinidad and Tobago (ffrench 1973), Panama (Ridgley 1976), Venezuela (Phelps and Meyer de Schauensee 1978),
and, most recently, Colombia (Hilty and Brown 1986).

Before these books appeared, not even trained ornithologists could reliably identify Neotropical birds in the field. Birdwatching as such was not
possible. Ornithological surveys were made down the barrel of a shotgun,
and the resulting study skins were shipped to museums. It is hardly an
exaggeration to say that until the 1970s nearly all we knew about Neotropical migrants in the winter was contained on the labels of hundreds of shot
specimens in the nation's museums. The broad outlines of winter ranges
were known, but that is about all. Such topics as diets, vocalizations, habitat preferences, social behavior, and territoriality had barely entered the
scientific literature. Quantitative information of any kind simply did not
exist.

With the appearance of modern field guides and the gradual decline of
shotgun ornithology, this impasse began to give way in the late 1960s and
early 1970s. After the first few pioneering reports had appeared in the literature, the study of migrants in the tropics suddenly became fashionable.
To the crypto-birdwatchers in the academic ranks, it became a respectable
excuse for escaping snowbound offices in midwinter. By the mid-1970s the
enthusiasm had snowballed into a minibandwagon, and scores of ornithologists were getting into the act, though little of their work had yet
found its way into print.

The sudden popularity of the subject, plus the awareness of a significant
accumulation of unpublished results, prompted Alan Keast of Queen's
University, Ontario, and Eugene Morton of the Smithsonian Institution to
organize a major symposium in the fall of 1977. This was held at the
Smithsonian's animal breeding facility at Front Royal, Virginia, and attracted 40 participants from the United States, Canada, and several Latin
American countries. The proceedings, edited by Keast and Morton, were
published in 1980 in a hefty tome that ran to 576 pages. Now, at last, there

was some quantitative information on which birds wintered where, and in what habitats. But this was 1980, eleven years after we had landed men on the moon.

The Geography of Migrants in the Winter

The main issue to which the participants at the Front Royal symposium addressed themselves was the basic one of where migrants spend the winter. Nearly half the reports are dedicated to providing simple descriptive statistics on the winter bird communities of tropical localities. One problem all these investigators had to resolve independently was how to conduct their surveys.

Since little such data had been gathered before, there were no standard methods. The spot mapping technique that is routinely used to census breeding birds cannot be applied to nonbreeding birds, because the underlying assumptions are violated in several ways. Many birds in the winter do not vocalize regularly or defend territories, few are associated in pairs, some are nomadic, others join flocks.

Neither was it practical to apply the methodology prescribed for conducting winter bird population studies in North America (Anonymous 1947, 1950). Many species are difficult to detect, much less to count, in the dense evergreen vegetation of the tropics. Observers from the north could instantly recognize black-and-white warblers, redstarts, and rose-breasted grosbeaks, but would often founder on the identifications of local species. Moreover, in the brevity of a between-semester break, time was of the essence. One did not have the leisure to set up measured plots and to conduct the repeated counts called for by the protocol set forth in *American Birds*. Instead, the displaced temperate ornithologist was obliged to improvise.

Perhaps because we all experienced the same difficulties and frustrations, a sizable fraction of the people who undertook to survey migrants in the tropics settled on the same two "quick-and-dirty" methods: transect counts and the capture of samples of birds in mist nets. Neither yields true population densities, that is, the number of individuals per unit area of habitat. Both rely on the presence of local resident species as a frame of reference against which to calibrate the abundance of migrants.

In one method an observer walks a transect, generally a road or path, through a particular type of habitat. He or she records all birds seen, and after a sufficient sample has been accumulated, the results are expressed as simple percentages of the total. In my own transect surveys, I tried to see at least 100 individual birds (not always an easy goal when birds are scarce). Since some species vocalize in the nonbreeding season and others do not, detecting birds by sound alone would have biased the result. I thus counted only those individuals that I saw well enough to identify by sight.

Unfamiliar resident species, provided I had a glimpse that would have sufficed to identify a familiar migrant, were included in the tallies as unknowns. A few unidentified sightings did not detract from the objective, which was to determine the proportion of migrants and the relative abundances of the individual species in each locality.

The results of such surveys are undoubtedly biased by a number of systematic errors. Conspicuous species, for example, are certain to be overrepresented. Noisiness, gregariousness, a tendency to select high, open perches or to be hyperactive, can all attract attention. At the opposite extreme, silent, skulky denizens of the understory are sure to be underrepresented.

To compensate for the bias inherent in visual surveys, many investigators have employed a second method: the use of mist nets. These are fashioned out of black nylon mesh reminiscent of hair netting, 12 meters long and strung between poles like a tennis net, but 2 meters high. It requires some old-fashioned sweat and toil to install them, but one can conquer even the most impenetrable tangles with a well-sharpened machete. Although nets can be arrayed in an infinite number of ways, I installed them end to end in a straight line. This standard method unambiguously defined one dimension of the area sampled. By operating 20 to 30 nets three or four consecutive days from dawn to dusk, I was usually rewarded with a sample of at least 100 different individual birds. Whenever possible, I tried to obtain samples of 100 or more birds by both visual count and netting at each locality visited. The data are presented in Figures 7.2 to 7.5. To flesh out the geographical picture, I have included published data of several additional investigators.

Certain patterns appear very clearly in the results. Regions close to the United States harbor large concentrations of migrants. Migrants can make up half or more of all birds present in parts of Mexico, the Bahamas, Hispaniola, and presumably Cuba. Although the proportions obtained within any country vary somewhat with habitat and elevation, in general, as one moves farther away from the United States, the relative abundance of migrants falls steadily. Some typical values are: Guatemala, Belize, 20–40 percent; Costa Rica, Panama, 10–30 percent; Puerto Rico, 10 percent; Guadeloupe, Trinidad, 1 percent; Venezuela, 1 percent; Ecuador, 1–15 percent; Peru, 0–5 percent. Migrants thus show a clear preference for the near over the far tropics.

Regarding the destinations of migrants, one should keep in mind that the distinction between the tropical and warm temperate regions of the hemisphere is entirely arbitrary. I have chosen to focus on the tropics because of our limited awareness of the conservation needs of the 250 species of North American birds that winter there. The fact remains, however, that still higher concentrations of migrants are found in our own southern

Fig. 7.2–7.5 Percentage of North American migrants in mist-net and transect samples at localities studied by the author. Symbols: M = mist-net sample; T = transect sample; P = primary vegetation; S = secondary vegetation (Fig. 7.2, Emlen 1980; Fig. 7.3, Waide et al. 1980).

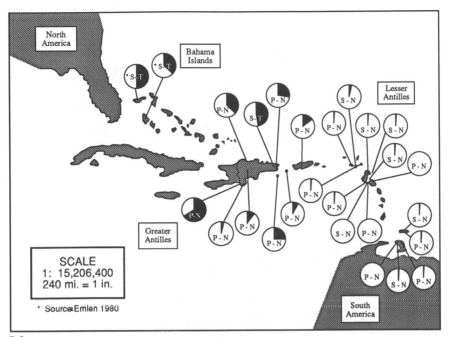

7.2

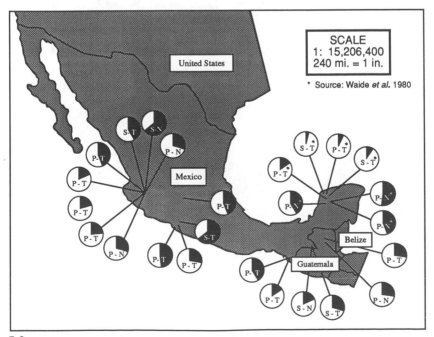

7.3

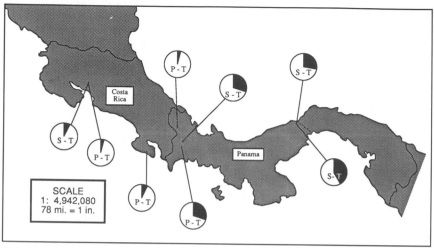

7.4

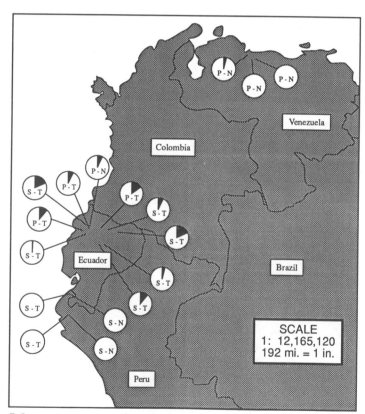

7.5

states. The proportion of migrants (here including any species wintering south of its breeding range) tallied in Christmas Counts in Florida and Texas ranges between 65 percent and 90 percent (*American Birds*). Some counts in these states report as many as 200 species, of which two-thirds may be migrants in the sense that they do not breed locally. The geographical zone in which migrant densities reach the highest levels is thus in our own country somewhat to the north of the actual tropics.

A second equally strong pattern is that species that breed only in the West tend overwhelmingly to winter in western Mexico. The reasons for this near unanimity of choice are probably proximity to the breeding ground and, as we shall see in Chapter 11, similarity of habitat.

A third, less obvious, pattern relates to the relative concentration of migrants on the breeding versus wintering grounds. The United States plus Canada north to the tree line represents an enormous area, approximately 16 million square kilometers. Within this vast region, the average species of long-distance migrant occupies a breeding range of several million square kilometers. But due to a caprice of geography, the near tropical region within which most species spend the winter comprises a far smaller area. Hence, many species do not enjoy the security of large geographical ranges in the tropics (see Table 7.2). Indeed, from the data presented above, it is easily estimated that more than half of all Neotropical migrants spend the winter in Mexico, the Bahamas, Cuba, and Hispaniola, which have a combined area of only 2.2 million square kilometers (Terborgh 1980). The populations of many species are thus highly compressed. In extreme cases, a species may be crowded into only a fifth or a tenth of the living space it occupies on the breeding grounds (Myers 1980).

The unsettling implication is that the felling of one hectare of rain forest for cattle pasture in Mexico or the Dominican Republic is equivalent in its effect to the construction of a 5 or 10 hectare shopping mall in Connecticut. Furthermore, the deforestation of a seemingly minor portion of the tropics, an event that might go almost unnoticed in the United States, could be devastating to one or another migrant species (one thinks again of the Bachman's warbler). Given the current pace of deforestation throughout Latin America, it is almost inevitable that other species are destined to follow the same fate.

Because migrant species are often localized on their wintering grounds, it does not suffice simply to note that more birds concentrate in the near versus the far tropics. An effective conservation plan must be minutely concerned with each species: precisely where it winters, what habitats it occupies within its winter range, and whether it accepts disturbed vegetation and second growth. But most urgently of all, we should be monitoring land use trends, country by country, to obtain advance warning of impending trouble.

Table 7.2 Principal Wintering Grounds of Neotropical Migrants

Guatemala / Mexico / Belize (2.11×10^6 km^2)

Flammulated owl	Lesser nighthawk	Ruby-throated hummingbird
Broad-tailed hummingbird	Rufous hummingbird	Allen's hummingbird
Calliope hummingbird	Western kingbird	Wied's crested flycatcher
Ash-throated flycatcher	Hammond's flycatcher	Dusky flycatcher
Gray flycatcher	Western flycatcher	Buff-breasted flycatcher
Violet-green swallow	Black-capped vireo	Bell's vireo
Gray vireo	Warbling vireo	Black-and-white warbler
Blue-winged warbler	Nashville warbler	Virginia's warbler
Colima warbler	Lucy's warbler	Olive warbler
Magnolia warbler	Black-throated gray warbler	Golden-cheeked warbler
Hermit warbler	Grace's warbler	Macgillivray's warbler
Yellow-breasted chat	Red-faced warbler	Hooded warbler
Wilson's warbler	Hooded oriole	Scott's oriole
Northern oriole	Western tanager	Hepatic tanager
Black-headed grosbeak	Blue grosbeak	Indigo bunting
Lazuli bunting	Clay-colored sparrow	

Central America (4.62×10^5 km^2)

Vaux's swift	Scissor-tailed flycatcher	Great crested flycatcher
Yellow-bellied flycatcher	Least flycatcher	Wood thrush
Yellow-throated vireo	Philadelphia vireo	Prothonotary warbler
Worm-eating warbler	Golden-winged warbler	Tennessee warbler
Yellow warbler	Black-throated green warbler	Chestnut-sided warbler
Bay-breasted warbler	Louisiana water-thrush	Kentucky warbler
Mourning warbler	Orchard oriole	Summer tanager

West Indies ($<2.35 \times 10^5$ km^2)

Roseate tern	Chuck-will's-widow	Black swift
Swainson's warbler	Bachman's warbler	Parula warbler
Cape May warbler	Black-throated blue warbler	Kirtland's warbler
Ovenbird	American redstart	

Table 7.2 *continued*

Northern South America[a] (3.6 × 10⁶ km²)

Swallow-tailed kite	Mississippi kite	Broad-winged hawk
Solitary sandpiper	Red phalarope	Wilson's phalarope
Northern phalarope	Franklin's gull	Sabine's gull
Elegant tern	Least tern	Black tern
Yellow-billed cuckoo	Black-billed cuckoo	Common nighthawk
Chimney swift	Eastern kingbird	Gray kingbird
Sulphur-bellied flycatcher	Acadian flycatcher	Willow flycatcher
Alder flycatcher	Western wood pewee	Eastern wood pewee
Olive-sided flycatcher	Bank swallow	Barn swallow
Rough-winged swallow	Cliff swallow	Purple martin
Swainson's thrush	Gray-cheeked thrush	Veery
Black-whiskered vireo	Red-eyed vireo	Cerulean warbler
Blackburnian warbler	Blackpoll warbler	Northern water-thrush
Connecticut warbler	Canada warbler	Bobolink
Scarlet tanager	Rose-breasted grosbeak	Dickcissel

Southern South America[b] (3.4 × 10⁶ km²)

Cinnamon teal	Swainson's hawk	Golden plover
Eskimo curlew	Upland sandpiper	Pectoral sandpiper
White-rumped sandpiper	Baird's sandpiper	Stilt sandpiper
Buff-breasted sandpiper	Hudsonian godwit	

Source: Rappole et al. 1983.
[a] Includes Venezuela, Peru, Ecuador, and Columbia.
[b] Includes Paraguay, Uruguay, and Argentina.

8 *Migrants in Passage*

Any seasoned observer of birds along the Atlantic seaboard knows very well that the fall migration is not simply a reversal of the spring's northward movement. Nearly every feature of the two migrations is different—the sequence of arrivals and departures, the key concentration points, and the duration of the migratory periods. The spring hawk migration, for example, goes almost unnoticed, but when the birds again return south, they pass in great numbers through migration funnels along the barrier islands of the coast and over certain ridgetops of the Appalachians. Many shorebirds are among the latest spring arrivals, not appearing in numbers on our beaches and tidal flats before late May. Yet some of these same species are the earliest harbingers of the fall retreat, returning to the coast as soon as mid-July. The length of their sojourns at our latitude varies correspondingly, being a mere two weeks or so in spring, but more than two months in the fall. Songbirds are not exempt from such seasonal idiosyncrasies. Bird listers, eager to tally more than 20 warbler species in a day, visit favored inland hot spots in the spring, but in seeking to repeat the feat a few month's later, obtain best results along the coast.

The radical difference in the behavior of migrants on their northbound and southbound trips have to do with migratory routes, the timing of arrivals and departures, and habitat preferences en route. Experienced birdwatchers know the details for their home regions by heart. But scientists are only now beginning to investigate the causes of these seasonal differences in migrant behavior.

MIGRATORY ROUTES

Migration is an energy-demanding process that requires a high state of physiological preparedness. The necessary hormonal conditioning is frequently mediated through changes in day length (Farner and Lewis 1971; King and Mewaldt 1981).

A blackpoll warbler preparing to fly nonstop from Maine to Venezuela, something it accomplishes in 80 to 100 hours, must, within the final few days before departure, store fat equal to 50 percent of its normal body weight (Nisbet et al. 1963; Griffin 1969; Pond 1978). It arrives in Venezuela nearly four days later in an emaciated condition with almost no reserve to spare. The risks involved in performing such a stupendous physical feat, from a human perspective, seem awesome. Everything has to be right—hormones, plumage, physical condition, fat load, and particularly the weather.

Birds accumulate in "staging areas" along the coast, laying down fat and awaiting just the right wind conditions—a strong front from the northwest. When such a front has passed by, the waiting birds arise in a massive "wave," usually just after sundown, and begin the almost impossible-to-believe task of flying more than 3,000 kilometers without food, water, or rest (Drury and Nisbet 1964; Williams et al. 1977; Torre-Bueno 1978; Torre-Bueno and Larochelle 1978; Larkin et al. 1979). One would think there must be an easier way.

Although the feat of flying nonstop over the Atlantic seems incredible, it has independently evolved as the route of choice in scores of species. We know this from various sorts of evidence, including the radar tracking of migratory waves, the amount of fat accumulated before departure, the common occurrence of dozens of migratory species every fall in Bermuda, Puerto Rico, and Antigua, and the near absence at that season of many of the same species on the southeast Atlantic coastal plain (Nisbet 1970; Hilditch et al. 1973; Richardson 1976; McClintock et al. 1978; Williams 1985).

It would seem much "easier" for these birds to continue down the coast to Florida, and then to make the comparatively short hop to the Antilles before launching across the Caribbean to South America. But this "easy" route is ignored by far too many species for the omission to be mere coincidence. What seems easy to us is evidently not so easy for the birds. Why not? The answer is not known in detail, but the circumstances provide a strong suggestion.

As summer draws to a close, a gathering front of birds begins to move southward across the continent. In general, the species that breed farthest north spend the least time on their nesting ground, as little as six weeks in the case of many shorebirds. Passerines normally take somewhat longer, but eight to ten weeks is commonplace. As northern species begin to drift south ahead of inclement weather, their numbers begin to accumulate, as snow before a plow blade. This gathering front quickly results in concentrations of birds that are far greater than the habitat normally supports (Holmes and Sturges 1975). This is particularly true at the end of the nesting season, when local populations are already swollen by the presence of large numbers of recently fledged juveniles.

If this process of snowballing accumulation were to proceed from north to south across the entire breadth of the continent, the numbers of birds that would arrive in October on the Gulf Coast would be truly fantastic. The migratory population of an entire continent would be concentrated in a few degrees of latitude. The collective demand for food presented by this hoard of birds, especially given that they would need to store fat for the trans-Gulf leg of their journeys, would be wholly unsupportable.

We can now see why what might seem like an "easy" way of migrating is not easy at all. In fact, relatively few migrants continue all the way down the coast, and the fall migration in Florida is notably unspectacular (Nisbet 1970).

Different species typically drop out at different points along the coast, a fact that has been well documented by volunteers operating a series of coastal banding stations. These stations are located in strategic migration "funnels" at such concentration points as Monomoy Island, Massachusetts; Cape May, New Jersey; and Cape Charles, Virginia. Many birds must forsake the coast for overwater routes at these natural jumping-off points, because the number of migrants, especially tropical migrants, seems to diminish southward. Beyond the North Carolina Capes, the flow becomes a mere trickle.

The progressive abandonment of the coastal route by southbound migrants may be related to resource levels. If the high prey densities needed to sustain rapid premigratory weight gain were to be found only in the Northeast, the pattern would make sense. But so far as I am aware, the data needed to test this idea have not been gathered.

Reversing the Flow: The Spring Return

In the spring we see a very different picture. Birds return to the East from the tropics via relatively short overwater hops across the Gulf from staging areas in the Yucatan Peninsula and the Antilles, or via the overland route through Mexico. Instead of hopping great distances in dramatic nonstop flights, most species filter slowly northward through the central and Appalachian states, taking as long as six weeks to reach their eventual destinations after arriving in the United States (Teale 1951). Throughout the period, the coast remains almost barren of migrants, except for shorebirds. Why is the spring so different?

No one has the definitive answer, but again, resources are probably a major factor. The main surge of Neotropical migrants moves northward in phase with the leafing out of the forest canopy. The timing is hardly coincidental, because the larvae of several species of defoliating insects hatch out in synchrony with bud break to take advantage of tender, protein-rich young foliage (Schneider 1980). For several weeks thereafter these (geometrid moth) larvae, commonly known as "inchworms," can be extremely abundant and in outbreak years can even strip the canopy of leaves while producing a continuous rain of frass (feces).

In the Middle Atlantic states, geometrids appear to be particularly abundant in oaks, because migrating warblers and vireos are strongly associated with these trees. The caterpillars can at times be so abundant that bird species that normally engage in other pursuits are prompted to get into the act. In the woods near Princeton, I have been surprised to see catbirds, grackles, and redwings scrambling clumsily about in the tops of tall oaks in quest of easy pickings. The banquet is so bountiful and obvious that we do not have to wonder what fuels the northbound migration.

Many of the species that move beyond New Jersey into the Northeast or Canada take advantage of the spring geometrid bloom. They can afford to proceed at a leisurely pace, because their northern destinations in mid-May are still bare of leaves and perhaps even snowbound. The advancing wave of spring sets the timing, and the penalty for arriving early could be severe.

This reasoning fails to account for the behavior of several migrants that stop to nest in the Middle Atlantic region. Several of these arrive considerably earlier, as early as late March, even though they appear to be as dependent on insect prey as the later arrivals—for example, tree swallows, phoebes, blue-gray gnatcatchers, pine and yellow-throated warblers, and Louisiana water-thrushes. It is the males that arrive first in a race to secure territories ahead of competitors. Undoubtedly there are insect resources we know little about that are targeted by these birds, but even so, they seem to be taking a calculated risk in arriving so early. Sharp frosts and wet spring snows are still a possibility, yet the birds routinely seem to weather these hazards.

Finally, some comments on shorebirds. Several species (for example, golden plover; hudsonian and marbled godwits; upland, buff-breasted, Bairds, stilt, and white-rumped sandpipers) follow a circular migration route—down the Atlantic coast in the fall and up through the Great Plains in the spring (Griffin 1964). The route is parallel to that traced by many songbirds, but the shorebird flyways are more widely separated and narrower. The factors that favor circular migration in the two groups of species are likely to be different.

Several of the shorebirds that follow a circular route prefer short grass or stubble to mudflats. The rest forage on bars and shores in the conventional manner. In either case, suitable habitat is abundantly available in the plains in spring, when water levels tend to be high and when, in the past, the grass had been reduced to stubble by the winter grazing of bison. Mowed and freshly plowed fields now provide alternatives to the no longer extant natural habitat.

The plains environment would not be so hospitable to shorebirds returning in the fall. Rivers would be at low ebb, and many of the countless pools and potholes that offer spring foraging would be dry or choked with vegetation. The late summer prairie would be rank with tall grasses and forbs, offering neither running space nor visibility to a terrestrial forager. With shorebirds, circular migration may be as much a matter of habitat as of resources.

In returning to their southern haunts, certain shorebirds may even outshine the blackpoll warbler as long-distance flying champions. This is not yet a proven fact, though the circumstances are highly suggestive. Golden plovers, hudsonian godwits, and upland, Bairds, and white-rumped sandpipers, among others, are known to fly south over the Atlantic Ocean (Richardson 1979). The main populations of these species accumulate in staging areas around Hudson Bay and then simply vanish. They then re-appear in southern South America, more than 8,000 kilometers away. In between they fail to appear in anything more than token numbers.

It is conceivable that they make the trip in one giant effort. If so, plovers and godwits would have to be able to match the feat of blackpoll warblers. Warblers and other small songbirds are comparatively slow fliers, traveling in level flight at velocities around 30–35 kilometers per hour (Schnell 1965). A warbler must maintain this speed for at least 80 hours to make the journey from Maine or Nova Scotia to the Caribbean (Larkin et al. 1979). Unlike warblers, shorebirds are designed for speed. Sandpipers and plovers have been clocked at 60–70 kilometers per hour, a velocity twice that achieved by a warbler (Tucker and Schmidt-Koenig 1977). If a plover could maintain this speed for the same 80 hours of flying time, it would be able to make the journey from Hudson Bay to the Rio de la Plata estuary in Argentina in a single hop.

Another noteworthy feature of shorebird migration is that the northbound and southbound trips of species that normally migrate along the coast—knots, dowitchers, ruddy turnstones, semipalmated sandpipers—are made at dramatically different rates. Returning adults of these and other species appear on beaches and mudflats along the East Coast as early as the second half of July. From a human perspective, they are scandalously irresponsible parents, because they leave their recently fledged young to fend for themselves in the Arctic. But we should not attempt to extend our sense of propriety to nature, because natural selection would not forgive such nonchalance if it did not result in optimal reproductive success. The fact that many species of shorebirds abandon their young in the Arctic indicates, for shorebirds at least, that benign neglect is an effective parental policy.

A few weeks later, young begin to appear among the adults along the coast, and shorebird numbers swell to a seasonal peak in late August and early September. The populations quickly spread out along the entire shoreline from Massachusetts to Florida and later begin a gradual retreat from the Northeast. Sizable numbers of birds of many species are present

FIG. 8.1 Buff-breasted sandpiper

for nearly three months from July through October, and stragglers commonly remain until even later.

The northbound trip follows an entirely different schedule. There are a few early arrivals, notably the sanderlings, pectoral sandpipers, and yellowlegs that appear as early as the end of March; but in general, shorebird numbers remain low until after the warblers have returned in May. Then vast numbers of birds suddenly appear for a climactic period that lasts barely two weeks. Virtually the entire East Coast populations of knots, ruddy turnstones, sanderlings, and semipalmated sandpipers pass through in this contracted period (Myers et al. 1987).

There is a very special reason why these shorebirds concentrate so spectacularly on the spring migration. It is to take advantage of the mass spawning of the horseshoe crab, an event that coincides with high tides accompanying the full moon. These bizarre relics of the Paleozoic emerge from the surf by the thousands to spawn on certain favored beaches.

The females first appear in the foam, each one pursued by several smaller males scrambling frantically to obtain a decisive grip on her spike-like tail. Slowly, almost imperceptibly, the tightly coupled pairs plow up the beach to just above the high tide mark, where the females scrape out a shallow depression in which to deposit their eggs. More males may crowd around as egg laying begins, adding confusion to an already chaotic scene. At the peak of an emergence, the beach can be so littered with immobile forms that there is hardly space to place one's feet.

Thus far I have described only part of this unforgettable spectacle. Birds constitute the other part, thousands and thousands of them—laughing gulls, ruddy turnstones, sanderlings, knots, semipalmated sandpipers, and others. They converge in chattering, swirling throngs to feast on the freshly laid eggs. The frenzied feeding is more than simple gluttony, it is an essential part of the migratory strategy of these birds. J. P. Myers of Philadelphia's Academy of Natural Sciences has estimated that a sanderling must consume 135,000 eggs in less than a fortnight in order to store enough energy for the flight to Hudson Bay, the next, but not the last, leg of its journey back to the Arctic (Myers 1986).

The special importance of the horseshoe crab spawning for shorebird survival has only recently been appreciated, thanks to Myers's pioneering work. Although the crabs occur all along the coast, there are only a few spots where they nest in great aggregations. Such aggregations are needed to generate food resources in sufficient density to fuel the rapid weight gain that a bird requires for its onward migration.

It now appears that the greatest shorebird concentration point on the Atlantic Seaboard is at the mouth of Delaware Bay, on beaches just a few miles northwest of Cape May, New Jersey. Myers estimates that 80 percent or more of the entire Atlantic population of red knots may assemble on just a few kilometers of shoreline (Myers et al. 1987). This presents a wonderful spectacle, but it also poses a serious threat to the shorebird population.

The critical shoreline is already being parceled out for summer cottages. Even more ominous is the possibility of an oil spill. Delaware Bay is the location of several major refineries, and heavily laden tankers arrive and depart every day. An accident at the critical season could decimate the crabs and birds alike, reminding us that migration is a chain whose strength is that of its weakest link.

9 *The Ecology of Migrants in the Winter*

WHICH SPECIES MIGRATE?

The farther north one goes in the temperate regions, the closer the answer to the question "Which species migrate?" becomes "All species," though by no means all migrants go to the tropics. Christmas Counts from such high-latitude outposts as northern Alaska, the Yukon, and the Northwest Territories report very few birds of any kind—ptarmigans, ravens, gray jays, boreal chickadees, and hoary redpolls being the principal terrestrial species. Considering that the landscape is covered with snow and ice, that temperatures are often far below zero, and that a dim glow of light may illuminate the scene for only an hour or two a day, it is astonishing that any birds at all remain to brave the winter.

When shivering in the far less awesome chill of January in New Jersey, I often extend my incredulous admiration to the tiny kinglets and chickadees that busily search the barren twigs of windblown trees for unseen morsels of sustenance. Obviously, there is more to getting through the winter than meets the eye.

The species that migrate to the tropics can be grouped into several categories, the largest of which is composed of obligate insectivores, species that feed on insect prey year around. These include nightjars, swifts, flycatchers, swallows, and most vireos and warblers. Why should these birds go to the tropics, when kinglets, which are no less insectivorous, manage to brave the snow and ice? A superficial answer is that the long-distance migrants feed on active insects (nymphs, larvae, and adults), whereas in the winter kinglets, brown creepers, chickadees and others subsist on the inactive forms of insects (eggs, pupae, and diapausing adults). It is a subtle point, but an important one.

Shorebirds universally forsake their Arctic breeding grounds for milder, but not necessarily tropical, climes. Many species pass the winter along the coasts of California and the southeastern states. The populations of most of these spill over into the tropics. Others—and here the division is quite sharp—seek perpetual summer by traveling all the way to temperate South America. These include the grassland specialists that winter in the pampas, whereas those that prefer tidal flats tend to have broad winter distributions (Myers 1981).

Most terns and a few gulls also go to the tropics, presumably because the fishing is better in ice-free water. Still, it remains a puzzle why certain gulls and terns stay in the north while others leave it far behind.

A number of raptors migrate beyond the United States, though again it is not an easy matter to make sense out of the pattern. Most kestrels stay, whereas most merlins leave. One common forest-living *Buteo* stays (the red-shouldered hawk), and the other leaves (the broad-winged hawk). The same can be said of prairie *Buteos*: the ferruginous hawk stays and the Swainson's hawk goes. Kites leave, except for the white-tailed, which is resident in California. In some cases, the choice of which leaves and which stays seems arbitrary, but probably it is not. The reasons for these dichotomies in behavior will someday be discovered.

Nectar feeders (hummingbirds) flee the north in search of flowers, though most of them winter on the fringe of the tropics in Mexico, where they take advantage of a profuse burst of flowering in what is the dry season there (DesGrange 1978; DesGrange and Grant 1980).

A final major category of Neotropical migrants is composed of dietary generalists, species that seek insects at all seasons but freely supplement their intake with fruit, nectar, or seeds. In this category we find some flycatchers, vireos, and warblers, plus thrushes, orioles, tanagers, and a number of finches.

Neotropical migrants are thus not readily distinguished by their diets. Some species in every one of the categories mentioned above, except nectarivores (hummingbirds), routinely winter in the continental climate of our middle tier of states. There is more to migration than simply the matter of food.

Neither does taxonomy provide a consistent predictor. Ever since I was a teenager, I have found it odd that the winter avifauna of the southeastern coastal plain included one or more of many of the migratory families. There was a flycatcher (phoebe), a swallow (tree), a *Catharus* thrush (hermit), a gnatcatcher (blue-gray), a vireo (solitary), and several warblers (pine, yellow-rumped, yellowthroat), even occasionally a goatsucker (chuck-will's-widow). It hardly seemed plausible that this was mere coincidence. Yet how could it be explained? Were these species for some reason especially cold-hardy? Perhaps so, but this couldn't be the whole story, because these birds have to find food in the winter environment.

Many of them seemed to have a special trick for coping with the worst spells of weather. The chuck-will's-widow might possibly hibernate during cold periods as its western relative the poorwill is known to do (Terres 1980); phoebes winter over running water, frequently at spillways, where the water never freezes and where the flying adults of aquatic insects emerge throughout the winter; hermit thrushes eat the berries of holly, greenbrier, and viburnum when not searching for insects in the leaf litter;

tree swallows and yellow-rumped warblers hawk insects on the wing except when it is below freezing, and then they resort to eating waxy bayberries (*Myrica* spp.: Wiley and Giampa 1978); pine warblers do what they do in the summer—search tufts of needles—but the trees they use are evergreen and probably harbor greater numbers of insects than the crowns of bare deciduous trees. The same can be said of the ruby-crowned kinglets, blue-gray gnatcatchers, and solitary vireos that winter in southern swamps, where there are several common species of evergreen trees and shrubs (Morse 1967).

The key to the puzzle thus seems to be food. Each species either has a reliable source of prey (phoebe, pine warbler) or has some alternative way of muddling through when it is simply too cold to find active insects (chuck-will's-widow, tree swallow, hermit thrush, yellow-rumped warbler).

The total number of species inhabiting our southeastern swamps and woodlands is about the same in summer as in winter (30-40), and in each season about half of the resident species are migrants (Gauthreaux 1982). The species that arrive for the warm season mainly depend on larval and adult insects, food items that are scarce in winter, and those that come for the cold season mostly depend on fruit and seeds, foods that are scarce in spring and early summer. Seasonal changes in the composition of the bird community thus seem to be tied to the annual cycle of food availability.

Cold per se may be less important as a determinant of where birds winter. Certainly this is the impression one gets in reading the annual Christmas Count issue of *American Birds*. Each year the reports abound with records of birds that are outrageously out of range—a blue-gray gnatcatcher in Newfoundland, a yellow-throated warbler on Cape Cod, a northern water-thrush in Connecticut, a Nashville warbler in New York, pine warblers in Michigan and Minnesota, and a Cape May warbler in Colorado (*American Birds* 1986). If these birds could not tolerate cold, they could never survive in these places until late December or early January, even in what might be considered a "mild" winter. Sometimes these misdirected waifs manage to survive the entire winter in mid-continent America, though usually it is in conjunction with a faithfully stocked feeder. Once again, our conclusion is that food, more than weather, dictates where species go to spend the winter.

Are Migrants Really Tropical Birds?

The question of whether migrants are really tropical birds never fails to inspire a debate any time ornithologists gather to discuss migration. Those with experience in the tropics often claim that flycatchers, warblers, and vireos are legitimately tropical birds, because many of them spend more than half the year on their wintering grounds (Rappole and Warner 1980; Smith 1980; Stiles 1983). Scientists with a more northerly orientation frequently take the opposite view: that long-distance migrants are temperate birds because the temperate zone is where they breed. They only go to the tropics to escape the rigors of winter. Who is right?

Both views are simplistic because neither takes into account how the current situation evolved. Let us take an extreme example: it would be ludicrous to imagine that blackpoll warblers, which breed in the boreal forest, suddenly began to migrate to Amazonia when the global climate began to cool at the onset of the Ice Age. It is similarly ludicrous to imagine that the ancestors of rose-breasted grosbeaks suddenly burst out of Colombia one particularly bad dry season to seek better breeding opportunities in southern Canada.

It is far easier, and far more realistic, to imagine that migratory behavior evolved gradually. There are plenty of examples to support a gradualist hypothesis. In North America there are scores of species that are partially migratory, having both resident and migratory populations—red-tailed hawks, flickers, blue jays, song sparrows, to name a few. In such species, the populations that nest to the north are normally the migrants. When they come south, they encounter their sedentary relatives. As a consequence, population densities become higher in the winter than they are in the summer.

But perhaps winter food supplies are not sufficient to support an expanded population. The simple option available to the migratory individuals is to continue farther south in a pattern known as "leap-frog migration" (Salomonsen 1955). The northern breeders then wind up spending the winter to the south of the southern breeders. This is what happens in the species mentioned above, and in many others as well, although further study of banded individuals is required to work out all the details.

To reconstruct a scenario under which this behavior might plausibly arise, let us imagine an incipient climatic deterioration, such as the one that accompanied the onset of the Ice Age. Winter conditions gradually become too severe for survival at high latitudes. Species that were permanently resident in these regions during warmer times may have been induced to wander when food supplies dwindled, as black-capped chickadees do from time to time. Perhaps by chance some individuals wandered south, where they encountered more benign conditions. These might have had a higher winter survivorship than those that stayed. If the tendency to wander south (as opposed to wandering in inappropriate directions) is at all genetically determined, these successful individuals would pass the tendency on to their offspring. In time the whole population would become "fixed" for the habit of southward migration.

This is one way for migratory behavior to evolve. Let us call it the "retreat hypothesis." It pertains to species that initially were resident at high latitudes prior to a cooling of the global climate, or an intensification of seasonality, such as occurs when the tilt of the earth's axis of rotation increases.

Just as plausible, however, is an alternative "advance hypothesis" that would apply to species initially resident on the fringes of the tropics, or at warm temperate latitudes (Cox 1968, 1985). Young birds that were seeking breeding territories might wander northward beyond the traditional geographical limits of the breeding population. If these first-time breeders were to find appropriate conditions, their reproductive efforts could be successful. But in keeping with their ancestry, they would be burdened with genes that prompted them to establish year-round territories. Hence, when the winter arrived, they might all perish.

Something very similar to this occurs regularly in the Carolina wren. The species commonly breeds as far north as Maryland, but in central New Jersey, where I live, it is normally absent. Nevertheless, if we have a succession of mild winters, Carolina wrens will appear and breed in the Princeton area. A few years ago the numbers built up so that I was reminded of my native Virginia. But then we had a severe winter with snow and a long period of subfreezing weather. Afterward, there was not a Carolina wren to be found anywhere in the area.

Carolina wrens inhabit year-round territories and are not known to migrate. Yet it is clear that the northern limit of their distribution is dynamic and can expand 100 miles or more in just a few years, provided the weather is conducive. What is lacking so far is any tendency for the northernmost individuals to pull back southward for the winter. Perhaps in time such a tendency may evolve.

Indications that such behavior may recently have evolved can be seen in a number of species of the Southwest. The famed birding that draws thousands of visitors every year to southeastern Arizona is largely due to such species—gray and black hawks, several hummingbirds, coppery-tailed trogon, thick-billed kingbird, painted redstart, olive warbler, hooded oriole. All of these species have tropical or subtropical ranges throughout most of which the individuals are permanent residents. Only at the extreme northern limits of their distributions (that is, northernmost Mexico and southern Arizona) do they display migratory behavior (Rappole et al. 1983). Should the earth's climate show a warming trend in the future, it is easy to imagine that these species could readily extend their ranges farther northward. In sum, migratory behavior can potentially evolve in response to either a warming or a cooling of the climate. In either case, it requires that an advantageous tendency to wander be given a directional component by natural selection.

Thus far, our speculations about the origins of migratory behavior in temperate birds provide an explanation only for partial migration. We are as yet a long way from understanding how golden plovers came to winter in Argentina, or how Connecticut warblers ever found their way to the Amazon basin. Long-distance migration is a greater puzzle, because there is no continuity between the breeding and winter ranges. Indeed, the breeding and wintering grounds may be an ocean apart, as in the case of the blackpoll warbler, which migrates over the Atlantic directly to South America from the northeastern states.

To induce long-distance migratory behavior there must be an intensification of the seasonal contrast between summer and winter. Seasonality at high latitudes depends on the angle of tilt of the earth's axis of rotation, as explained above. When this angle increases or decreases, as it is known to do in 41,000 year-long cycles, the contrast between the seasons varies accordingly (Hays et al. 1976; Lockwood 1979). One might predict in the absence of seasonality that all breeding species would be resident, as they are in climatically uniform parts of the tropics. Were seasonality to increase, more and more species would be obliged to accommodate to the changes through migration—or to die out if appropriate behavior did not evolve. In an extreme case of seasonality, such as is experienced in the Arctic, nearly all species are obliged to migrate.

Gradually increasing seasonality of the global climate can lead, through incremental steps, to long-distance migration, as the separation between optimal breeding and wintering grounds becomes ever greater. The effect of exaggerating seasonality will be to increase the migratory distance traveled by species conforming to either the "retreat" or "advance" models.

As a note of explanation, the reader should be aware that seasonality is independent of annual mean temperature. In other words, a change in the tilt of the earth's axis of rotation does not alter the total amount of solar radiation received annually at the surface. If the axis of rotation were perpendicular to the orbital plane, the climate would resemble that of April all year long. Alternatively, the global climate can experience cooling or warming phases, as it has done through the Ice Age (Pleistocene), without concomitant change in the degree of seasonality experienced at any point.

ONCE IN THE TROPICS, WHERE THEN?

Migration may be necessary for a temperate zone breeder to escape the combined effects of cold, short days, and food scarcity, but once a bird has arrived in the tropics, that should be enough. The inimical features of the temperate winter have been left behind. Further travel could only entail greater risks—the possibility of encountering a tropical storm, or of meeting predators in unfamiliar surroundings, or simply of succumbing to exhaustion. Nevertheless, dozens of species fly all the way across the Northern Hemisphere tropics to winter in the Southern Hemisphere. In doing so, they travel about twice as far as they would if they stopped in Mexico or the Antilles, as so many other species do. One has to presume that these birds receive some compensating benefit for undergoing the additional cost of flying so far.

In the game of natural selection, costs and benefits are measured in the components of Darwinian fitness—survival and reproductive success. Since reproduction is in abeyance in the nonbreeding season, we can be confident that survival is what is at stake. It seems contradictory, but it almost has to be true: birds that go to the Southern Hemisphere assume greater risks and fly farther to increase their likelihood of surviving until the next breeding season. How can we rationalize this paradox?

There are two classes of explanation of this behavior, and both of them probably apply, but to different species in different degrees. One is that by flying farther some species succeed in avoiding factors that negatively affect their survival in the near tropics. The other possibility is that the Southern Hemisphere tropics offer something that positively enhances survival. What might these factors be?

We have already seen that approximately half of all Neotropical migrants winter in Mexico and the Antilles, and that relative to the size of the breeding ground, this is a very reduced area. Populations are consequently highly compressed, a fact that must engender severe intraspecific competition: for food sources, territories, social rank in flocks, and so forth (Lack 1968; Fretwell 1980; Gauthreaux 1982; Greenberg 1986). If survivorship is negatively density dependent (meaning that the greater the number of individuals in a locality, the less any one is likely to survive), a bird, especially a low-ranking individual, might do better to avoid concentrations of its own species (Morse 1980). This could encourage a gradual expansion of the winter range, should other factors not intervene.

In fact, several specialized species do have unusually extensive winter distributions. Some examples are the black-and-white warbler, which feeds nuthatchlike on trunks and branches, and the northern and Louisiana water-thrushes, which hunt insects along quiet and rushing water courses, respectively. All three of these warblers spread out over most of Mexico, all of Central America and the Antilles, and a sizable portion of northern South America. Few other terrestrial migrants are so ubiquitously distributed in the winter.

A second reason for bypassing the near tropics in selecting a wintering site could be to avoid the competition of other species, particularly close relatives (Cox 1968, 1985). In vireos, warblers, and *Empidonax* flycatchers, closely related species show a striking tendency to winter in geographically separate regions, or to separate by habitat or elevation within a region (Barlow 1980; Fitzpatrick 1980; Keast 1980; Terborgh and Faaborg 1980). Take, for example, the genus *Wilsonia*. Wilson's and hooded warblers winter through much of Mexico and Central America, but hooded warblers mainly occupy forest interior, whereas Wilson's warblers inhabit scrub, edges, and early second growth and are common at higher elevations as well as in the lowlands. The Canada warbler, like the hooded, winters in forest interiors, but in South not Central America.

A similar though more complex situation is found in the genus *Vermivora*. The Bachman's warbler winters (wintered?) in Cuba; the blue-winged warbler in the lowlands of southeastern Mexico, Guatemala, and Honduras; and the golden-winged warbler in southern Central America and the northern Andes. The winter behavior of the Bachman's warbler is undescribed, but blue-winged and golden-winged warblers habitually search for insects in curled dead leaves that are caught in vines and twigs. Greenberg (1987) has shown that on a per-leaf basis, curled dead leaves, relative to live leaves, conceal ten times the biomass of arthropod prey. Although Bachman's, blue-winged, and golden-winged warblers do not overlap geographically with one another, members of this trio overlap extensively with another geographically exclusive trio: the orange-crowned, Nashville, and Tennessee warblers. These last three do not forage especially in dead leaves, but pursue a different winter specialty—taking nectar from flowers (see below). The orange-crowned warbler winters mainly in the southern United States and on the Mexican plateau, the Nashville in eastern Mexico and in Guatemala, and the Tennessee warbler abounds from southwestern Mexico, south along the Pacific slope of northern Central America, then throughout southern Central America into Colombia.

Further examples of the geographical separation of winter ranges are to be found in closely related species of a number of genera: *Dendroica* and *Oporornis* warblers, *Piranga* tanagers, *Catharus* thrushes, *Tyrannus*, and *Myiarchus* flycatchers, and so on. It is difficult to prove in any particular case that the segregation of related species into geographically or ecologically distinct wintering grounds is a consequence of competition, but the number of cases is so great that the circumstantial evidence is persuasive (Greenberg 1986).

Even if one assumes that interspecific competition is the root cause of these patterns, it is not clear what factors determine the outcome. Does one species winter to the north of another because the habitat or food supply is more appropriate to its particular ecology, because of historical accident, or because one species is capable of dominating the other and forcing it to winter in a less desirable area (Cox 1968)? We have no way at present of distinguishing among these possibilities.

There are nevertheless reasons to suppose that the geographical locations of winter ranges are not rigidly fixed and that species may be capable of responding quickly (in an evolutionary sense) to new circumstances. The limits of breeding distributions are usually sharply demarcated, presumably because males and females must be able to find each other, and because the requirements for breeding are more exacting than for wintering. Winter ranges are not so precisely delimited, as anyone who has participated on Christmas Counts is keenly aware. The same fuzziness of winter range boundaries is also apparent in species that winter in the tropics (Greenberg 1986).

While studying winter birds in the West Indies, I have frequently encountered species that normally winter elsewhere, mainly in Central America. Among these, I can recall prothonotary, golden-winged, magnolia and hooded warblers, and rose-breasted grosbeak. All of these birds were hundreds of kilometers out of range, and yet I have no reason to suppose that they did not successfully return to the breeding ground. Similarly, several species that winter in the Antilles are found in small numbers along the coast of the Yucutan peninsula—for example, parula, Kirtland's, yellow-throated, Cape May, and prairie warblers (Paynter 1955; Russell 1964). It would be extraordinary indeed to discover a species nesting so far from its regular haunts.

The high frequency with which out-of-range individuals are encountered in the winter suggests that winter ranges are constantly being subjected to the test of natural selection. Unconventional wintering grounds are being tried out by thousands of individual birds each year. The survival of these vagrants is undoubtedly below the mean for the population that winters within the conventional range. Nevertheless, if ecological conditions somehow changed for the better outside the traditional range, or if a few individual birds happened upon a region in which survival was higher than average, a shift in the winter distribution of the species could follow, perhaps in only a few years (Terborgh and Faaborg 1980).

A case in point is the dickcissel, which in recent years has begun to appear in sizable numbers in Central America, whereas traditionally it wintered principally in the natural grasslands (llanos) of Colombia and Venezuela (Fretwell 1980). Winter ranges are thus not a static feature of a species' biology, but instead are maintained from year to year through the dynamic process of natural selection. It is via this mechanism that we can understand how some species have "discovered" winter ranges that are thousands of kilometers away from the breeding ground.

Let us return to the question of why a species might profit from going as far as the Southern Hemisphere. Even though southern Mexico, Central America, and the Greater Antilles are well within the geographical tropics, these regions are nevertheless affected by an annual climatic cycle. Roughly speaking, the period we call "winter" in temperate North America corresponds to the dry season in the Northern Hemisphere tropics.

Numerous studies have shown that the availabilities of fruit and insects, the two most important classes of food resources for birds, reach their lowest levels in the dry season (Janzen and Schoener 1968; Robinson and Robinson 1970; Janzen 1973; Buskirk and Buskirk 1976; Wolda 1978; Foster 1982). These resources do not become abundant again until April or May, at the approach of the wet season. By then most migrants have left for points north. Hence the winter is not a time of abundance in the near tropics; to the contrary, it is the time when the availabilities of food resources are at their lowest levels. A similar situation prevails in the southern United States, though fruit stocks are high at the beginning of winter (Baird 1980; Stiles and White 1986).

The preceding discussion suggests that birds pay a price for wintering in the near tropics. They must abide the presence of high densities of their own species, and of many other migrant species as well, and they must find adequate food resources at a time of general scarcity. The fact that so many species do remain in the near tropics suggests that the disadvantages of going farther south must be pronounced, that is, if all other things are equal. Very likely, all other things are not equal.

There is probably a major advantage to be gained for certain species in migrating to the Southern Hemisphere. The advantage derives from the fact that there the seasons are reversed. November through March is a time of scarcity in the Northern Hemisphere, whereas in the Southern it is a time of plenty (Terborgh 1983, 1986). Fruit and insect abundances reach their peak values for the year during this period, and resident species are nesting. If the residents can obtain enough to feed themselves and a clutch of nestlings as well, a migrant should not be pressed merely to feed itself. Moreover, when it is ready to begin the northward return trip, the resources needed for rapid weight gain would be on hand.

There may be another advantage of going to the far tropics as well. South America is a huge continent, comparable in size to North America, and the main part of it is tropical. The intraspecific crowding experienced by any species that winters in Mexico or the Antilles is relieved by going to South America. Numerically prevalent species, such as the red-eyed vireo and blackpoll warbler, when dispersed over the vastness of Amazonia, become practically invisible (Pearson 1980). I have searched for these myself in Ecuador and Peru; they are there, but relatively hard to find. Intraspecific competition within so large an area is effectively nil. Interspecific competition is probably not, because Amazonia harbors the world's richest avifauna (Terborgh 1985). In the southern tropics migrants must compete more with residents, in the northern tropics with other migrants. The balance may be a toss-up, but the relevant parameters have not yet been measured (Greenberg 1986).

The impression one gains from observing migrants in Amazonia is that the species traveling so far are a select lot. Many of them feed on resources that reach peak levels with the onset of the southern rainy season. One such resource is flying insects (Terborgh et al. 1986). These provide sustenance for Mississippi kite, common nighthawk, chimney swift, wood pewee, alder flycatcher, purple martin, barn swallow, and bank swallow. Fruits, especially of lauraceous trees, are another. These are avidly sought by sulphur-bellied flycatchers and eastern kingbirds, whereas veeries and gray-cheeked and Swainson's thrushes feed on smaller, sweeter berries in the forest understory (Fitzpatrick 1982). Red-eyed vireos probably eat fruit too, as do black-whiskered vireos, though little is known of their winter ecology. A third example involves the yellow- and black-billed cuckoos, both specialized caterpillar eaters. Caterpillars suddenly become abundant as trees replace their leaves with the arrival of the rains. Coincidentally, both cuckoos appear in the southern tropics at just the appropriate time. For these and the other species mentioned above, the opportunity to exploit seasonally abundant resources seems to offset the hazards of migrating to a distant continent.

Numerous authors have suggested that migrants choose habitats and geographical ranges in response to the opportunity to exploit seasonally abundant resources (for example, Morton 1971, 1980; Hilty 1980; Tramer and Kemp 1980; Waide 1980). When this statement is made in reference to fruit and insect resources in the northern tropics, it is contradicted by the published data on resource levels. An alternative interpretation is that migrants concentrate in the near tropics, not because resource levels are especially high, but because their own metabolic requirements are at a minimum. With the benefit of 12-hour days in which to search for food, and only self-maintenance at stake, even low resource levels may be adequate. If so, then access to higher resource levels may not, except perhaps in the special cases described above, compensate for the costs of traveling to a more distant destination.

Thus far my remarks on food resources have been restricted to fruit and insects, two classes of resources that drop to low levels in the Neotropical dry season. There are other classes of resources, however, that do not conform to the same temporal pattern of availability.

In semiarid environments, seeds are produced at the end of the wet season and are maximally available somewhat later when they mature. Given this seasonal schedule, it would not make sense for any granivore (seed eater) to migrate to the southern tropics, and in fact, none do. Seed abundance in the southwestern deserts, and presumably on the Mexican plateau as well, is at a maximum after the end of the summer rains (Pulliam and Brand 1975). The winter consequently begins with a bountiful supply on hand. As the stocks dwindle, flocks of sparrows and finches may roam from site to site in search of remaining pockets of abundance (Cody 1971). Since rainfall in the desert is highly variable from year to year, so is the annual seed crop. This results in great fluctuations in the numbers of sparrows and finches that winter at a given site in successive years (Dunning and Brown 1982). The challenge faced each fall by sparrows and finches is in locating areas that received higher than average rainfall during the previous summer.

Nectar is another resource that does not fit the fruit and insect pattern, as many prominent trees, shrubs, and vines of the northern Neotropics flower during the dry season (Janzen 1967). Birds that feed on nectar can consequently enjoy the benefits of exploiting a seasonally abundant resource without traveling to the southern tropics (DesGranges and Grant 1980). In fact, no Neotropical migrant that routinely feeds on nectar crosses the equator.

The use of nectar as a seasonally abundant resource presents an especially interesting case. Hummingbirds and some western orioles are essentially the only North American birds that regularly exploit nectar sources during the breeding season. But on the wintering ground, a number of others become avid nectar feeders, including tanagers, eastern orioles, and warblers (Beehler 1980; Schemske 1980).

Four warbler species specialize on nectar as a winter food resource. These probably interact competitively, because they occupy contiguous but basically nonoverlapping geographical distributions. Cape May warblers, the only *Dendroica* in the group, inhabit the Bahamas and Greater Antilles; orange-crowned warblers are abundant at high elevations in the Mexican mountains; Nashville warblers replace them at lower elevations in northern and central Mexico and in the Caribbean lowlands; and Tennessee warblers abound from southwestern Mexico south through Central America to Colombia. Wherever there are dense aggregations of certain flowers, such as *Combretum fruticosum* (a liane) or *Luehea seemanii* (a tree), one can see the local representatives of this quartet of species engaging in supplantings and chases over access to the richest concentrations of flowers (Emlen 1973, Bahamas; Beehler 1980, Panama; Schemske 1980, Costa Rica). When *Combretum* vines are flowering in January, nearly all the Nashville or Tennessee warblers one sees (depending on the region) are strikingly red-faced from the brightly colored pollen.

Migrants show other kinds of opportunistic feeding behavior, in addition to visiting flowers. I have already mentioned that a number of flycatchers and vireos regularly consume fruit in their wintering areas (Leck 1972; Leck and Hilty 1968; Morton 1971, 1973, 1980; Fitzpatrick 1982), in addition to more traditional fruit eaters such as thrushes, tanagers, and finches (Rybczynski and Riker 1981).

Another kind of opportunism is seen in the migrants that follow swarms of army ants. The attraction is not the ants themselves, which are inedible to most birds, but the spiders and insects that are the ants' prey. The swarms move relatively slowly, so that many potential prey are able to escape by taking wing or fleeing on foot. Often the escape is only temporary, because once routed from their hiding places, the desperate fugitives become easy marks for the birds that invariably attend the swarms. A number of tropical birds (dubbed "professional ant followers" by E. O. Willis) are obligate commensals of army ants, since they seldom if ever forage away from swarms (Willis and Oniki 1978). Other tropical residents and migrants, such as hermit and Swainson's thrushes, attend swarms on a more casual basis, especially when few of the highly aggressive "professionals" are present (Willis 1966; Greene et al. 1984).

Feeding behaviors, such as those described in the above paragraphs, should not be considered unusual or bizarre, but rather as aspects of the normal ecology of each species, an ecology that is practiced for the six or seven months out of each year that most long-distance migrants spend in the tropics. The fact that we do not see these behaviors during the relatively shorter periods that the birds spend on the breeding grounds probably reflects only the lack of suitable opportunities. Nectar, caught-up dead leaves, and army ants are not readily available in the temperate or boreal forest. What we see when we observe species for only the part of the year that they spend in the north is an impoverished sampling of their full ecological repertoires. The recent "discovery" of these additional behaviors is only a reflection of a historical tendency to ignore migrants when they are not in our own backyards.

10 *Territories and Flocks*

One of the joys of the temperate spring is noting the return of bird song to the silent woods of winter, as new voices blend into the chorus with each passing week. Connoisseurs delight in distinguishing the separate lines, just as a seasoned concertgoer knows English horn from oboe.

The occasion for all this vocal activity is the establishment of breeding territories. Male birds arrive first from the south and, with dual purpose, announce their claims. First, they must warn neighbors and potential rivals of their willingness to defend their holdings, and second, they must make their eligibility known to late-arriving females. The fervor of these vocal efforts soon begins to wane, as females choose mates, and as the males themselves become engaged in domestic activity. By August the party is over, and the quiet of the woods is broken only by the droning of cicadas and an occasional die-hard red-eyed vireo.

Territoriality is so ubiquitous a mode of social organization that it permits the use of a standard method for censusing North American breeding birds (see Chapter 3). The few exceptions—species that do not hold territories, such as turkeys, grouse, quail, and woodcock, or colonial species, such as swifts and bank swallows—are rarely counted with precision in these censuses. In practice, the exceptions are so few that they are generally ignored.

Scores of species that defend territories while breeding, abandon them and adopt other life-styles in the off-season. These changes in habits are as familiar as the winter flocks of crows, blackbirds, and sparrows that wander from field to field in search of grain, or as the mixed bands of chickadees and other small birds that roam the winter woods. Only a small minority of species continue to maintain exclusive territories throughout the year.

If territories are the convention among breeding birds, then to almost an equal degree, flocks become the convention during the remainder of the year. Gulls, waterfowl, and shorebirds join in flocks, as do finches, swallows, and jays. Why the predilection for flocks? It will help to answer this question about temperate birds before we return to the tropics, because the situation is more complicated there.

BIRDS OF A FEATHER: WHY DO
THEY FLOCK?

Perhaps the most familiar flocks are the mixed parties of chickadees, titmice, and other species that glean the bare twigs and branches of our winter woods. So commonplace are these bands that one might assume their social workings to be well understood. But scientists frequently have a blind spot for the obvious. Although more erudite ornithological topics, such as the lice birds carry under their feathers, have been studied in detail, these flocks have only recently been subjected to serious investigation. To casual observation, the mixed parties seem to be informal gatherings of the birds resident in a wood. Studies of color-banded individuals have now shown that such flocks actually possess a high degree of internal organization (Smith 1984; Sullivan 1984).

The central membership is made up of chickadees and titmice. The same individuals band together every morning and are soon joined by a host of followers. Each such chickadee coalition maintains a definite territory that it defends against the intrusions of neighboring bands. Follower species are often less tightly associated with the territory and may freely pass from one group of chickadees to another. A relatively scarce, large species such as the hairy woodpecker may join in the activities of several flocks, while maintaining a territory of its own against other hairy woodpeckers.

Ornithologists have long wondered why these and other flocking birds show such an affinity for one another's company, but the analysis needed to demonstrate the probable cause of the behavior was not begun until recently (Bertram 1978; Pulliam et al. 1980; Sullivan 1984).

In a study of winter mixed flocks in New Jersey, Kim Sullivan, a Rutgers University graduate student, was able to discriminate the roles of leader and follower in a simple but elegant series of experiments. Noting that chickadees or titmice were nearly always the first to give an alarm at the approach of a potential predator, she challenged the flocks under controlled conditions by flying a model sharp-shinned hawk into their midst, while a tape recorder registered the response (Sullivan 1984). The recordings decisively confirmed her previous impression, namely, that the chickadees and titmice gave alarms before other species. She then showed that follower species (such as downy woodpeckers and nuthatches) instantly reacted to these alarm calls when they were played back through a speaker at times when no danger was apparent. The followers thus seem to be gaining an advantage by associating with chickadees, since the chickadees provide an early warning system against predators.

The benefits proffered by the apparently magnanimous chickadees did not stop at this. Dictating her observations into a tape recorder to assure accurate documentation of the time sequences, Sullivan observed the foraging behavior of downy woodpeckers when they were associated with chickadees and when they were foraging alone. Solitary downies spent more time (11 percent) with their heads up, as if scanning the horizon for approaching predators. In contrast, when the same birds were associated with flocks, they foraged much more intently, pausing to raise their heads only 3 percent of the time. Not only are followers warned of predators while participating in mixed flocks, but they "feel" secure and can dedicate themselves more continuously to the business at hand.

Are chickadees so altruistic in their relations with follower species that they bestow these benefits free of charge? Under the stern winnowing of natural selection, such benign generosity would not be rewarded. The chickadees must benefit somehow by the presence of their followers, though just how remains a matter of speculation.

One guess is that they are exploiting what is known in the jargon of evolutionary biology as the "selfish herd effect" (Hamilton 1971; Vine 1971). The idea is simple: by being at the center of the flock, the chickadees would normally not be the first to be sighted and attacked by a hawk. One would thus expect the followers to bear most of the brunt of predation, though no one has yet demonstrated this.

But suppose it was true. Are the followers being duped by the leaders? What is going on? Actually, it is most likely that both parties benefit. By joining in flocks, *all* the participants lower their risk of being killed in a surprise attack (Bertram 1978; Landeau and Terborgh 1986). It does not matter that the followers may suffer a higher rate of predation than the chickadees; they nevertheless benefit in relation to the risk they would take by foraging alone. Benefits are realized by both parties, exemplifying a type of evolutionary arrangement known as a mutualism.

What about the many species that go to the tropics? Until recently there was a complete dearth of published information on how these species lived on the wintering ground. Many are still unstudied. Nevertheless, what we do know indicates that the winter behavior of tropical migrants is highly varied. Some join in mixed flocks, others in single-species flocks, and still others are solitary or territorial. In general, the proportion of flock joiners is not as high as in the north, but the prevalence of territoriality is greater. Hummingbirds, for example, are solitary and often defend shifting feeding territories consisting of a clump of nectar-producing flowers. Nightjars are usually solitary, and so are most hawks and many flycatchers. Other species, such as swifts and swallows, forage in their customary loose aggregations, and waterfowl, gulls, terns, and shorebirds behave in the tropics the way they do anywhere else. The most interesting situations arise when we look at wintering songbirds.

WINTER TERRITORIES IN THE TROPICS

As mentioned earlier, studies on the behavioral ecology of migrants in the tropics did not begin until the 1960s. The pioneer in this field was Paul Schwartz, a native of upstate New York who went to Venezuela as a refrigeration engineer. He soon became intrigued by the bird life and began to pursue serious studies on his own. Eventually, he obtained a position in the Venezuelan government service as a wildlife biologist and dedicated the rest of his life to building a library of tropical bird song recordings.

One of Schwartz's first and best-remembered accomplishments was a banding study of the northern water-thrushes that wintered in a large city park in Caracas (Schwartz 1964). At the time people naively imagined that migrants wandered through the tropics like so many party hoppers, enjoying a life of unrestrained leisure and plenty until it was time to come back home and go to work. Schwartz discovered that this uninformed impression was badly mistaken.

Each year in October, arriving water-thrushes would chase and battle one another to gain control over exclusive territories on low-lying terrain bordering a stream that ran through the park. This came as a complete surprise, because migrants were not known to engage in any kind of territorial activity in the winter.

It was not the only surprise to come out of Schwartz's work. He discovered that the territories were held, not by pairs but by individuals, suggesting that in the winter males and females act as rivals rather than as partners. This was a completely unexpected finding, one that seems to set the stage for understanding some entirely different issues, as we shall see below.

Schwartz's contribution had still another side, one that more than the others has required a readjustment in our thinking about the role the tropical environment plays in the lives of migratory songbirds. He determined that the same individuals returned to the park year after year, often to precisely the same territories. The implication is that good territories are scarce and valuable. Once a bird succeeds in establishing itself, it gains a certain psychological advantage over rivals, as long as it remains within its territory. Presumably so as not to lose this advantage, individuals may return to the same territories for their entire lives.

This is why maintaining high-quality habitat in the tropics is a matter of crucial importance to migratory birds. If a bird loses its territory to ''development,'' it has lost its most vital asset—the source of security that assures its overwinter survival. Often there will be nowhere else to go.

Precisely this point has been demonstrated by John Rappole and Eugene Morton (1985) in some highly relevant research. These ornithologists have been studying the effects of habitat alteration on the densities and behavior

of overwintering migrants in one of the last remaining forested areas of
Caribbean Mexico—the Serrania de los Tuxtlas in southeastern Veracruz
State. With the help of Mexican university students, they have banded over
a thousand birds, including migrants of 24 species.

They initiated the study in 1974–75 in a 5-hectare plot of forest that was
contiguous with what was then an extensive region of primary forest. They
determined that many species of migrants held defended territories in this
forest, among them wood thrush, worm-eating warbler, hooded warbler,
and Kentucky warbler (Rappole and Warner 1980). By color banding the
birds, and then observing their activities when free in the forest, they were
able to determine how many individuals occupied the study plot and the
sizes of their territories.

Five years later, in 1980, they returned to the site and found it drastically
altered. The original 5 hectares had been carved up into a patchwork of
fields and forest fragments, and the surrounding primary forest had been
pushed back hundreds of meters, so that the plot had become an island. It
now contained a pasture (1.7 hectares), a tract of partially felled forest (0.7
hectare), a cornfield (0.6 hectare) and an area of thick undergrowth along
a stream (0.2 hectare). Less than 2 hectares of the original forest remained.

Obtaining permission from the squatters who now had possession of the
land, they repeated the measurements that they had made five years earlier.
The total number of birds that occupied the 5 hectares had fallen significantly. This applied to migrants as well as to residents, in spite of the fact
that the area now contained substantial amounts of edge and scrub, types
of vegetation that have repeatedly been described as good habitat for
migrants.

Not only had the populations of many species fallen below their former
levels, but the individuals present now occupied larger territories, suggesting that the quality of the habitat had diminished as well. In 1975, for
example, there had been 12 hooded warblers resident on the plot, each of
which occupied an average of 0.3 hectare. In 1980 only five hooded warblers were present, and the average territory size had increased to 1.0 hectare. Similarly, magnolia and Wilson's warblers defended territories of 0.2
to 0.4 hectare in 1975, but in 1980 the same species were using areas of 1
hectare or more.

Other species, such as the black-and-white warbler and worm-eating
warbler, had abandoned the plot altogether. These species, as well as some
others, typically join mixed foraging flocks on the wintering ground, just
as brown creepers and golden-crowned kinglets do in the temperate forest.
But in the absence of chickadees, the mixed flocks in coastal Veracruz are
led by tawny-crowned and gray-headed greenlets, members of the vireo
family. Apparently the 1.8-hectare fragment of forest that remained on the
plot was too small to support a greenlet flock, since these key species were

missing, along with the migrants that habitually accompany them (Rappole and Morton 1985).

What happens to all the migrants that are displaced from their territories when forest is cleared to make cornfields or cattle pasture? Rappole and his colleagues are currently attempting to answer this question by attaching tiny radio transmitters to wood thrushes. In the Los Tuxtlas region, where huge areas have been deforested within the last few years, they find wood thrushes that show two types of behavior—territorial residents and nonterritorial wanderers. Residents are distinguished by living in mature forest and by remaining (until the batteries powering their transmitters fail) within 50 meters of the point of capture. Nonresidents generally leave the vicinity shortly after release and are rarely found again, since they usually outdistance the range of their transmitters.

The few nonresidents that were later relocated were found in disturbed vegetation along a nearby river. At least two of them were killed by raptors, because their beeping radios were later recovered from telltale scatterings of feathers. It seems likely that territories confer multiple benefits—greater security to their owners, as well as a defended food supply.

The discovery of territoriality in overwintering migrants has raised some questions no one thought to ask before. On their North American breeding grounds, virtually all migrant landbirds except swifts and swallows are territorial, so territoriality is taken for granted. Moreover, the diversity of behaviors that would be needed to undertake a comparative study is lacking. The issue becomes a matter of interest on the wintering ground, because now some species show territoriality and others do not.

TERRITORIES AND THE SINGLE FEMALE

Let us consider as an example four flycatchers that winter in the vicinity of the Cocha Cashu Biological Station in Amazonian Peru (Fitzpatrick 1982). Two, the eastern wood pewee and the alder flycatcher, establish individual territories where the birds remain resident throughout the northern winter. The other two, the sulphur-bellied flycatcher and the eastern kingbird, are nonterritorial and can frequently be seen in monotypic flocks, especially the eastern kingbird. All four hold conventional territories in the summer, so why do we find this difference in the winter?

It appears to be a matter of diet. The first two species are insectivorous throughout the year, whereas the other two switch on the wintering ground to a diet that is largely composed of fruit (Morton 1971; Fitzpatrick 1982, 1983).

The distinction is a critical one because of the way the two types of resources are distributed in the environment. Insects and other arthropods tend to be dispersed in the habitat. If the vegetation is more or less uniform,

Fɪɢ. 10.1 Eastern kingbird

one hectare will contain about as many as the next. Fruit, on the other hand, tends to occur in concentrated patches. A large crop may provide a superabundance for a time, but later the same habitat could offer nothing. Frugivores are thus obliged to be opportunistic and only rarely show territoriality. The erratic comings and goings of cedar waxwings are a familiar example.

In order to understand why insectivores are territorial, we have to imagine how a bird exploits its environment. Within the space of, say, a hectare, there is certain to be variation in the quality of the habitat—spots where the foraging is reliably good and spots where it is chronically poor (Gradwohl and Greenberg 1981). For a sallier such as a pewee, a territory is likely to have a few good perches and many that are not so good. But a bird will not learn to concentrate its efforts on the good spots and to ignore the poor ones until it becomes thoroughly familiar with an area.

Here is where a territory has special value to its owner. By excluding other members of its species, the owner maintains exclusive rights over the good foraging spots and capitalizes on its hard-gained knowledge of where they are (Terborgh 1983). Were it to wander around at random, it would spend most of its time foraging in poor sites, and like the unfortunate wandering wood thrushes in the deforested Tuxtla Mountains, it might be less prepared to evade predators. For these reasons, nearly all forest-dwelling insectivorous birds are strongly territorial.

Wintertime territoriality entails an unconventional twist, as Paul Schwartz found with his northern water-thrushes. In such species, true feminine equality prevails. It is not a chivalrous equality, granted by acquiescing males, but a militant equality, hard-won through belligerence. Females must compete on equal terms with males for possession of patches of real estate that are crucial to survival.

There are some species in which the females are externally indistinguishable from males, northern water-thrushes being a prime example. They are the same size and bear the same plumage characteristics. In these, we can presume that the contest is one of equals, except for one important detail—behavior. Male and female sex roles are often strongly divergent during the breeding season. Males arrive earlier and devote much time and energy to establishing, defending, and advertising possession of the joint territory through song. In the meantime, the females lead much less conspicuous lives and perform more than their share of the work in nest building and incubating. Later, after the young have fledged, males assume a more domestic mien, curtailing their singing activity shortly after dawn to devote themselves to feeding and leading the still dependent juveniles (Robinson 1981).

Changes in behavior through the seasons and the differentiation of sex roles are hormonally mediated, though the details have been worked out for only a few species, a leading example being the common canary (Nottebohm 1981). Undoubtedly, other hormonal changes are involved in the inducement of female territorial behavior on the wintering ground.

Going back to the wood pewees in Peru, we can ask about the way in which territories are established and maintained. One is always apprised of the arrival of pewees in October, because they sing incessantly, right through the middle of the day, when other birds tend to be quiet. The winter song is distinctly peweelike, but it is not the song they sing in North America. It consists of detached notes, similar to the "pee" or "wee" parts of the refrain that gives them their name. The birds appear to be solitary, and we suspect, though it has not yet been proven, that females are singing on a par with males. If so, this is a new twist—a bird that is silent at nesting time but engages in territorial song during the winter.

There are many species in which the males and females hold separate winter territories, but the winter vocalizations are more in the category of "notes" than of "songs." Northern and Louisiana water-thrushes defend their winter domains with their characteristic "chips," and so do hooded and Kentucky warblers. Vocal advertisement of territories with true song appears to be unusual, though not unique to the pewee. Crested flycatchers in Panama also call vigorously from their forested retreats. Further examples will certainly come to light in future studies.

There are many species in which the males and females are not identical in size or plumage. In some of these, redwings being a well-studied example, the sexes partially segregate for the winter, either in different habitats or by concentrating in different geographical regions (Dolbeer 1982). When there is geographical segregation, the males as a rule winter farther north, presumably to obtain the advantage of an early arrival on the breeding ground (Fretwell 1980; Pearson 1980; Myers 1981).

Recently it has been discovered that male and female hooded warblers segregate by habitat in the Yucatan Peninsula (Lynch et al. 1985). Males and females vigorously defend territories, periodically announcing themselves with a loud "chip." For a while Lynch and his colleagues were baffled, because they failed to find females in the primary forest habitat believed typical for the species, even when they used mist nets to capture the birds for banding. The mystery was resolved when they set their nets in brushy abandoned cornfields. Here they found females, but no males.

In the hooded warbler the males are slightly larger (10.8 versus 10.1 grams) and more boldly patterned than the females, and are presumably dominant to them in a contest. This might suggest that males were monopolizing the remaining primary forest habitat in the region, now that it is becoming scarce. If so, the females could be left with no other recourse than to spend the winter in disturbed and semiarid habitats, where, like the nonterritorial wood thrushes in the Tuxtlas, they might experience reduced survival. Differential overwinter mortality could then result in a serious deficiency of females on the breeding ground.

This disturbing possibility has now been tested by Morton and his colleagues (1987). Working along habitat boundaries where winter territories of the two sexes came into contact, the investigators removed male hooded warblers from territories adjacent to or surrounded by territories occupied by females. In no case did the females expand into the space left vacant by the missing males, implying that the use of different habitats by male and female hooded warblers is truely a matter of preference rather than of aggressive monopolization of the prime habitat by males. Nevertheless, the case provides a warning of the kind of threatening situation that could develop as the amount of wintering habitat in the tropics continues to be reduced by deforestation.

With regard to the complex issue of sexual differences in plumage, the work of Lynch et al. (1985) has revealed a heretofore unsuspected relation to female territoriality. Female hooded warblers show a wide range of variation in the plumage around the head. At one extreme, considered to be the typical female pattern, the crown is olive and the face and throat are yellow. In some intermediate birds, the border between the olive and yellow is enforced with a black edging that extends as a thin necklace across the throat, whereas in other more extreme individuals, major portions of the crown and throat are black, closely mimicking the more intense pattern of adult males. Lynch and his colleagues found that these malelike females often hold territories in primary forest, whereas dull-plumaged females were nearly always in scrub habitats. It is now known that the progression of female plumages described above is unrelated to age, and that each bird retains a particular plumage throughout life. With the continuing reduction in the amount of primary forest habitat available on the wintering ground, females with malelike plumage seem to make up a diminishing fraction of the population (E. S. Morton, personal communication).

Some migrants participate in yet another kind of territorial system, akin to that practiced by the flocks of chickadees and their followers that glean our northern woods. The tropical equivalents of these bands are made up of insectivorous species with names that often reflect their resemblance to northern counterparts—antshrikes, antwrens, antvireos. Membership in these flocks adheres to a strict quota of one family per species (Munn and Terborgh 1980; Gradwohl and Greenberg 1981). Color-banding studies have shown that once a bird becomes an established member of such a flock, it tends to remain with it for years, presumably for life (Munn 1985; Greenberg and Gradwohl 1986). Day after day throughout the year the same individuals assemble to forage together, a situation remarkable for its stability and continuity.

The species that participate in these flocks possess a unique form of mutual territoriality (Munn and Terborgh 1980). All flock members recognize the same set of territorial boundaries, so that in effect the flock, rather than its component pairs, possesses the territory. It is not yet known how these mutual territories are established, but they may form around a pair of the lead species, which in Amazonian Peru is one of two species of antvireo of the genus *Thamnomanes* (Munn 1986). When neighboring flocks happen to meet, there is a sudden outburst of vocal activity, as the male and female of each pair posture and display to their counterparts in the opposing group.

Several species of migrants are regular participants in these tropical mixed flocks while in their winter homes. A few migrants even appear to be obligate flock members, just as many of the permanent residents are. Among these can be counted the blue-winged, golden-winged, worm-eating, chestnut-sided, and Canada warblers (Greenberg and Gradwohl 1980; Greenberg 1985; Greenberg 1987). While in these flocks, the northern visitors obey the local rules, distributing themselves as single individuals or pairs. This is an important point because it implies that the number of migrant individuals the tropical wintering ground can support is limited by the number of mixed flocks of resident insectivores. When the habitat is disturbed or fragmented, as it has been in the Tuxtlas Mountains of Mexico, so that the resident flocks can no longer maintain themselves, the flock-dependent migrants are excluded as well.

The social limitation of migrant densities in tropical mixed flocks poses an interesting question in itself. The behavior was first noticed by Greenberg and Gradwohl (1980), who found that Canada warblers migrating through Panama often occurred in such flocks as pairs. They suggested that perhaps the birds migrated as pairs, thereby maintaining long-term pair bonds that could continue through the year.

Since Greenberg and Gradwohl proposed this idea, I have had occasion to observe Canada warblers on their wintering grounds in Ecuador, and on migration in New Jersey. In Ecuador, males and females did not occur together in pairs, and in fact seemed to concentrate at different elevations. At 1,300 meters, 11 out of 14 individuals encountered were females, whereas at 1,600 meters, three out of four were males. During migration in New Jersey, the rule of males first, females later seems to hold. There is no doubting Greenberg and Grahwohl's observations, but a different explanation is likely. If male Canada warblers will not tolerate another male in a flock, and females likewise will not tolerate other females, the effect would be to limit flock membership to single birds or pairs. A reduced level of intersexual aggression would permit pairs to coexist temporarily while they fed in the protective company of a mixed flock.

Fig. 10.2 Canada warbler

HAVING reviewed the cases of northern water-thrushes, pewees, hooded warblers, and Canada warblers, we can now appreciate that northern birds display a wide range of territorial behaviors on the tropical wintering grounds. Why a system that seems so simple and straightforward on the breeding ground has become so diversified on the wintering ground is a question that has barely been asked by ornithologists and one that merits far more study. For our purpose, it is essential to appreciate that some of these territorial systems, particularly the segregation of males and females into distinct habitats, and sex-limited membership in flocks, have important implications for conservation.

BACK TO THE CASE OF THE FRUIT-EATING FLYCATCHERS

Finally, let us return to the eastern kingbirds and sulphur-bellied flycatchers that abandon their territoriality on the wintering ground. Both of these flycatchers become avid fruit eaters in the nonbreeding season. Upon arrival in their Amazonian winter homes, both species encounter somewhat larger tropical relatives, the tropical kingbird and the streaked flycatcher, respectively. In one-on-one combat, the migrants would not be able to wrest control of a fruit tree from one, much less a pair, of their intensely territorial tropical counterparts, but this potential hindrance is circumvented by a behavioral tactic. The migrants travel in flocks. I have watched 50 or 60 kingbirds pour into the crown of a single tree and begin snatching fruits. The resident tropical kingbirds are obliged to hold their fire, because against such odds any defense would be futile (Fitzpatrick 1983). The sulphur-bellied flycatcher engages in similar tactics, though its flocks are typically much smaller.

The adoption of fruit eating and gregariousness as a winter strategy enables these two migrants to overcome the competition of tropical counterparts, but it seems to impose some additional behavioral requirements, especially in the case of the eastern kingbird. The species is the most abundant North American migrant in eastern Peru from the end of September through early November, a period that coincides with the fruiting peak of their favorite lauraceous trees. Later in the season, ripe lauraceous fruit becomes relatively scarce, and the big flocks of kingbirds disappear. A scattered few individuals remain for the rest of the winter, but the bulk of the population moves elsewhere.

Perhaps kingbirds follow a kind of circular migration route at the southern end of their journey, tracking the lauraceous fruiting peak from one part of Amazonia to another. At present we can only guess that this is what they do. This, and much more, remains to be discovered about how migrants have adapted to the tropics.

11 *A Glimpse at Some Tropical Habitats*

To the uninitiated, the word *tropics* often carries the connotation of steamy jungles teeming with malevolent pests and awash with debilitating fevers. In reality, tropical landscapes are as varied, and often as beautiful, as any one sees in the temperate regions. The vegetation may be lush and dense, but so may it be in some temperate environments. Perhaps it is the palms, vines, and epiphytes that create the exotic flavor of tropical vegetation. But once the novelty of these unfamiliar plant forms has worn off, tropical habitats can be seen to be as distinct and varied as those in the observer's homeland. The word *jungle* then ceases to have any meaning, just as it has no place in the botanical lexicon.

The environments in which North American migrants spend the winter are at least as varied as those in which they breed. Chilly mountaintops in Mexico, limestone scrub in the Antilles, the vast grasslands or llanos of Venezuela and Colombia, mangroves in Panama, cloud forests on the slopes of the Andes, the forbidding thorny fastness of the Paraguyan chaco, even Tierra del Fuego—all provide a retreat for one species or another (see Figure 11.1).

A visitor viewing migrants for the first time in one of these environments would find both the expected and the unexpected. He or she would be reassured to note that most species choose winter homes that bear some obvious resemblance to their summer habitats. Louisiana water-thrushes course along clear pebbly streams, yellow-throated warblers creep around pine boughs, willow flycatchers sally from willowlike plants along rivers, and dickcissels throng to the grasslands and ricefields of the llanos. But a visitor would also find some disconcerting exceptions, such as indigo buntings in flocks of hundreds along Yucatan roadsides; eastern kingbirds, also in large flocks, feeding on avocadolike fruits in the canopy of the Amazonian rainforest; and chimney swifts darting over the Peruvian coastal desert.

There is another surprise when one finds species in seemingly incongruous combinations. A rainforest in the Dominican Republic, for example, might have Cape May warblers and gray-cheeked thrushes from the boreal forest; black-throated blue warblers, and redstarts from the Appalachians; and parula and worm-eating warblers from the eastern lowlands. There is nothing sacrosanct about the "communities" of species we find breeding together, for they recombine in many ways during the months they are beyond our purview.

It is also surprising to find so many species together. Rich eastern deciduous forests commonly harbor four to six warbler species, but perhaps due to the geographical congestion of the wintering grounds, one may find eight, ten, or even (in western Mexico), 15 warbler species in a single homogeneous habitat (Hutto 1980). We now see that not only are the populations of individual species geographically concentrated in the winter, but the species may also be crowded into communities of extraordinarily high diversity. Once we realize this, we can appreciate that many tropical habitats, from a conservation standpoint, are even more precious than our own.

Figures 11.2 through 11.21 present a pictorial review of some of the tropical habitats used by overwintering migrants, proceeding generally from north to south. The photos, more effectively than words, convey an impression of the richness of the biological world to the south of our borders. The captions offer comments on the importance of each habitat to migrants, which migrants were found in it, and its current conservation status.

ACCOMMODATION TO CHANGE: ARE PRIMARY HABITATS NECESSARY?

We have seen that migrants pass the winter in a diverse array of environments—high and low, wet and dry, both north and south of the equator. As time goes on, many of these natural vegetation formations are being transformed by relentless economic pressures.

The magnificent pine and fir forests of the Mexican cordilleras are being felled to build houses in the crowded cities, and the once extensive evergreen forests of Mexico's Caribbean lowlands have been reduced to mere fragments to provide pasture for an ever-expanding market for beef. Lowland dry forests in Guatemala are being cleared for cotton growing and to raise winter crops, such as melons, for the North American market. Much of the natural vegetation of Cuba and the Dominican Republic has been replaced with sugarcane fields. In Jamaica, Guatemala, Panama, and other countries, coffee growing to supply export markets has drastically reduced the amount of mid-montane forest available to migrants. Lowland rainforests in Honduras, Panama, and Ecuador are being replaced with banana plantations, again for export to richer countries in the north. African oil palms are changing the landscape in Costa Rica, Ecuador, and elsewhere. Mid-elevation cloud forest has been discovered to offer a propitious climate for dairy farming in Costa Rica, Colombia, and Ecuador. And in the future there looms the truly grim prospect that many of these countries will

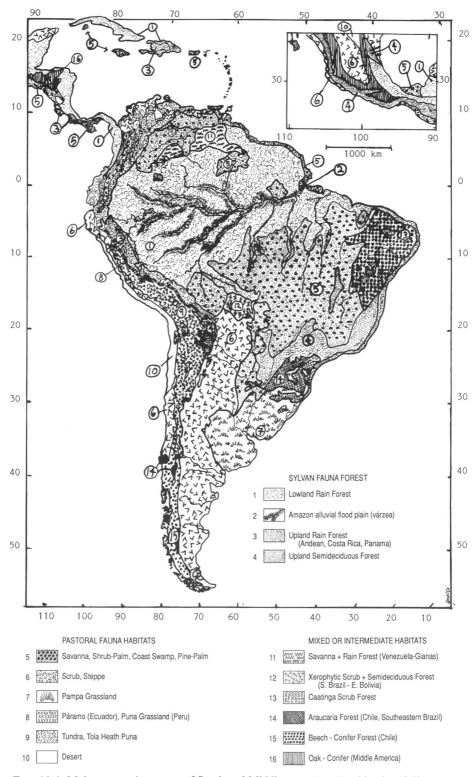

SYLVAN FAUNA FOREST

1   Lowland Rain Forest

2   Amazon alluvial flood plain (várzea)

3   Upland Rain Forest
     (Andean, Costa Rica, Panama)

4   Upland Semideciduous Forest

PASTORAL FAUNA HABITATS

5   Savanna, Shrub-Palm, Coast Swamp, Pine-Palm

6   Scrub, Steppe

7   Pampa Grassland

8   Páramo (Ecuador), Puna Grassland (Peru)

9   Tundra, Tola Heath Puna

10   Desert

MIXED OR INTERMEDIATE HABITATS

11   Savanna + Rain Forest (Venezuela-Gianas)

12   Xerophytic Scrub + Semideciduous Forest
      (S. Brazil - E. Bolivia)

13   Caatinga Scrub Forest

14   Araucaria Forest (Chile, Southeastern Brazil)

15   Beech - Conifer Forest (Chile)

16   Oak - Conifer (Middle America)

FIG. 11.1 Major vegetation zones of South and Middle America (Hershkovitz 1969).

Overwinter Habitats of Neotropical Migrants

FIG. 11.2 Princeton students Terry Root and David Wilcove in oak woodland, Volcan Colima, Jalisco, Mexico. This habitat is extraordinarily rich in migrants. One can see mixed flocks containing up to 15 species of warblers, including painted redstart, olive warbler, red-faced warbler, black-throated gray warbler, plus orioles, flycatchers, vireos, grosbeaks, and tanagers.

Fɪɢ. 11.3 Primary pine—fir forest at high elevation in the Sierra Madre del Sur, Guerrero, Mexico: Rivoli's hummingbird, ruby-crowned kinglet, hermit warbler, Townsend's warbler, western tanager.

FIG. 11.4 Princeton University field camp in *Pinus hartwegii* forest high on Volcan Colima, Jalisco, Mexico: Rivoli's hummingbird, Williamson's sapsucker, brown creeper, golden-crowned kinglet, olive warbler, hermit warbler.

FIG. 11.5 Princeton student Margaret McFarland folding mist net in relict alder forest near timberline on Volcan Colima, Jalisco, Mexico: blue-throated hummingbird, calliope humming-bird, broad-tailed hummingbird, rufous hummingbird, Allen's hummingbird, hermit thrush, orange-crowned warbler, MacGil-livray's warbler, hepatic tanager. In spite of being in a national park, this site was actively being logged and grazed by cattle while we were there, and numerous spent shotgun shells on the ground provided ample evidence of hunting.

Fɪɢ. 11.6 View of the narrow coastal plain of the Lesser Antillean island of St. Kitts, with St. Eustatius in the distance. The fertile volcanic soil is intensively utilized for sugar cane: no migrants here.

Fɪɢ. 11.7 Only the steep upper slopes and ridges of St. Kitts and other volcanic islands in the Lesser Antilles retain natural vegetation: parula warbler, Cape May warbler, black-throated blue warbler.

FIG. 11.8 Most of what little lowland vegetation remains in the Antilles is found in rugged karst (limestone) topography too steep or rocky for cultivation, such as this hill in central Puerto Rico: black-throated blue warbler, American redstart, ovenbird, Louisiana water-thrush.

FIG. 11.9 Land slumping is a predictable consequence of deforestation on steep slopes in the humid tropics (Puerto Rico).

FIG. 11.10 Primary stand of Caribbean pine in a national park in the central cordillera of the Dominican Republic: black-and-white warbler, yellow-throated warbler, palm warbler, yellow-rumped warbler.

Fɪɢ. 11.11 Except for two relatively small parks, the mountains of the Dominican Republic and adjacent Haiti have been almost entirely denuded of their natural vegetation.

FIG. 11.12 Dry forest in its leafless condition in January when many migrants are present, Guerrero, Mexico: broad-billed hummingbird, ash-throated flycatcher, western flycatcher, black-capped vireo, warbling vireo, black-and-white warbler, Nashville warbler, painted bunting.

FIG. 11.13 Tropical thorn scrub near Azua in the southwestern Dominican Republic: prairie warbler. Although a rather minor habitat for North American migrants except in western Mexico, thorn scrub is being widely degraded by tree removal for charcoal production and overgrazing by goats.

FIG. 11.14 Primary lowland evergreen forest at Tikal National Park, Guatemala: least flycatcher, wood thrush, blue-gray gnatcatcher, yellow-throated vireo, black-and-white warbler, worm-eating warbler, blue-winged warbler, magnolia warbler, hooded warbler, American redstart, orchard oriole, summer tanager.

FIG. 11.15 Luxuriant mid-elevation Andean forest in the Quijos Valley of Ecuador: olive-sided flycatcher, Swainson's thrush, caerulean warbler, blackburnian warbler, Canada warbler, summer tanager.

FIG. 11.16 Ridge-top elfin forest in the Luquillo National Forest, Puerto Rico.
Elfin forests are nearly devoid of migrants.

FIG. 11.17 Princeton tropical ecology class observing birds in the cloud forest of El Triunfo Reserve in Chiapas, Mexico. Cloud forests in general harbor few migrants. Here we found broad-winged hawk, vaux's swift, Townsend's warbler, and Wilson's warbler.

FIG. 11.18–11.19 Black (left) and red (right) mangrove forests in Santa Rosa National Park, Costa Rica: prothonotary warbler, Tennessee warbler, northern water-thrush. Mangrove forests are being felled for the manufacture of paper and charcoal, or removed to make room for impoundments used in shrimp culture.

FIG. 11.20 A Princeton University field course visits the wildlife refuge at Palo Verde, Costa Rica: blue-winged teal, sora rail. Marshes such as these are being widely drained for rice cultivation.

FIG. 11.21 A high Andean marsh near Cusco, Peru: cinnamon teal, Wilson's phalarope.

have to devote major portions of their national territories to biomass planta-tions for alcohol production to reduce the cost of petroleum imports, as Brazil is already doing. When this happens, what will become of the migrants?

Not all of them will disappear, that is certain. Some species seem to benefit from disturbance; others, to varying degrees, adapt to it; and still others, we hope a minority, will decline in proportion to the disappearance of primary habitats. If we are not to blunder blindly into this future, we should make an effort to establish which species can adapt to disturbance and which cannot. Only then can we begin to define priorities.

THE IMMEDIATE CONSEQUENCES OF DEFORESTATION: TWO EXAMPLES

Winter travelers in the New World tropics commonly remark on the conspicuous abundance of migrants in early successional habitats, such as gardens, hedgerows, brushy pastures, and young second growth (Karr 1976; Terborgh 1980). Observations of this type have led at least one au-thor (Monroe 1970) to the sanguine conclusion that ''opening up'' the tropical forest could even lead to an increase in the capacity of the land-scape to harbor overwintering migrants. If this were true, we could all rest comfortably and leave the tropical countries to cope with their own conser-vation problems.

But an impressionistic assessment, even if correct, should not be taken at face value without probing its implicit assumptions. Among the hidden assumptions, two are particularly crucial: first, that migrants in general would benefit, and second, that the new ''habitats'' generated by defores-tation would be more conducive to migrants than the original forest. We shall see that neither of these projections is valid. To illustrate the point, let us proceed with a pair of concrete examples.

An Ecuadorian Cattle Pasture

In 1985 I surveyed migrants in the Quijos Valley of Ecuador. It is mag-nificent terrain on the eastern slopes of the Andes. Lush cloud forests sweep down from misty, unseen heights to roaring whitewater torrents in deep canyons below. It is the land of cock-of-the-rock and quetzal, breath-taking in its scale and beauty, but formidable of access.

The Ecuadorian government has recently completed a road down the Valley to service a pipeline carrying oil from its eastern fields. When I was there in early 1985, the road was carrying a steady flow of settlers into the region, and scattered openings were beginning to punctuate the forested vistas. It is at this incipient stage in the modification of an erstwhile wilderness that one has the best opportunity to make "before" and "after" comparisons.

A representative area of natural forest contained a dazzling array of bird species, far too many to discover and enumerate in the span of a brief sojourn. Migrants were present in addition to the myriad residents, but in the verdant gloom of the cloud forest, birds of any kind were frustratingly difficult to find. It took me most of three days to accumulate an adequate sample of sightings, a hard-won goal in the brief bursts of sunlight between showers.

Yet my perseverance was rewarded. Migrants represented 16 percent of the tally. The species present were olive-sided flycatcher, Swainson's thrush, blackburnian, caerulean, golden-winged, and Canada warblers, redstart, and summer tanager—a set of birds with real class.

A few miles farther along the road, I found a narrow footpath that led sharply down a slope into one of the newly established clearings that are beginning to dot the landscape. Venturing forth, I was pleased to find that the peasant owner of this plot was cheerful and accommodating, and that his dogs were not prohibitively aggressive.

FIG 11.22 Olive-sided flycatcher.

On a slope that was somewhat gentler than the rest, he was preparing pasture for a nascent herd of Brahman cattle. The forest had been cut and burned less than two years before, as one was reminded by the many charred snags that projected incongruously from the lush grass. Here, in the "after" setting, birds were conspicuous. They flew up from the edge of the path and sallied out from the many naked snags. Migrants seemed plentiful too, but *which* migrants? Not one of the species I had seen in the nearby cloud forest was in that pasture.

The total diversity of species was drastically diminished, to a mere 15 or 20 from the 150 or more that had inhabited the original forest. Gone were the colorful cocks-of-the-rock, tanagers, trogons, and hummingbirds. Flycatchers and seedeaters took their places in the pasture. As for migrants, the proportion remained about the same—18 percent—but there was only one species, the western wood pewee, instead of eight. Apparently the rough-hewn opening on the mountainside provided good conditions for hawking flying prey, for pewees were there by the dozen, sallying out from the sun-bleached branches of forest ghosts.

The lesson to be drawn from this example is a general one. When natural habitats are modified to serve human purposes, they lose the structural complexity and botanical richness that are required to maintain highly diverse bird communities. It may indeed be true that the *proportion* of migrants is unaffected by clearing the primary forest, but the total number of birds, and certainly their diversity, is bound to decline. That the birds are more conspicuous only creates a seductive illusion.

A Yucatán Milpa

To reinforce the point, let us examine another case in a very different setting: the hot, low limestone plain of the Yucatán Peninsula. Mayan farmers have occupied this land for centuries, hacking little cornfields known as milpas out of the scrub and abandoning them a few years later in the classic pattern of slash-and-burn swidden agriculture. In time, the exhausted milpas return to forest, closing the cycle.

In the late 1970s Robert Waide, then a graduate student at the University of Wisconsin, investigated the effect of this time-honored agricultural practice on migrants. He selected six sites near the archaeological zone of Becan in southeastern Campeche. Three were old milpas, abandoned for one, two and five years, and three were forested, representing late stages in the regeneration cycle. Using mist nets to capture large samples of birds at each site, he obtained the results shown in Table 11.1.

Migrants are numerous in the Yucatan and constituted a third or more of all birds present in the habitats sampled by Waide. At the six sites combined, he captured a total of 985 birds, of which 502 (51 percent) were migrants of 25 species. The three early successional (milpa) sites averaged

TABLE 11.1 Mist Netting Results from Early and Late Successional Habitats in the Yucatán Peninsula

| Species | Abandoned milpas | | | Regenerated forest | | |
	1 year	2 years	3 years	Becan	Chicanna	Buena Noche West
Local residents	44	186	99	36	55	63
Ruby-throated hummingbird	4	0	2	0	0	0
Empidonax flycatcher	1	5	9	6	1	2
Gray catbird	0	7	3	0	0	0
Wood thrush	2	0	0	4	5	0
Swainson's thrush	0	0	0	0	1	0
Gray-cheeked thrush	0	0	1	0	0	0
White-eyed vireo	0	1	8	4	5	2
Black-and-white warbler	0	0	1	4	1	4
Worm-eating warbler	0	0	0	1	0	1
Yellow warbler	0	4	8	0	0	0
Magnolia warbler	2	0	9	3	3	7
Black-throated green warbler	0	0	0	0	1	0
Ovenbird	0	2	2	2	1	3
Northern water-thrush	0	0	3	0	0	0
Kentucky warbler	0	0	0	7	6	9
Yellowthroat	3	21	5	0	0	0
Yellow-breasted chat	0	1	0	0	0	0
Hooded warbler	1	0	1	1	3	4
American redstart	0	0	3	0	1	1
Blue-winged warbler	0	0	0	0	1	0
Orchard oriole	0	30	0	0	0	0
Rose-breasted grosbeak	0	3	0	0	0	0
Indigo bunting	37	164	44	2	0	1
Painted bunting	1	14	2	0	0	0
Dickcissel	0	1	0	0	0	0
Percent migrants	54	58	51	49	35	35
(without indigo bunting)	24	32	37	47	35	34

Source: Waide 1980.

55 percent migrants, and the three late successional (forest) sites averaged 39 percent migrants.

As can been seen at a glance, however, the migrant population in the milpa sites predominantly consisted of indigo buntings, which, as mentioned before, form large itinerant flocks in the winter. To include such flocks along with species that occur in ones and twos can result in a distortion of the sample. If indigo buntings are removed from the tallies, the milpa sites are then seen to contain a proportion of migrants (33 percent) that is no greater than that found in the forested sites.

Waide's results show clearly that migrants differ in their acceptance of disturbed environments. There are species such as ruby-throated hummingbird, catbird, yellowthroat, orchard oriole, rose-breasted grosbeak, indigo bunting, and painted bunting that seem to prefer the early stages of regrowth.

We can identify a second group of species that occupies mature habitat only: wood thrush, worm-eating warbler, Kentucky warbler, hooded warbler. These are species that face severe problems in the future as deforestation continues to eliminate suitable habitat.

Finally, there are species possessing a high degree of versatility that can tolerate, though not necessarily at equal densities, both early and late successional habitats: *Empidonax* sp. (mostly least flycatchers in the Yucatán), white-eyed vireo, magnolia warbler, ovenbird. Such species may suffer declines, but probably will remain with us, even in the event of total deforestation of their winter ranges.

From these two examples, it is obvious that "opening up" the tropical forest does not automatically benefit migrants. The contrary impressions of earlier authors, although accurately reflecting their observations, were concerned more with quantity than quality. Disturbed habitats in some regions do support higher densities of migrants than undisturbed primary vegetation, but it is seldom true outside of lowland Amazonia that disturbed habitat supports more species (Fitzpatrick et al. in press). Furthermore, it has recently been pointed out that past comparisons of migrants in primary forest versus second growth, many of which were conducted with mist nets set on the ground, neglected the forest canopy. Now that special attention has been given to the canopy, it has also been found to harbor considerable numbers of migrants (Greenberg 1981; Loiselle 1987).

The take-home message one derives from this is that disturbance nearly always leads to simplified communities. This was especially evident in the Ecuadorean cattle pasture, but was also apparent in the comparison of abandoned Yucatán milpas to regenerating forest. Had Waide included an active milpa as a control, he might have found it to be little more attractive to migrants than the Ecuadorean pasture.

True, one might retort, but in a slash-and-burn rotation system most of the land is fallow. If the cycle length is 20 years, then perhaps only 5–10 percent of the landscape is under cultivation at any time. The remaining 90–95 percent is undergoing succession and remains as suitable habitat for a wide range of migrants.

Although this argument might literally be true, it overlooks some important facts. First, as we have seen, the migrant species that use early successional vegetation are not the same as those that inhabit primary forest. The argument assumes the equivalency of all migrants, an assumption that many would be reluctant to accept. Second, slash-and-burn agriculture is on the way out and soon will be as obsolete as the shocks of corn that used to add an autumnal flavor to the landscape in my youth. In the ever more crowded world we live in, intensive, rather than extensive, agricultural practices are, of necessity, the current trend. Any realistic model of the future is therefore better represented by the Ecuadorean cattle pasture than by the abandoned milpas in Mexico. This future does not bode well for migrants, even if they are only catbirds and yellowthroats.

BEFORE VERSUS AFTER: WHERE DEFORESTATION HURTS THE MOST

In order to project current trends into the future it would be valuable to obtain information of several kinds. First, we need to know where migrants go to spend the winter. The answer, as we have already seen, is that they go nearly everywhere in the hemisphere south of the United States, but that they are most concentrated in the near tropical regions. Second, within each biogeographical region, we need to know which habitats are most crucial. Deserts, for example, harbor few migrants, whereas mangroves harbor many. Finally—and this is most critical to predicting the future— we need to know which habitats are being modified most rapidly and which migrant species are being most severely affected by the particular mode of land use to which each habitat is being put. The changes brought about by human utilization of the landscape can be drastic or relatively benign. To illustrate this more concretely, I shall again offer a pair of examples, representing what can be regarded as a worst-case and a best-case situation.

Worst Case: Mangroves

The once extensive mangrove forests of the Pacific lowlands of Ecuador have been entirely obliterated. They were first exploited for fuelwood and charcoal and later removed entirely to make room for large-scale impoundments used in the commercial propagation of shrimp. Since shrimp are unable to complete their life cycle in these impoundments, they must be restocked as larvae after each harvest. Ironically, the nursery ground of the shrimp was in the erstwhile mangrove forest, so larval shrimp can no longer be obtained in Ecuador.

Instead, Ecuadorean shrimp growers by the dozens go across the border to Peru to seine larvae for stocking their impoundments. Their rudimentary encampments dot the shores of shallow bays and estuaries that are still lined with mangroves. But to heap irony upon irony, shrimp culture has been catching on in Peru, and clearing for the installation of impoundments has already resulted in the loss of more than 50 percent of that country's mangroves.

We are obviously witnessing a self-limiting process here, a fact of which the Peruvian government is well aware. Yet one doubts that much will be done about it. First, most land in Peru is held without title under laws that strongly favor de facto possession. Removing someone from land he or she has already "developed" is almost unthinkable and certainly would not stand up to judicial process. Second, the political unpopularity of reining in a burgeoning industry, especially one that offers employment to a major sector of the local population, would be overwhelming.

From the political point of view, much the easiest course to take is to do nothing. The situation will resolve itself when there is no longer any resource to exploit. The collapse of the industry, with all the attendant hardship for the local population, will be regarded as an act of nature, and no politician will be held to blame. As is so frequently the case with the management of renewable resources, the future is sacrificed to immediate political expediency.

Soon there may be no mangroves in either Peru or Ecuador. The loss will have only minor repercussions on North American bird populations, because few migrants go so far south. Nevertheless, mangroves in other countries farther north are coming under increasing pressure, not only for shrimp culture, but for use as fuelwood and building materials. Recently I learned of plans to launch a paper-making industry based on Central American mangrove forests. Regarded as otherwise worthless, mosquito-ridden swamps by most local residents, with many of them in the common domain, there are few restraints to their continuing destruction. The rapidly eroding mudflats that remain in their place are inimical to small songbirds. Think of this next time you see a northern water-thrush or a prothonotary warbler.

FIG. 11.23 Prothonotary warbler

Best Case: Coffee Plantations

Not all land-use scenarios are as bleak as the case of mangroves. Some agricultural practices are compatible with the maintenance of high populations of migrants. This was first impressed on me many years ago when I conducted some tally counts on coffee and cacao (chocolate) plantations in the Dominican Republic.

In the Western Hemisphere, coffee and cacao are commonly grown under shade. The wild progenitors of today's cultivated varieties are plants of the forest midstory, requiring partial sunlight but subject to stress when fully exposed. In cultivation, both are grown in a vertically structured environment, with a superimposed canopy of a species (usually a legume) that provides a suitably light shade. When properly managed, plantations remain productive for many years and the overtopping shade trees can attain impressive stature. To the passing traveler with an untrained eye, a mature coffee or cacao plantation can easily be mistaken for a natural forest.

Coffee and cacao plantations make good migrant habitat. The two-tiered structure is conducive to the diverse foraging tactics of a multispecies community. In the plantations I studied in the Dominican Republic, there were ovenbirds on the ground, Louisiana water-thrushes along the streams, black-throated blue warblers and redstarts in the coffee or cacao understory, and parula, black-throated green, and Cape May warblers in the canopy. As migrant habitat, the man-made vegetation served almost as well as the native forest. I say almost because there were two common migrants to the Dominican Republic that I never found outside of primary forest: the worm-eating warbler and the Bicknell's (gray-cheeked) thrush. Thus, even the best-case scenario for artificial vegetation falls short of perfection.

Most common land-use practices in the Neotropics result in situations somewhere between those of the two examples just cited. Tropical landscapes often appear chaotic to eyes accustomed to the orderliness of temperate agriculture—patchworks of land in use and in various stages of disuse. Where much of the land is held by individual small farmers and peasants—as in Mexico, Guatemala, and Jamaica—the improvised disorder works to the benefit of migrants, since they can seek their varied feeding requirements in a heterogeneous mosaic of fields, hedges, brush, and copses of taller tress.

Where modern industrial-scale agriculture has taken over—as in Cuba, the Dominican Republic, and parts of Mexico, Honduras, and Panama—the result is not a happy one. Limitless expanses of sugarcane and bananas are no better for migrants than the cornfields of Illinois are for upland sandpipers and prairie chickens.

12 *Which Are the Crucial Habitats?*

We learned in the previous chapters that migrants tend to concentrate in the near tropical regions, such as Mexico and the Greater Antilles, and that more species are generally found in undisturbed primary habitats than in their man-modified derivatives. Still, if one were to jump to the conclusion that all habitats in the Antilles harbor high densities of migrants, or that migrant densities are low everywhere in central and southern South America, one would be mistaken. The actual patterns of distribution are more complicated than this; certain climates and certain types of vegetation seem to be preferred and others eschewed, and preferences seem to change as one goes from north to south. The details of these patterns deserve our scrutiny, because any future plan to conserve migrants will have to take them into account. But first it will help to appreciate the relationships between tropical habitats and climates.

TROPICAL CLIMATIC GRADIENTS

The sun in the tropics passes high overhead every day of the year, a climatological fact that precludes the wide seasonal swings in day length and temperature we experience in the temperate regions. This does not mean that tropical climates are aseasonal, only that the seasonality experienced is not of the same kind as at higher latitudes. Temperatures remain nearly constant throughout the year, but rainfall may vary sharply.

Large portions of the New World tropics experience a regular annual alternation between wet and dry seasons. The wet season normally coincides with ''summer,'' the period when the sun is most directly overhead. Regular dry seasons occur when the sun is in the opposite hemisphere. But some areas are inherently wetter than others.

Annual rainfall can vary from a few centimeters, say, in the Guajira Peninsula of northern Colombia, to over 10 meters in the upper San Juan Valley of western Colombia. Risking a mild oversimplification, one can say that as annual rainfall increases, so does the length of the wet season. That is because the rainfall experienced in the wettest month of an otherwise dry climate is comparable to the average monthly rainfall in a much wetter climate. Specifically, areas receiving 500–1,000 millimeters per year will tend to have three to four wet months and eight to nine dry months, areas receiving 2,000 millimeters per year will tend to have about seven wet and five dry months, and areas receiving over 4,000 millimeters have virtually no regular dry season. Seasonality and rainfall are thus very closely associated and can, to a first approximation, be considered as a single climatic variable.

The second major climatic variable in the tropics is temperature, but as associated with elevation rather than with season. Annual mean temperature decreases steadily at the rate of about 5 degrees Centigrade with each 1,000 meters of ascent. With mean temperatures of 26–27 degrees Centigrade at sea level, at this rate one reaches the line of perpetual snow at about 5,000 meters (16,000 feet).

To appreciate the full spectrum of tropical environments, we should consider all possible combinations of rainfall and temperature. Fortunately, this daunting prospect is amenable to simplification, because tropical mountains tend to be relatively well watered. Thus, although one must be acutely concerned with rainfall in considering lowland environments, in the mountains it is mainly temperature (elevation) that is of concern.

Wet versus Dry Habitats in the Lowlands

The use of semiarid environments by migrants varies regionally. John Faaborg and I (1980) found that austere thorn scrub in the southwestern Dominican Republic held only 3 percent migrants (mostly prairie warblers), whereas better-watered lowland vegetation types elsewhere in the country contained from 25–66 percent migrants. In contrast, Richard Hutto (1980) found a very high 55–60 percent migrants in thorn scrub in western Mexico, although the total density of birds was low. The disparity in the two sets of results seems best explained by the fact that the Mexican sites were occupied by western species, such as black-throated gray and MacGillivray's warblers, whereas only eastern species occur in the Dominican Republic. It would be surprising indeed if eastern species were to congregate in the desert for the winter.

Christmas Counts taken in various parts of Mexico invariably report high frequencies of migrants, regardless of whether the locality is high or low, wet or dry. A large fraction of the birds that breed in our Great Plains and Great Basin are known to winter on the Mexican plateau, though quantitative, scientifically gathered data are scanty. Around Ciudad Guzman in Jalisco, for example, I found large flocks of chipping, clay-colored, and lark sparrows in agricultural fields and hedgerows. The situation may be much the same over most of interior Mexico.

South of Mexico, semiarid regions are confined to restricted geographical pockets. One of these occurs in northwestern Costa Rica in the province of Guanacaste. Although hardly larger than an average-sized Texas county, Guanacaste deserves special mention, for it provides the winter home of most of the world's scissor-tailed flycatchers.

The use of dry habitats can also be transitory, as has been found in the semiarid zone of northern Colombia and Venezuela (Russell 1980; Bosque and Lentino 1987). There, a number of eastern species (especially gray-cheeked thrushes, redstarts, and blackpoll warblers) are present through the end of the rainy season (November–December), but then leave for parts unknown when the trees began to lose their leaves. Again, this is in contrast to the situation in western Mexico, where appreciable numbers of migrants (17–24 percent) remain in tropical deciduous forest throughout the leafless period (for example, solitary vireo, warbling vireo, blue-gray gnatcatcher, Virginia's warbler; Hutto 1980).

Nevertheless, migrants in lowland Mexico clearly prefer moister habitats. Two gallery forest sites studied by Hutto supported populations of 154 and 257 migrant individuals per hectare (64 percent and 70 percent of all birds present), whereas thorn scrub and deciduous forest, respectively, supported average migrant densities of 12 and 21 individuals per hectare. Of course, one must bear in mind when making such comparisons that gallery forest is extremely limited in aerial extent relative to thorn scrub and deciduous forest, so that, overall, the latter two habitat types may shelter greater numbers of individuals.

Farther south, in the coastal desert and deciduous forest of northwestern Peru, the only North American migrants I found were occasional flocks of chimney swifts. Similarly, in the leafless deciduous forest at Turiamo in northern Venezuela, migrants represented a scant 2 percent of 446 birds captured in mist nets (Terborgh and Faaborg 1980).

The overall picture is easily summarized. Highly seasonal tropical environments are much used by western migrants in Mexico and Costa Rica, but largely ignored by eastern species in the Antilles and northern South America.

Moister environments, supporting semideciduous or fully evergreen lowland tropical forest, are (or were) distributed from northeastern Mexico east through the Antilles and south through most of Central America and northern South America (see the map in Figure 11.1). It is these greener, shadier types of vegetation that are sought out by migrants of eastern provenance. Since over 150 species are involved, I will be able to describe only broad trends.

The most salient of these has already been emphasized, namely, the tendency for migrant densities to be highest in Mexico and the Antilles and to decline as one proceeds southward. Beyond this, it is important to note that individual species may be strikingly localized within the evergreen forest region, and that no species occurs ubiquitously. The most localized species, of course, are potentially the most vulnerable. I shall return to this point below.

Tropical Mountains

There is fully as much variety in the mountain vegetation to the south of our borders as there is in the lowlands. Viewing ridge upon ridge of spruce, fir, and pine in the Sierra Madre of Mexico, one could easily imagine the Rockies. At slightly lower elevations there are broad slopes of oak, juniper, and madrone, highly reminiscent of Arizona or Southern California. In truth, the highlands of our Southwest offer merely an impoverished sampling of the splendid biological richness of the Mexican cordillera.

Farther to the south, in Costa Rica or the Andes, the elevational sequence of vegetation zones is radically different from that in Mexico. From the foothills up to about 1,500 meters is what can be called lower montane forest. It resembles lowland forest except that the trees are seldom as large, and the understory tends to be more crowded. The next higher zone, extending to 2,500 or even 3,000 meters, is widely referred to as cloud forest, for nearly every day it lies shrouded in mist. The abundant water encourages lesser plant growth forms, such as mosses, ferns, and orchids, to grow on every available surface. Knarled trunks, huge-leafed Philodendrons, tree ferns, and bamboos fill out the scene, giving it a mysterious, storybook look. Going still higher, the forest gradually loses stature, and the mosses and ferns give way to multihued lichens. Near the timberline one confronts an impenetrable barrier of low, profusely branched crowns. Called *bosque enano* (dwarf forest) in Spanish and elfin forest in English, these mountaintop thickets are made cheerless and forbidding by an almost perpetual drizzle. Only in rare moments when the sun appears through a break in the clouds can one fully appreciate the kaleidoscopic beauty of this hidden world.

Montane habitats are home to large numbers of migrants. This is uniformly true from Mexico south into the Andes. At the northernmost limits of the tropics in central Mexico, high densities of migrants are found at all elevations from sea level to near the timberline (Hutto 1980). Farther south, migrants are conspicuously more abundant in montane habitats than in the lowlands.

Migrants made up less than 1 percent of the birds in lowland evergreen forests on both the Pacific and Atlantic slopes of Ecuador, whereas they made up 15 percent of all birds sighted or netted around 1,500 meters on both slopes. John Fitzpatrick, Scott Robinson, and I (in press) have reaffirmed this result for the eastern slope of the Peruvian Andes. The reasons for the unbalanced distribution of migrants into montane versus lowland habitats are obscure, but the pattern itself is unquestionably real.

In referring to montane habitats, I have thus far neglected to mention the elevations above 2,000 meters (6,500 feet). Migrants are relatively common in Mexican fir, pine, and alder forests even at 3,300 meters (11,000 feet), but perhaps these should be regarded as southern extensions of the temperate zone. Such an interpretation would be in accord with the majority of species wintering there—Williamson's sapsucker, brown creeper, golden and ruby-crowned kinglets, orange-crowned and yellow-rumped warblers, and others. All of these winter abundantly within the United States. But one also finds Townsend's and hermit warblers, which do not, so latitude clearly exerts an influence, in addition to the character of the habitat.

This situation changes to the south of Mexico. Mountaintops are no longer garbed in pine and fir but in cloud and elfin forest, habitats unlike any encountered in North America. In both southern Central America and in the Andes, I have found migrants to be scarce or lacking above 2,000 meters.

In some localities, the upper elevational limit of migrants is sharply defined. One particularly well-studied site at which this is true is the cloud forest reserve of Monteverde, in Costa Rica. Migrants of many species abound in the evergreen forest zone just below the reserve entrance. Only a few vertical meters higher in the true moss-draped cloud forest, they are suddenly very scarce (Tramer and Kemp 1980). In two days of birding there in January 1986, I found only an occasional golden-winged warbler. I had very much the same experience at other high-elevation sites in Panama, Venezuela, and Ecuador. The chilly, damp heights of humid tropical mountains are eschewed for the more propitious climes at mid-elevation.

This is unfortunate, for our own species also finds optimum conditions in the mid-elevation zone. Virtually throughout the tropics, the belt between 500 and 1,500 or 2,000 meters is under siege. It is almost entirely gone on the Pacific slope of Central America and is currently undergoing rapid development on the less desirable pluvial slopes of the Caribbean drainage. The central Andes of Colombia are entirely deforested within these elevations, and what areas remain in the western and eastern Andes are going fast. The pace of change has been a little slower in Ecuador and Peru, but the lapse of another generation will serve to close the gap. The migrants that winter in these tropical mountains are under threat. Those that cannot adapt to artificial conditions, such as dairy farms and coffee plantations, should already be considered endangered.

A WORD ABOUT THE SOUTHERN PAMPAS

There is yet another set of species whose situation merits this gloomy judgment: the several shorebirds that winter on the grassy plains of the Argentine and Uruguayan pampas. These include the stilt, buff-breasted,

Fɪɢ. 12.1 Upland sandpiper

and upland sandpipers, golden plover, and hudsonian godwit, as well as
the nearly extinct eskimo curlew. The populations of at least four of
these—eskimo curlew, buff-breasted and upland sandpiper, and hudsonian
godwit—are known to be drastically lower now than in the relatively recent
past. The pampas of the southern cone of South America are that continent's counterpart of our Great Plains. History is now in the process of
repeating itself.

Our plains were settled first by cattlemen who were later displaced by
farmers. The conversion of our long-grass prairie to cropland is now so
complete that only tiny patches of it remain untouched by a plow. Species
that were once abundant, such as the prairie chicken and bison, have become curiosities, confined to a scattered few refuges where they are on
view to the public. They are no longer fixtures of the general landscape.

Argentina and Uruguay are experiencing the same course of events. Famous for gauchos, *parrillada*, and ornate silver spurs, the Wild South lives on in people's imaginations, just as does the Wild West, with its cowboys and Indians, to a public overseas who knows us only through movies and cigarette ads.

Our image of Argentina is equally outdated. Cowboys there now drive pickup trucks, just as they do in Wyoming. What were once endless seas of waving grass are now seas, just as endless, of corn and wheat. The pampas have gone the way of Illinois and Kansas, a process that has been dramatically spurred by tax and other economic incentives.

Argentina lives, as it did in the past, from its food exports, but the return from an acre of corn or soybeans is so much greater than from an acre of range that there is no contest. Even marginal lands are going under the plow to provide vital foreign exchange for an economy in trouble (Myers and Myers 1979). The upshot of these trends for the curlews, godwits, plovers, and sandpipers that have used the southern plains for millennia is obvious. They are destined to go the way of the prairie chicken, but perhaps to even greater extremes, because the conservation movement in Argentina has not yet achieved the vitality it enjoys in the United States.

OVERVIEW

Every habitat mentioned in this chapter is being reduced with each passing year, but the situation of some is clearly worse than that of others. I would like to be able to offer a quantitative evaluation of the current status of each in the form of statements as "Of an initial X square kilometers of lower montane forest in southern Central America, Y square kilometers or Z percent remain intact," but until a few weeks before this work was due at the publisher's, no such data had been published. I am now able to report that data in just this form are available for Costa Rica, but that the results represent a bleak picture (see Table 12.1). Eighty-three percent of the country's original forest cover had been removed by 1983. This included the total loss of several entire life zones, for example, tropical dry forest and premontane moist forest. As is typical everywhere, the habitat that remains is the least suited to human occupancy—wet and pluvial forest on steep slopes at middle and higher elevations. As we have seen, much of this is not optimal migrant habitat either.

As for the current status of habitats in other regions south of the United States, I can only offer qualitative judgments that are admittedly no more than educated guesswork.

Let us return to our starting point and consider the status of mangroves. Peru and Ecuador aside, my impression is that mangroves have not yet been heavily exploited in most of the countries of Central America and

TABLE 12.1 Costa Rica: Change in Forested Area by Life Zone, 1940–83

Life zone	Total map area	1940 forest area[a]	1961 forest area[a]	1961 forest rate	1981 forest area	1981 forest rate	Total loss (%life zone)
Tropical							
Dry	3733	427	—	(9.1)	—	—	100
Moist	9903	5205	1695	(4.8)	9	(16.4)	>99
Wet	11,517	9726	7582	(1.3)	2816	(8.8)	78
Premontane							
Moist	3659	847	110	(3.6)	—	(16.7)	100
Wet	12,005	8799	5710	(1.8)	2244	(12.4)	81
Rain	4341	4100	3514	(0.9)	2155	(4.9)	50
Lower montane							
Moist	127	<1	—	—	—	—	100
Wet	925	515	215	(3.2)	127	(5.6)	86
Rain	3576	3446	3114	(0.6)	2336	(3.4)	35
Montane							
Wet	38	18	—	(9.1)	—	—	100
Rain	1165	123	1067	(0.2)	793	(3.7)	32
Total area	50,990	34,206	23,035		8711		
Average clearing rate				(1.8)		(7.7)	

Source: Sader and Joyce 1988.

[a] Areas given are for primary or near primary forests and do not include regeneration or secondary vegetation.

northeastern South America. Yet because mangroves occupy a limited area and are concentrated in a few critical spots along coasts, they are vulnerable. Any form of industrialization, the worst specters being shrimp aquaculture and paper manufacture, can quickly eliminate the mangroves from an entire region, as the experience in Ecuador has shown. The long-term economic argument for conserving mangroves as hatchery and nursery grounds for many commercially important shellfish and scale fish species should be compelling. The danger is that expediency and local politics can overwhelm the logic of any long-term rationale.

Tropical Dry Habitats

The vegetation of the seasonal lowlands of western Mexico and Costa Rica is in the late stages of being wholly taken over for human purposes. D. H. Janzen, an eminent ecologist with 20 years of field experience in this region, estimates that less than 2 percent of the tropical deciduous forest that once existed in Mexico and Central America is still intact. Worse yet, only 0.09 percent of it has conservation status. Fortunately for our purpose, most of the species that winter in deciduous forest are able to adapt to degraded vegetation.

The situation of tropical lowland evergreen forest is more complex, because it occurs over a much wider area. In some regions it is almost entirely gone, as in Cuba, Haiti, and the Dominican Republic. The daily exertions of hundreds of chainsaw operators is guaranteeing that a similar situation will soon exist in southeastern Mexico. Sizable areas of forest remain in the Caribbean lowlands of Central America, but these are also under pressure (Figure 12.2). Only in Amazonia and the Guianan region does there seem a realistic prospect that large blocks of natural vegetation will persist into the next century (Myers 1980). Veeries, gray-cheeked thrushes, red-eyed vireos, and Connecticut warblers are safe for the time being.

Montane habitats present a mixed picture. Most of the high-elevation conifer forests in Mexico have been logged, but not clear-cut, and are under sustained yield management. As long as current management practices remain in force, there will continue to be large areas of young and middle-aged pine and fir for kinglets, creepers, and hermit warblers. Farther south, the situation can only be described as bleak. The zone of high migrant density between 500 and 1,500 meters is currently being deforested at a greater rate than any other environment we have considered. This is true in every mountainous country from Guatemala to Argentina. We appear to be heading for an emergency here.

Another emergency is upon us in the pampas, where prairie grassland soon will be as scarce as it is in Iowa. The fates of many of the shorebirds that winter there are tied to the grasslands.

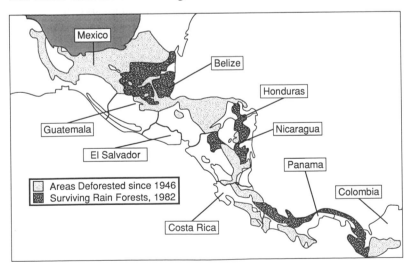

Fɪɢ. 12.2 Deforestation in Central America (*Tropicus*, Winter 1988, p. 4).

A Blue List for Migrants in the Tropics

Each year *American Birds* publishes an update of what is known as the "Blue List," a compilation of species known or suspected of being in trouble in some portion of their breeding ranges. The list serves the purpose of providing an early warning system to focus attention on potential conservation problems at the first possible moment.

In a similar vein, I present here a list of Neotropical migrants that deserve special attention, not always because of concrete data suggesting that they are in difficulty, but because they occupy geographically restricted winter ranges (see Table 12.2). Many may be holding their own perfectly well, others may even be increasing, but because the pace of change in many tropical countries is so much faster than it is in our own, serious situations could develop almost overnight.

The list includes 45 species, 26 of western or central affinities, 14 that breed mainly or exclusively in the East, and five passage migrants from the Arctic. Western species are heavily represented, because so many of them winter in relatively small areas in western Mexico.

Mexico consequently stands in first place as the most significant winter destination of these potentially endangered species. Of the 45, no fewer than 27 winter primarily in Mexico. Another five go to the Bahamas and Greater Antilles, three to southern Central America, four to the northern Andes, and six to the pampas.

The inclusion of species on the list is in no way definitive or final. Many of these species are very poorly known on their wintering grounds. The general outlines of winter ranges are known from specimens collected earlier in the century, but in some cases relevant ecological data are almost entirely lacking. There remains a lot of work to do in gathering the missing data: habitats occupied, elevational distributions, population densities, use of second growth and other nonnatural vegetation, and more. If we wait for professional scientists to provide all these data, we shall not have what we need soon enough. Here then is another area in which serious nonprofessionals can make important contributions to conservation.

TABLE 12.2 Migrants Having Geographically Restricted Winter Ranges

Locality	Principal natural habitat	Accepts disturbed habitat?
Northern and central Mexico		
black-chinned hummingbird	thorn scrub, galleries	yes
rufous hummingbird	pine-oak woodland	yes
Allen's hummingbird	pine-oak woodland	?
blue-throated hummingbird	pine-oak woodland	?
Botteri's sparrow	dry grassland	?
black-chinned sparrow	desrt scrub	?
Western Mexico		
calliope hummingbird	pine-oak woodland	?
broad-billed hummingbird	thorn scrub, galleries	?
dusky flycatcher	oak scrub	?
gray flycatcher	arid scrub, galleries	yes
black-capped vireo	desert riparian	yes
Bell's vireo	desert riparian	no
gray vireo	arid scrub	?
Virginia's warbler	oak woodland	no
colima warbler	pine-oak woodland	?
Lucy's warbler	desert riparian	no
black-throated gray warbler	oak woodland	yes
hermit warbler	fir forest	no
red-faced warbler	pine-oak woodland	no
Scott's oriole	desert scrub	?
black-headed grosbeak	pine-oak woodland	yes
lazuli bunting	riparian woodland	?
Southeastern Mexico/Guatemala/Belize		
Swainson's warbler	evergreen forest	no
blue-winged warbler	evergreen forest	?
Nashville warbler	evergreen forest	yes
golden-cheeked warbler	oak-juniper woods	no
hooded warbler	evergreen forest	no
Greater Antilles and Bahamas		
Bachman's warbler	evergreen forest	?
Kirtland's warbler	?	?
Cape May warbler	evergreen forest	yes
black-throated blue warbler	evergreen forest	yes
prairie warbler	deciduous forest	yes
Southern Central American lowlands		
scissor-tailed flycatcher	deciduous forest	yes
chestnut-sided warbler	evergreen forest	no
Southern Central American highlands		
Philadelphia vireo	montane forest	yes

TABLE 12.2 *continued*

Locality	Principal natural habitat	Accepts disturbed habitat?
Northern Andes, middle elevations		
cerulean warbler	montane forest	no
Blackburnian warbler	montane forest	yes
Canada warbler	montane forest	yes
scarlet tanager	montane forest	yes
Argentine pampas		
golden plover	shores, grassland	yes
Eskimo curlew	?	?
upland sandpiper	grassland	no
stilt sandpiper	marshes	no
buff-breasted sandpiper	grassland	no
Hudsonian godwit	shores, marshes	yes

Sources: rufous, Allen's, blue-throated, calliope, and broad-billed hummingbird: Des Granges 1978; dusky and gray flycatcher: Fitzpatrick 1980; black-capped, Bell's, and gray vireo: Barlow 1980; Virginia's and colima warbler: Hutto 1980; golden plover, upland, stilt, and buff-breasted sandpiper, and Hudsonian godwit: Myers, 1980.

13 The Whys and Wherefores of Deforestation

The perpetuation of migratory bird populations presents a special challenge because their continued well-being depends on the health of the environment over the entire Western Hemisphere. Migratory routes can be likened to closed chains in which the links represent critical habitats or staging areas. The loss of just one link in the chain can prove disastrous to a species, even if the other links remain intact.

Since species vary greatly in the habitats used during breeding, wintering and on stopovers, and in the routes taken in between, it is very difficult to draw sweeping generalizations about what should be done. Virtually every habitat is important to one species or another. The corollary is that it is impossible to alter *any* natural habitat on a large scale without affecting some migrant for better or for worse. Usually it is for worse.

This should not be taken as a categorical argument against change. In a dynamic society, change is inevitable. We should, however, be aware that changes in the environment entail costs as well as benefits. As a society, we have historically focused almost exclusively on benefits, while ignoring the costs. It is time we began tallying the costs, because they have been considerable.

As for the future, it is important to keep in touch with the rates and directions of ongoing change. We cannot reverse the past, but we can in principle control the future. If we care about the future, then we should do everything rationally possible to learn about it in advance. Herein lies the value of science. It is the business of science to make predictions.

The process of rational analysis begins with the gathering of facts. It continues by putting the facts to use in making predictions. In the simplest case, the predictions are mere linear extrapolations of current trends. Once predictions have been made, the process ends with evaluation. Are the projected changes desirable or undesirable? How are anticipated benefits to be weighed against calculated costs? These are value judgments that only society can make. It is the job of the scientist to provide the facts and projections from which society can arrive at its judgments.

Needed facts on migratory birds are frequently missing, as nearly every chapter of this book has made clear. To make specific predictions about future trends in migratory bird populations, we need more information than is currently available. This is elementary, but up to now we have hardly begun to gather the crucial base-line data. A number of suggestions have been offered as to how serious amateur ornithologists can contribute to the gathering of these data.

We should be making informed judgments, but generally have not done so because heretofore the needed information has not been available, either to scientists or to the public. We could rationally come to the conclusion, for example, that the benefit of mechanical corn pickers to society outweighs the cost, as represented by the loss of Kirtland's warblers and black-capped vireos to cowbird parasitism. If that is what our political process should determine, then so be it. My concern is that we are making such choices without even being aware that they are being made. In this case, the American public is generally uninformed, first, that Kirtland's warblers and black-capped vireos are seriously threatened with extinction and, second, the reasons why. An uninformed public cannot make reasoned judgments. Hence, as a scientist, I have felt compelled to speak out.

Conservation is essentially a debate over land-use policy, because land-use patterns determine the blend of habitats available to support wildlife. If we were ever to arrive at a state in which the entire landscape of the United States was taken over by urban development or cornfields, we would obviously have no wildlife left at all. A few densely populated nations are already close to reaching this condition. To maintain wildlife there must be some compromise been the needs of nature and the needs of humans. The conservation movement has vigorously sought to establish a national concensus on where the balance between these two needs should lie. Although there is as yet no general agreement, few Americans would assert that nature deserves no place at all. We are clearly evolving toward a national compromise, even though no one can say just where it will eventually lie.

Many tropical countries have only barely begun their own national debates. If we were to take the creation of Yellowstone National Park in 1872 as the starting point in our national debate (Runte 1979), it can be appreciated that we have made progress, but that it has taken a long time. The concern we must have for birds that migrate to the tropics is that they spend half the year or more in countries where the equivalent landmark conservation legislation was enacted much closer to 1972 than to 1872. It is clear that there is a long way to go in achieving national conservation consensuses in these countries too, but given the rapid pace of environmental change, there does not seem to be enough time.

In the following pages I discuss land-use patterns, especially as they relate to deforestation, first, from the perspective of U.S. history and, second, from the perspective of what is currently happening in much of tropical America.

DEFORESTATION IN THE UNITED STATES:
WHY WE STILL HAVE FORESTS

In the year 1800 settlement in the United States was confined to a narrow strip along the Atlantic seaboard. Daniel Boone had discovered the fertile bluegrass plains of Kentucky only 30 years before, and large-scale migration across the Appalachians had not yet begun.

A century later, colonization of the North American continent was essentially complete. Several transcontinental railroads linked the coasts, Oklahoma had been opened to settlers in 1889, and San Francisco was a thriving port city. The 60 million bison that had roamed the Great Plains at the beginning of the century had been reduced to a pitiful remnant of fewer than a hundred by its end. The open frontier had closed, and immigrants from Europe were flocking to industrial jobs in the cities rather than to virgin lands in the West.

The presettlement limits of forest in the United States are well known from the records of early travelers and surveyors. These records permit one to estimate the "original" extent of forested land in the 48 states at roughly 950 million acres (Clawson 1979).

The activities of settlers over the first 200 years of our nation's history hardly made a perceptible dent in this total (see Figure 13.1). Indeed, it was not until after the Civil War that land clearing began on a large scale west of the Appalachians. According to one estimate, the area of forest cleared annually increased from 2 million acres in 1860 to over 9 million acres by 1907 (Greeley, in Clawson 1979). By the time of World War I we had nearly completed the blitz of the East. In only 60 years about 400

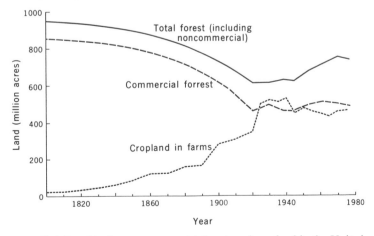

FIG. 13.1 Land in forest, commercial forest, and cropland in the United States, 1800 to 1975 (Clawson 1979).

million acres of virgin forest had fallen to the ax. This history is now being repeated in tropical America at comparable rates.

At no time during the heyday of logging in the United States was the East ever completely deforested (see Table 13.1). This is because the wave of exploitation took more than 100 years to pass from the Atlantic seaboard to the remotest bastions of the southern Appalachians and the north woods. Logged-over land was often allowed to return to trees, particularly in mountainous areas and where the soils were poor. The low point in the East was reached shortly after the turn of the century at a total forested area of around 350 million acres, approximately half of the estimated presettlement area. Since then, eastern forests have recovered slightly to a current coverage of about 385 million acres. Much of the increase has come from the abandonment of marginal farmland, although some areas, such as the bottomlands of the lower Mississippi and the peripheries of major cities, have suffered net losses during the interval.

Not only has the area in forest increased in recent decades, but the maturity of our forest estate has increased as well; net growth has exceeded harvests since about 1945 (Clawson 1979). The extent of forested land in the United States today (including the West, but excluding Alaska) is about 60 percent of what it was in presettlement times. We have not eliminated our forests because we were blessed in having superior agricultural lands

TABLE 13.1 Forest Area in the United States by Region, Precolonial Times to 1977 (in thousands of hectares)

Region[a]	Pre-colonial	1872	1920	1945	1963	1977	% of precolonial forest left in 1977
New England	38,908	17,415	25,708	31,092	31,886	32,460	83
Middle Atlantic	69,610	24,406	28,678	34,260	35,177	39,017	56
Central	170,560	80,967	60,182	69,271	70,073	67,700	40
South	298,640	203,591	177,865	174,631	206,397	193,715	65
Lakes	104,320	29,186	57,100	55,700	54,334	50,887	49
West	340,830	95,509	129,584	225,271	239,652	230,889	68
Total US	1,022,000	451,108	479,117	590,225	637,519	617,414	60

Source:Powell and Rappole, 1986.

[a] New England includes Maine, New Hampshire, Vermont, Massachusetts, Rhode Island, and Connecticut; the Middle Atlantic region includes New York, New Jersey, Pennsylvania, Delaware, and Maryland; the central region includes Ohio, Indiana, Illinois, West Virginia, Kentucky, Tennessee, Iowa, Missouri, eastern Kansas, and eastern Nebraska; the South includes Virginia, North Carolina, South Carolina, Georgia, Florida, Alabama, Mississippi, Arkansas, Louisiana, eastern Texas, and eastern Oklahoma; the Lakes region includes Michigan, Wisconsin, and Minnesota; the West includes Idaho, Montana, Wyoming, Colorado, western South Dakota, New Mexico, Arizona, Utah, Nevada, California, Oregon, and Washington.

in the largely treeless Great Plains. Had we not acquired the Louisiana Purchase from the French in 1803, the history of our forests might have been different. One can confidently say that the history unfolding now in the countries to the south of us will not parallel ours.

DEFORESTATION SOUTH OF THE BORDER

Development has taken a different course in Latin America and has been propelled by different forces. The earliest European settlements, in Santo Domingo, Panama, and Mexico, began 100 years before the Pilgrims landed at Plymouth Rock.

At first the impetus was gold, not freedom from persecution, and a gold rush seldom leaves culture, enlightenment, and prosperity in its wake. Settlers did trickle in after the gold frenzy abated, but at a much slower rate than in North America.

In Mexico, Guatemala, Peru, and Bolivia, a landed gentry gained wealth and status through ruthless exploitation of native populations, creating a rigid caste system that endures even today in forms both subtle and overt. Elsewhere, as in Hispaniola, Jamaica, Brazil, and Venezuela, in the absence of sufficiently numerous or tractable native peoples, black slaves from Africa were the instrument of enrichment. In both cases, the result was similar a stratified, rural based society whose captains lived in indo lent luxury as absentee landlords in the capital cities. In this stagnant and viscous milieu, upward mobility depended more on having the right genes and social connections than on hard work and ingenuity, and opportunity did not exactly beckon. Immigrants poured into North America by the millions, while the countries to the south lay dormant.

This dormancy persisted for nearly 400 years and was finally broken by forces from the outside. The industrialization of the north created a demand for primary materials—copper, tin, and later petroleum—at the lowest possible cost. Along with rising prosperity in Europe and North America came burgeoning markets for tropical agricultural products—sugar, coffee, cocoa, and bananas. It was the stimulus of this economic pull that attracted new blood and investment to the region and that began to rouse it from its somnolence.

Meanwhile, there had been no impetus to propel the colonization of the rainforest, the great frontier of tropical America. The climate was uncomfortable and the soils were poor. And beyond these deterrents, the land did not yield products that appealed to palates conditioned in Europe. Diseases such as malaria and yellow fever were rampant and essentially untreatable. Under these conditions, the reward for colonizing the jungle was the likely loss of 30 years from one's life span. The European population of Latin America consequently looked only to mountains or semiarid coastal regions for their livelihoods, and the vast evergreen forests of Central and South America lay practically untouched.

The period since World War II has seen the overturning of this status quo. Two related factors were decisive in bringing about the changes. First, a global antimalaria campaign, spearheaded by the World Health Organization, plus the advent of an effective yellow fever vaccine, lifted the pall of fear and suffering that had inhibited the settlement of vast forested hinterlands. And second, the population bomb exploded in the Third World. Millions of penniless and illiterate peasants failed to find jobs in the cities or land in the comfortable highlands that had for so long been the bastion of the region's landed gentry. Faced with no other alternatives, they flooded into wilderness that no one had previously wanted and began to hack out pitiful little plots such as the ragged Ecuadorean cattle pasture described in Chapter 11. Mountain slopes and fertile valleys in the foothills region of Central America and the Andes drew the first waves of settlers. The steamy Caribbean lowlands of Central America and the Amazon basin have held out as the last frontier. But even these are disappearing fast. Ours was a frontier of opportunity; this is a frontier of desperation.

Ironically, the people of Latin America do not want to colonize the humid tropical forest. To be sure, there are a few rugged individualists, as there are in any society, whose psyches compel them to a life of self-reliance in remote outposts where no man is their master. But such people are a tiny minority, and the wilderness is big enough to accommodate them. The great majority of the immigrant peasants who are felling the region's forests would far rather have steady jobs and live in the city. But the cities are crowded with thousands of others who, like themselves, cannot find work. Most of the peasants I have met in the region's jungles have tried life in the city and failed to become established. With all other avenues closed, the forest beckoned as the last resort.

The life of a peasant settler in the rainforest is not an enviable one. To find unclaimed land, he is often forced to travel far from existing roads and settlements. Great hardships are consequently forced upon him. There is often no school for his children and no doctor, should someone in the family fall ill. The chances are that he will try to produce a cash crop such as coffee or cacao, but he is obliged to proceed without adequate knowledge of how to care for a plantation and with no capital to buy fertilizers, pesticides, or genetically improved stock.

Vicissitudes are commonplace. An epidemic can sweep through his plants and wipe out the accumulated capital of several years' labor. And markets for export commodities are notoriously unstable. The choice of what to plant is usually based on market values of the day, but several years later when a plantation begins to bear, the economic conditions have often changed. Finally, should all these hazards be overcome, and our farmer succeeds in harvesting a crop, to sell it he must then carry the sacks for many miles, on his back or on the backs of burrows, to reach the nearest roadhead. A middleman and his truck will meet him there, offering the lowest possible price. Not being able to walk the many additional miles to the city, the farmer has no alternative to accepting what he is offered.

This is not a life you or I, or any sane person, would aspire to. Those who enter upon it are not mindless of its drawbacks. That is why most would prefer to live in the city with steady jobs and access to schools and doctors for their children. But to be in a city without a job, in a country where social welfare programs are unknown, is to starve. Life may be harsh in the forest, but at least one can plant a garden, raise some chickens, and go to bed every night with a full stomach. The keys to conservation in Latin America are thus jobs and people—more of the former and fewer of the latter. The present trends are leading to disaster.

In traveling through the Neotropics one can hardly fail to notice that there is a close relationship between human population density and the state of the countryside. The most lightly populated countries, such as Surinam and Guyana, are cloaked in primary forest, whereas at the opposite extreme are impoverished nations such as Haiti and El Salvador, where hardly an acre of natural habitat remains (see Table 13.2). As population densities approach and exceed 100 persons per square kilometer, people begin, in desperation, to spread into the farthest and least desirable corners of the landscape—cold, mist-shrouded mountaintops, hot, impenetrable thorn scrub. No place is too forbidding or remote to escape the pressure of the landless unemployed.

Never was I so acutely struck by this as when I climbed to the top of the Sierra de Baoruco in the southwestern Dominican Republic. At the time (1970) both the Dominican Republic and its neighbor, Haiti, had populations of about 5 million. The Dominican Republic, however, has about twice the area of Haiti, and its population is more concentrated in urban centers. The land is consequently under somewhat less pressure, and a few exciting wild areas remain within its borders.

One of these is the Sierra de Baoruco. It is wild because the land is inhospitable to anyone wishing to engage in shifting agriculture, or even goat herding. It is karst terrain, which, in geological jargon, means that it is built of limestone. In the tropical climate the limestone weathers rapidly and is carried away in runoff so that soil fails to accumulate on the surface. The entire landscape is thus constructed of exposed bedrock, weathered in an incredibly jagged "dogtooth" fashion. Razor-sharp points and ridges outline little water-smoothed depressions, giving the surface a pocked appearance. Countless fissures and crevices lead to unseen caves below and offer shelter to bats, iguanas, and scorpions. Rainwater disappears instantly into this underground labyrinth, eventually finding its way to the

TABLE 13.2 Population Projections for some Neotropical Countries

	1986 population in millions	Annual % increase	Per capita GNP (1983) (US$)	Year population reaches 100/km²	Years remaining
Brazil	143	2.3	1,870	2064	78
Colombia	30.0	2.1	1,410	2025	39
Costa Rica	2.7	2.6	1,070	2011	25
Cuba	10.2	1.1	1,435ᵃ	1997	11
Dominican Republic	6.4	2.5	1,160	*	*
Ecuador	9.6	2.8	1,420	2025	39
El Salvador	5.1	2.4	680	*	*
Guatemala	8.6	3.1	1,110	1994	8
Guyana	0.8	2.2	560	2136	150
Haiti	5.9	2.3	290	*	*
Honduras	4.6	3.2	670	2014	28
Jamaica	2.3	1.8	1,270	*	*
Mexico	81.7	2.6	2,180	2020	34
Nicaragua	3.3	3.4	880	2024	38
Panama	2.2	2.1	2,110	2045	59
Peru	20.2	2.5	1,040	2060	74
Surinam	0.4	2.0	3,390	2172	186
Trinidad and Tobago	1.2	1.8	6,830	*	*
Venezuela	17.8	2.7	3,830	2047	61

Source: Kent and Haub 1987.
ᵃ Cuba GNP for 1980. Source: Ehrlich and Ehrlich 1986.
* Already surpassed the density of 100 persons/km².

sea through anastomosing passages. None of it ever reemerges on the surface.

In spite of the austerity of this environment, it supports a varied and exotic vegetation of tall cactuses and evergreen shrubs. Where normally they would lie buried in the soil, roots crisscross the bare limestone everywhere, until plunging into one of the ever-present fissures, presumably to tap a source of groundwater somewhere below. From a mountaintop the landscape looks green and inviting, though on closer inspection its deterrent features are obvious.

In the Dominican Republic, the deterrence operated effectively (at least through 1975, when I last visited the country). The broken-glass limestone surface served as an absolute barrier to barefoot peasants. In a few days it can reduce the best made boots to tatters. Livestock cut their hooves and avoid walking on it. Moreover, the absence of surface water seemed to preclude the establishment of homesteads, because the region experiences a prolonged dry season each year. A few charcoal burners had penetrated the karstic terrain around its edges, but the entire peninsula between Enriquillo and Pedernales was practically devoid of population.

Having driven through more than 100 kilometers of this to reach the Sierra de Baoruco, I was totally unprepared for the sight that met me when I arrived at the top. The peak I had ascended was only a few kilometers from the Haitian border. As far as I could tell, the same type of karstic terrain extended indefinitely on the other side, as does the Sierra de Baoruco itself, though in Haiti it is known as the Morne La Selle. On the Dominican side, the greenness of a thick carpet of vegetation extended south all the way to the sea, broken only by a winding mine road. Not a single habitation or clearing interrupted the continuity of the scene.

On the Haitian side, there was no vegetation. The border sharply divided the scene, a boundary between green and gray. The landscape on the other side was naked and bleak. Even more to my astonishment, when I scanned with binoculars, I could see that the bare rock in Haiti was dotted with houses, not just a few, but many, as far as I could see.

To this day I cannot imagine how people manage to eke out an existence in that unsympathetic landscape. The first wave was probably composed of charcoal burners who removed the hardwoods to make briquets to sell in the city. In the normal sequence in such places, the charcoal burners are followed by goatherds, whose flocks can take advantage of the lower, younger growth that springs up after the trees have been felled. But on the Haitian side there did not seem to be enough vegetation left to support even goats, though perhaps across the distance I was missing details. After the charcoal burners had finished their work, whatever remained standing was later consumed as fuelwood. After this second phase had run its course, what could possibly remain to support human life? I still don't know.

At 215 per square kilometer, the population density in Haiti is the second highest in the hemisphere, trailing only El Salvador at 250 per square kilometer (see Table 13.2), and the rate of urbanization is among the lowest. Haiti is a good example of what the future may hold, because demographically it is a generation or two ahead of other countries. Haiti's vegetation has been reduced to bedrock and El Salvador has no natural vegetation left either, though the hilly interior that shelters guerrilla insurgents has regrown to scrub.

These two countries have come to the end of the road as far as their natural environments are concerned. Can other countries be far behind? If we take the 100-persons-per-square-kilometer criterion as our guide, we see that the answer is no. The Dominican Republic, Jamaica, and Trinidad-Tobago are already over the threshold. At current rates of increase, Cuba, Guatemala, Costa Rica, and Honduras have less than 30 years remaining. Of the nine countries mentioned above, all but Trinidad-Tobago are located in the near-tropical region of high migrant densities.

For the short term, the outlook for these countries is a continuation of current trends. In spite of migration to the cities, the absolute number of rural peasants continues to increase, putting ever greater pressure on undeveloped land. Although birth rates are beginning to show hopeful signs of decline in several nations, the demographic profiles of nearly all tropical American countries are so bottom heavy (half the population under 16), that one or more doublings in population size are inevitable, even if, beginning tomorrow, all new mothers refrained from having more than two children. Given these harsh realities, nothing short of a miracle could prevent one country after another from going over the 100-persons-per-square-kilometer threshold. When this happens, the remaining natural habitat is doomed, and along with it the essential requirement for overwinter survival of many songbird species.

THE BALANCE BETWEEN TEMPERATE AND TROPICAL HABITAT

The Situation on the Home Front

In Chapter 6 we examined bird population data from the Great Smoky Mountains and failed to find definite indications that tropical migrants are in decline. If tropical deforestation is going to result in such severe consequences for migrants, why aren't the signs already apparent? Although there may be more than one answer to this question, the most critical factor is certain to be the balance of habitat available for occupancy in the temperate breeding ground versus the tropical wintering ground.

The landscape of the United States has undergone a profound transformation since presettlement times. Among other developments, the amount of forested land in the East has been reduced by nearly half, the tall-grass prairie has been almost entirely put to the plow, and desert riparian woodlands in the Southwest have been systematically cleared for flood control and irrigation projects. The effect of these changes on bird populations, although largely undocumented, must have been nothing less than drastic. Although we do not know the magnitude of these changes, there can be no doubt that North America today harbors far fewer breeding pairs of migrants than it did when the Pilgrims landed at Plymouth Rock.

If we were to take presettlement time as our frame of reference—that is, a condition representing a millennia-old equilibrium between breeding ground and wintering ground—we must ask about environmental change in North America *relative* to that in the tropical countries to the south. The historical discussion above indicates that major environmental change in North America preceded that in most tropical countries. (I am here disregarding the partial deforestation of Central America by Amerindians in pre-Columbian times on the grounds that by the beginning of the historical period of interest, circa 1800 to the present, most of Middle America had again returned to natural vegetation; Powell and Rappole 1986.) Given the truth of this statement, the environmental deterioration of tropical America will have to "catch up" with that in North America before any effects of deforestation are detectable. Apparently, we have not yet reached the catch-up point, except perhaps in the case of the Bachman's warbler.

How far do we have to go in the case of other forest-dwelling species? I ask specifically about forest-living species because there are many of them, and because there is a legitimate question of evaluation involved. If one were to ask about the species that originally inhabited the tall-grass prairie instead, the answer would be that the wintering ground is unlikely to be a matter of concern, because the loss of breeding habitat probably exceeds 90 percent. (An exception is found in the shorebirds that winter on the Argentine pampas.) For forest birds we can wonder what current population sizes are relative to those in precolonial times.

To obtain a crude index of the current U.S. population of forest-dwelling migrants one might simply compare, as we did above, the extent of forested land in the East today to the amount presumed to have been present in precolonial times. This simplistic approach is certain to lead us astray, because it contains at least three significant sources of error:

1. Much of today's forest is immature, that is, undergoing regeneration following lumbering or the abandonment of agricultural land. Regenerating forests do not support bird populations commensurate with those of mature forests (see Table 13.3). Indeed, the data suggest that

TABLE 13.3 Diversity and Density of Breeding Birds with Plant Succession in the Georgia Piedmont

Age of plant community (years)	No. of breeding bird species	No. of breeding pairs
1–2	2	15
3	2	40
15	8	105
20	13	127
25	10	83
35	12	95
60	24	163
100	23	233
150	22	224

Source: Johnston and Odum 1956.

100 years is required for the full recovery of bird numbers. Logging cycles are seldom this long, so little of today's forest is in a mature state.

2. An estimated 40 percent of the eastern forest estate is contained in fragmented suburban and rural woodlots (U.S. Department of Agriculture, in Powell and Rappole 1986). We have already seen in Chapter 2 that such woodlots support drastically reduced numbers of migrants.

3. Large areas of erstwhile hardwood or mixed pine-hardwood forest in the Southeast have been converted to even-aged pine plantations. Encompassing many millions of acres of both private and public (National Forest) lands, commercial forests dominate the landscape of a number of southeastern states.

Pines of several species are grown in orderly rows. When judged ready for harvest, large blocks are clear-cut. The tracts are then replanted after "site preparation," which can mean various things—chaining the ground to remove palmetto, burning the slash, treatment with fertilizers, weed killers, etc. Under the most intensive forms of management, genetically uniform trees develop as a "crop" in an environment that is almost as rigorously controlled as that of a cornfield. Other species of plants (for example, hardwood saplings, shrubs) that might compete with, and hence retard, the growth of the pines are kept to a minimum.

These southern pine plantations are a biological desert. One finds a few pine warblers, cardinals, and towhees, but little else. The diversity of mammals, reptiles, and amphibians is similarly depressed, not to mention that of native herbaceous plants (that is, wildflowers). Although classified as "forest" in land-use surveys, pine plantations are hardly better as habitat for migrants and other wildlife than the Iowa cornfields we discussed in Chapter 7.

The 60 percent of the United States east of the plains that appears in official statistics as "forest" is thus surely a gross overestimate of the amount of prime migrant habitat. A generous appraisal would be that, on average, a hectare of today's eastern forest harbors half the density of migrants that Fawver and Wilcove counted in their virgin plots in the Great Smoky Mountains. Taking into account a 40 percent reduction in the total area of eastern forests, the fragmented and early successional state of most of today's forest, and the prevalence in the South of biologically sterile pine plantations, one concludes that the current populations of forest-living tropical migrants are probably no more than a quarter of their presettlement levels. This creates a potentially dangerous situation, because it implies that we may have to wait until three-quarters of the tropical wintering ground has been degraded before we begin to obtain concrete evidence that something is amiss. By then the amount of time remaining until the final quarter has been destroyed may be precariously short.

The Situation in the Tropics

We may now be approaching the turning point in this balance. This can be judged from a comparison of forest cover trends in the United States versus Middle America (see Figure 13.2). According to the best available

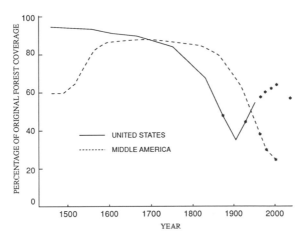

FIG. 13.2 Percent of original forest cover remaining in the United States and Middle America since 1500 (Powell and Rappole 1986).

estimates, primary forest in Middle America and the Greater Antilles that has not been protected in parks will have been completely removed by the year 2000 (Myers 1980). The situation with regard to tropical forest in South America is generally better than that in Middle America (see Figure 13.3), but apart from the Andean region, the density of migrants in South American forests is very low. Most of these seek edges or areas of disturbed vegetation along river margins and so are unlikely to be affected in proportion to the loss of primary forest. The Andean region, in contrast, is undergoing very rapid development, and its forests contain many migrant species that are unable to maintain their full densities in disturbed vegetation. And as noted above, the situation of the shorebirds that winter in the Argentine pampas is already desperate.

Clearly, if the present rate of deforestation of tropical America continues unchecked, it will lead to consequences no U.S. citizen could desire. What can be done? In the final chapter I offer some suggestions. The social, political, and economic factors responsible for deforestation are many and complex. Affecting a turnabout in the current thinking of politicians, planners, and bankers toward development in the tropics will not be easy, and the effort will require the participation of many institutions, both governmental and private. The important thing for now is that we begin to face up to a future that is coming faster than we realize and that we think seriously about steps the United States can take as a nation to mitigate the worst-case scenario.

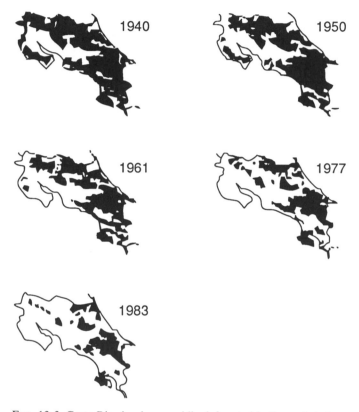

FIG. 13.3 Costa Rica has been rapidly deforested in the period since 1940, and by the year 2000 will have virtually no natural forest remaining outside of parks and reserves (Alfaro et al. 1985).

14 Conservation in the Tropics

The pattern of land use in the United States has changed little in the last forty to fifty years (Clawson 1979). Barring unforeseen developments, we can anticipate that the total areas committed to cultivated crops, forest, pasture, and the like will remain about the same in the coming decades. The relative stability of the land-use situation in our own country contrasts markedly with the situation of flux that exists in most of the developing countries to the south. These countries are going through the transition from rural, agricultural-based economies to modern industrial-commercial economies, just as we did a century ago. And they are doing it with the same reckless disregard for renewable resources that we showed at the corresponding time in our own development.

If we are concerned about conservation in the countries to the south, it should be our most fervent wish to promote and facilitate the urban-industrial development of their economies. As I said earlier, almost no one in Latin America wants to be a subsistence farmer; it is a life-style that offers no hope of progress and security. Anyone who can break out of it will do so. All that is required is opportunity.

We could be instrumental in providing that opportunity if we were to alter the thrust of our foreign-aid policy. Instead of promoting further agricultural development on fragile, marginal lands, as the World Bank and our Agency for International Development (AID) programs have been doing for decades, the international development agencies should encourage urbanization and improved efficiency of agriculture on lands capable of sustaining it. Some recent policy shifts in these two organizations suggest that we may now be moving in a more positive direction (Holden 1988).

Nearly all the people in what we regard as "modern" Western societies live in cities. That is why, in places such as the United States and Canada, we still have a countryside to enjoy. Even in crowded Europe, nations such as France and West Germany maintain a substantial portion of their national territories in forest cover. Other countries might be happy to follow this route, but in our assistance programs we sometimes seem to be pushing them in the opposite direction. The ill done by this tendency is compounded by the tropical countries' impractical attitudes toward development.

GOOD INTENTIONS GONE AMISS

In Peru, through our AID program, we are financing the construction of "highways of penetration" into virgin lands at the foot of the Andes (see Figure 14.1). A road designed to open up the Pichis and Palcazu Valleys is under construction at this writing. I predict that this project will backfire, because the areas being opened up are ideal for growing coca, the plant from which cocaine is extracted. This is precisely what has happened in the case of some previous road-building projects in which the United States participated, for example, in Peru's Apurimac and Huallaga Valleys. These two valleys are now the leading centers of cocaine production in Peru, if not in the world. The intent and the result of assistance programs are not always concordant.

Should the Pichis-Palcazu project unfold as planned, it would allow thousands of landless peasants to "colonize the jungle," thereby establishing Peruvian sovereignty and authority over a region that hitherto has been wilderness and alleviating temporarily some of the overwhelming population pressure that exists in the Andean highlands.

FIG. 14.1 The building of "highways of penetration" leads to the clearing of broad swaths of land paralleling the roadway. Often such lands are ill suited to permanent agriculture and are soon abandoned (Norris 1988).

Once translocated to the forested foothills at the base of the Andes, the colonists have limited options. A lucky few will be assigned tracts on more or less level terrain on the floor of one of the narrow valleys. Many others, perhaps the majority, since there will not be enough prime valley floor locations to go around, will invade as squatters on steep slopes.

Each colonist begins work by felling and burning a block of forest, usually no more than 2 to 4 hectares to start. He then plants a mixed garden of manioc and plantains, with perhaps some corn and beans. This is the first necessity, for he has no money and must feed his family. Once these subsistence crops are in, he then has time to think about a cash crop.

In a remote trans-Andean valley, where transportation to the outside world is prohibitively expensive, the choices are few. Coffee and cacao are almost the only possibilities available, because they are the only agricultural commodities appropriate to the climate that are valuable enough to compensate the cost of transporting them to the nation's seaports. These, of course, lie across the Andes on the Pacific coast. Thus it is a marginal situation at best, because most of the farmer's potential profit goes to pay the trucker. Even if he is prudent and industrious, he has little prospect of getting ahead under these circumstances—unless, of course he switches to producing coca.

Without knowing it, our farmer is caught in a far more pernicious marginality, one that has to do with the relative rates of growth in the underdeveloped and developed worlds. Being burdened with enormous external debts, there are countries like Peru all over the globe that are struggling to find ways of earning foreign exchange. Having rural-based populations, and being in possession of only rudimentary technologies, such countries naturally look to agricultural export commodities to rescue themselves from the humiliating specter of international bankruptcy. The hidden pitfall in this policy is that what may be a good strategy for one country, or two, becomes a calamity when it is followed by many.

Throughout the underdeveloped world, population growth rates range between 2 percent and 4 percent per year. The economies of such countries must grow at still higher rates if there is to be any per capita progress at all. Now, if a country's economic growth is premised upon increasing the production of agricultural export commodities, there must be a market for these commodities. But agricultural commodities are consumed as food, and markets for them cannot grow faster than the population of consumers.

The crux of the matter is that the population of consumers is hardly growing at all. The population of Europe has already stabilized, and that of North America is growing at only 1 percent per year (Brown and Jacobson 1986). The expectation of future expansion of the hard currency market for tropical agricultural commodities therefore cannot exceed 1 percent per year. How, then, can scores of poor Third World countries, the popula-

tions of which are growing at 2–4 percent a year, hope to work themselves
out of debt by selling agricultural commodities to the First World? Obviously they can't. All they can do is compete with each other, thereby depressing the price of the commodities they wish to sell. Little wonder then
that commodity prices have already fallen 30 percent in the 1980s (*The
Economist* 1988). This is a self-limiting proposition that offers no promise
either to the lending agencies that are supporting rural development in the
Third World or to the recipient countries themselves.

SUBSIDIES FOR DEVELOPMENT: THE PRICE OF
FALSE ECONOMIES

The Brazilian government has for decades been financing schemes to
encourage settlement of the country's vast and sparsely populated Amazonian hinterland. Nearly everything that has been tried so far has failed to
lead to sustainable development, requiring the scrapping of a succession of
policies (Goodland and Irwin 1975; Fearnside 1980). At the root of these
failures is the poor quality of the region's soils, only 15 percent of which
have been judged suitable for supporting sustained agriculture (Wambeke
1978; Smith 1981; Sanchez et al. 1982).

That the colonization of nutrient-deficient rainforest soils is both ecologically and economically foolhardy can be seen by the results of efforts
to promote cattle ranching in the Amazon. Primary forest is cleared on a
large scale, often hundreds of hectares at a time. After burning off the
fallen trunks and branches, the land is sewn with various species of exotic
African grasses. The ash, or at least that portion of it that is not swept into
the heavens during burning, supplemented with nutrients released from
decaying trunks, at first produces a vigorous growth, giving the appearance
of healthy pasture. For a time, cattle grow and reproduce well, but after
only three to five years the nutrients contained in the original forest are
depleted, the fragile soil becomes compacted by the pressure of hooves,
and the pastures become choked with weeds (see Figure 14.2). At this
point ranchers either sell out or move their animals to new pastures prepared by felling more virgin forest (Buschbacher 1987). In the state of
Pará, a focal area for cattle development in the 1970s, more than 50 percent
of the pastureland had been degraded by the invasion of woody growth,
and 85 percent of the ranches had failed by 1978 (Hecht 1983).

This process has already resulted in the abandonment of millions of hectares of land. The biological capital once contained in the original forest
cover has been squandered, along with its essential stores of mineral elements. The common practice of annual burning to suppress weeds and to
encourage new growth aggravates soil compaction, frequently leading to
loss of the entire A horizon (topsoil) through erosion (Scott 1975, fide

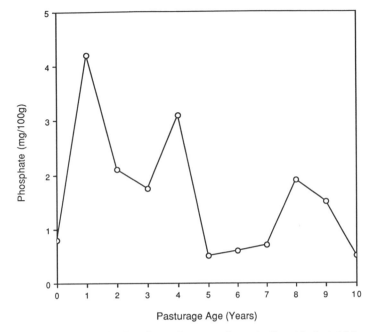

FIG. 14.2 Available phosphorus increases dramatically with the initial burning of the felled rainforest, and then falls to a lower level after about five years. Phosphorus has been found to limit pasture growth in several parts of the Amazon, including Paragominas on the Belém-Brasília Highway. Low levels of phosphorus result in poor pasture growth regardless of the levels of other soil fertility indicators (Fearnside 1980).

Groom 1984). The land now persists in an exhausted condition that will render it useless for either cattle or timber for perhaps another 100 years (Jordon 1986; Uhl and Saldarriaga 1986).

These are the environmental costs. Now what about the benefits? Estimates of beef production in Amazonian Brazil have been derived in various ways by different investigators, but most fall in the range of 26–44 kilograms per hectare-year over the five-year lifetime of a pasture (Smith 1978, fide Groom 1984; Fearnside 1979). Even if we take the high end of this range, it represents an uneconomic use of land when contrasted with a 1980 global average grain harvest in the developed world of 2.6 tons per hectare, and 1.5 tons per hectare in the developing world (Barr 1981). The direct monetary benefit to the rancher comes to less than $20 per hectare-year, or roughly $100 by the time the pasture is ready for retirement (Groom 1984).

It hardly sounds credible that anyone would bother to clear primary forest for a gain of merely $100 per hectare. In fact, it is not credible; the whole scheme operated on a false economy.

Bent on vindicating the massive investment it had made in constructing the Transamazonian Highway system, the Brazilian government offered heavily subsidized loans to investors willing to launch ranching operations. What then happened in many cases was that the recipients of these loans invested most of the money in enterprises unrelated to cattle raising, thereby realizing rates of return that handsomely exceeded the interest rates on the subsidized loans. To create the appearance of legitimacy, a portion of the loan money was employed to clear forest in what can only be described as sham operations. Fortunately, the Brazilian government has recently discontinued the subsidies.

If the world's remaining tropical forests are not to be converted to wasteland, both national and international lending agencies must begin to refuse politically motivated loan requests and concentrate on economically viable projects. The colonization of marginal lands does not offer a long-term solution either to overpopulation or to underproduction of basic foodstuffs. Nearly everywhere on earth, soils that are truly capable of supporting sustained agriculture have already been settled. Future gains in agricultural output can best be made by increasing yields on these inherently suitable soils, rather than by destroying marginal lands (Ledec and Goodland 1989).

WHAT CAN BE DONE?

The picture I have painted does not abound with optimism. Yet it does contain optimistic elements, even if they are as yet mere glimmers of hope.

Latin America is urbanizing rapidly and will do so even more rapidly if its international solvency is not held hostage to the increased production of agricultural export commodities. If there were jobs, as there have been, for example, in Venezuela because of oil revenues, people would flock to the cities. Seventy-five percent of Venezuela's population lives in urban areas, the highest rate in Latin America, and Venezuela's countryside is still relatively intact (Myers 1984). Urbanization offers the only hope for taking pressure off the land and salvaging any remnant of tropical nature through a future in which the population sizes of most countries are certain to double or quadruple.

Further development of fragile marginal lands in the humid tropics, in the absence of technologies for sustaining productivity over the long run, will only result in more needless waste, and the coincident extinction of species. The soils of the humid tropics are among the poorest on earth; this is the principal reason the world's rainforests have remained largely intact until the present century. To be sure, there are tropical lowland areas where sustainable agriculture can be practiced, as for example where there are alluvial or volcanic soils, but most such regions have long since been settled. What remains now, at this late stage in the colonization of our planet, are lands of last resort.

The 85 percent of Amazonia that is underlain by poor soils should be held in forest reserves and not opened to colonization, at least not with the inadequate technology currently available (but see Sanchez and Benites 1987). Allowing settlers to enter will only lead to the destruction of huge areas of forest and the eventual abandonment of a degraded landscape. This mistake has been made so many times in so many countries that there is no rational excuse for repeating it.

One way to slow down the destruction is simply not to build roads into regions that are inherently unsuited for long-term occupancy. Road construction proposals should be required to pass hardheaded cost-benefit analyses based on real, not phantom benefits. Most of all, road building should not be undertaken for purely political reasons, as has so often been the case heretofore. New roads are an easy excuse for politicians who, unable to create legitimate jobs for thousands of unemployed heads of families, offer them bogus opportunities to "colonize the jungle" (see Figure 14.3).

Road construction opens avenues of access to impoverished and unprepared city dwellers or highlanders who are completely ignorant of the methods of tropical agriculture. Lacking capital resources, they simply follow those who entered before them in the time-honored pattern of slash and burn. Where governments offer assistance loans, the efforts of these colonists may be directed toward the production of cash crops or to establishing family cattle ranches. In any case, in the absence of sustainable technologies, the end result is the same: exhaustion of the soil and eventual abandonment of the land. There is no natural end to this vicious cycle other than the final destruction of all remaining primary tropical forest.

Conservationists must devise an action plan for breaking this cycle. The most crucial and controllable element in the cycle is roads. It may sound patronizing to recommend a moratorium on road building in areas of primary tropical forest, because national governments make the decisions on where and when to build roads. Or so one might suppose. What is not so obvious is that many road-building projects in developing countries are financed by international agencies. AID, the World Bank, and other international assistance organizations finance roads. The loans are made at the request of the recipient countries, but these requests, as we have seen, are more often based on political than on economic criteria.

What practical alternative is there to the continued colonization of fragile marginal lands? There can be no answer other than to increase the productivity of land that is already under cultivation. The potential gain in output can be enormous. The transition to high-yield agriculture has al-

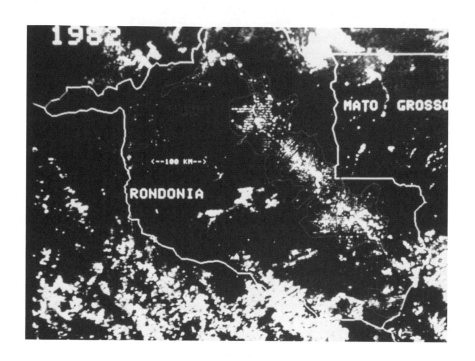

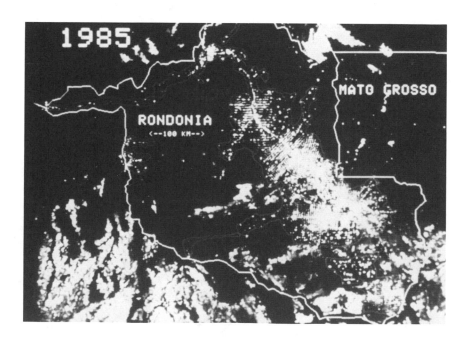

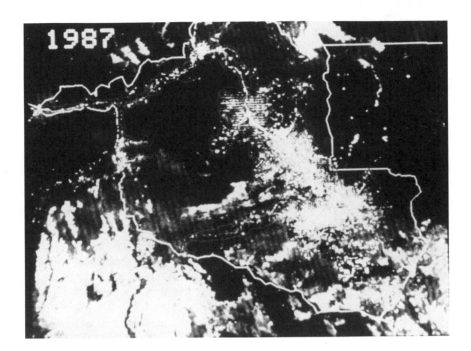

FIG. 14.3 These satellite images show the state of Rondônia, in the southern part of Brazilian Amazonia. Settlers are allocated plots measuring 2,000 meters by 500 meters aligned on roads built by the government at 5-kilometer intervals. The images indicate the speed and scale of forest clearing: about 30 percent of the area was deforested within seven years. If the present accelerating rate of deforestation persists, Rondônia may well lose most of its forest within just another decade (NASA Goddard Space Flight Center, Greenbelt, Md.; courtesy of Dr. C. J. Tucker).

ready been accomplished in some Third World countries and must be actively promoted in the rest (Greenland 1975; Plucknett and Smith 1982).

India was suffering severe food shortages in the mid-1960s, and some were predicting apocalyptic famines by 1975 (Paddock and Paddock 1966; Ehrlich 1968). Yet these famines have not materialized, and India has achieved self-sufficiency to the point of being able to export small quantities of rice. This remarkable accomplishment has been achieved without significantly expanding the amount of land under cultivation; indeed, India is already so heavily populated that it has virtually no empty land available for further settlement.

The example of India should be a lesson for the lending agencies. They have a herculean task ahead in promoting further increases in the world's food supply, but underproduction is chronic in many countries, and this can provide the necessary potential for future gains.

There is often a simple but unpublicized reason behind the chronic underproduction of basic foodstuffs one finds in so many Third World countries. This is that there are disincentives to investment in improved agricultural production. These disincentives take the form of low and unpredictable prices. In an effort to curry favor with the urban masses that are viewed as their principal constituencies, governments subsidize the prices of basic food commodities to urban consumers—flour, milk, sugar, cooking oil, etc. The agricultural work force is constituted of semiliterate rural peasants who wield little political power, so national leaders tend to ignore them. Farmers are thus obliged to sell at government-sanctioned prices that can fail to cover the costs of production.

In Europe and North America it is the producer that is subsidized—through price supports, land bank programs, government-supported storage facilities, export subsidy programs, and the like. Given these incentives, the farmers of the developed countries produce at the limits of efficiency, and even crowded countries such as Holland and Denmark are significant exporters of agricultural products. In the developed countries, parliaments debate the chronic problem of agricultural surpluses, not of shortages.

In the Third World, underproduction frequently results from the perverse practice of subsidizing consumption rather than production. Leaders are frequently too timid to take the politically risky course of allowing commodity prices to reflect the cost of local production. It is far more expedient to buy cheap grain produced abroad at much higher efficiency. But this leads to a vicious cycle of ever widening gaps between domestic consumption and supply. Politically handcuffed agricultural ministers, unable to stimulate production through price incentives, mistakenly look to forested regions as potential future breadbaskets and are deaf to the unwelcome advice that the soils are unsuitable. If this situation is to be rectified, economics will have to provide the decisive arguments.

The Future of Tropical Forests

What then can be done with the world's remaining tropical forests? One might like to see them protected as parks, but it would be wholly naive to suppose that governments will approve the permanent idling of major portions of their national territories. Tropical forests will have to be put to use, just as have nearly all temperate forests. Parks cannot be counted on to shelter large numbers of migrants in the future. Even in our own country, where we are rightfully proud of our conservation heritage, parklands account for less than 5 percent of our national territory. In tropical America, the average commitment to parks is considerably less than this. Even in the most wildly optimistic vision of the future, it would be hard to imagine that overpopulated developing countries would be willing to commit more than 10 percent of their territories to protecting wildlife. This means, of course, that 90 percent of the land will be committed to other purposes. We must focus on this 90 percent in contemplating the future survival of migrants, because if it is all converted to cropland, cattle pasture, and degraded wasteland, the prospect of wholesale extinctions is unavoidable (Ehrlich and Ehrlich 1981; Myers 1986).

Forestry is an extensive use of the land and as such brings in relatively low returns. Planners thus tend to discount forestry in favor of more intensive kinds of development. Being economists, they base their projections on the current discount rate, a practice that forces them to take a short-term point of view. This often leads to policies that jeopardize the long-term future.

Let us consider once again the attempts to develop a cattle industry in the Brazilian Amazon. An economist would consider only the short-term profit of $100 per hectare realized over the five-year productive life of the pasture. The cost of idling that hectare of land for the ensuing 100 years would not be taken into account. If the accounting were done in a responsible fashion, that is, in a way that placed a weight on the future equal to that on the present, there can be little doubt that the analysis would favor forestry over ranching. Tropical forests on poor soil grow slowly, but even at low growth rates it is not much to ask that profitability exceed $100 per century. At today's prices, one good mahogany tree can be worth over $1,000, even in markets near the source.

As a solution to the tropical deforestation problem I advocate the development of tropical forestry as a serious commercial alternative to agriculture on fragile marginal lands. We devote about half of our national territory to forest production. Even overcrowded Japan does this. European countries retain smaller but nevertheless appreciable proportions of their land in forest. The only rational and consistent policy is to urge tropical countries to do the same.

Sustainable Productivity under Multiple-Use Management

A sensible model for the management of forest lands in the tropics is the one we have applied to our own National Forest System since the days of its illustrious founder, Gifford Pinchot. Appointed by President McKinley in 1898 as chief of the bureau that would become the U.S. Forest Service, Pinchot was a man of wisdom and perspective. Profoundly distressed at the unrestrained plundering of the American virgin forest he had witnessed in his youth, Pinchot went abroad to study forestry in Europe. The virgin forests of that continent had been felled hundreds of years before, and the notion of sustained productivity was already well established in the management of secondary forests there. Shortly after Pinchot returned to the United States, he persuaded the government that the country would soon face a major shortage of timber unless it began to manage its forest estate with more foresight.

Pinchot's greatest contribution to posterity was in establishing the multiple-use concept as the cornerstone of the Forest Service's management philosophy. At the heart of this concept is the recognition that public forestlands have more than one political constituency (Wilderness Society 1986). They are not simply to be exploited for the commercial benefit of the timber industry. Other interests, both commercial and noncommercial, must expressly be accommodated in each forest's management plan. Major constituencies are found in the millions of Americans who use National Forests for recreational activities—hunting, fishing, hiking, camping, river running, even birdwatching. Protection of watersheds for downstream users is another legal obligation of National Forest managers, as is the preservation of our native flora and fauna. Unfortunately the preservation of flora and fauna is usually the last of the statutory mandates to be taken into account in the drawing up of management plans, because plants and animals don't vote.

The genius of the multiple-use concept is in its inherent flexibility. This allows it to apply to a wide range of circumstances and to adapt to changing climates of opinion. Issues, such as whether or not to permit clear-cutting and how much National Forestland to designate as wilderness, are open to public debate and subject to congressional review. Forests tend to be managed more for production and less for recreation and wildlife in states in which the timber industry is big business. This has been carried to an extreme in some southeastern states, where entire National Forests are operated as high-yield tree farms—an egregious abuse of Pinchot's concept.

Nevertheless, the political mechanism for correcting such abuses is inherent in our democratic system.

Although we began to manage our public forestlands under the multiple-use concept many years ago, other countries have been slow to follow suit. This is especially true in the tropics, even though many tropical countries are naturally forested. In spite of the intrinsic suitability of climate and terrain, the development of responsible forestry programs has been a matter of the lowest priority to the governments of developing countries. Throughout tropical America, forestry departments are typically understaffed, underfunded backwaters of government that devote their meager resources to fostering plantations of pine and eucalyptus on land that once supported highly diverse mixed forest. To an even greater extreme than in the tree farms of our South, the replacement of natural forests with tree monocultures in the tropics results in drastic losses of biological diversity (Terborgh and Weske 1969).

Tree plantations will not save the day for tropical migrants. The practice of what is known as "mixed silviculture" could. In principle, mixed silviculture entails the management of seminatural forests for a multiplicity of commercially valuable products (Wyatt-Smith 1987). If mixed silviculture could be practiced under the multiple-use concept, it would vindicate the intrinsic value of biological diversity and oblige managers to accommodate watershed protection, recreational potential, wildlife, and other values in their planning. If managed according to scientifically enlightened and forward-looking criteria, forests could potentially provide the same benefits to the residents of tropical countries as our forests do to residents of the United States.

The most straightforward and effective means of redirecting forestry practices in tropical countries would be to require our foreign assistance programs to sponsor mixed silviculture projects as philosophically in keeping with our domestic forest management policy. To support the replacement of natural forests with tree plantations is, by analogy, as hypocritical as the practice of allowing U.S. companies to sell abroad environmental toxins such as DDT and dioxane, which are banned as public health hazards in our own country.

CONSERVATION OF MIGRATORY BIRDS AND THE U.S. CITIZEN

Environmental change does not come without consequence for wild plants and animals. Changes that pose major threats to the continued survival of many migratory birds are occurring both in North America and in the tropics. Some of these changes are essential to the welfare of our own species, but others are not. The environment is our natural heritage, the source of our wealth and well-being. Yet it is frequently overexploited or abused, as if its value were only in the present. Any society that allows this attitude to prevail for long will find itself paying a heavy price in the future.

One such price could be having to endure the loss of further bird species from the North American fauna. Unregulated hunting and logging in the eighteenth, nineteenth and early twentieth centuries cost us the Labrador duck, Carolina parakeet, passenger pigeon, and heath hen. The ivory-billed woodpecker, Bachman's warbler, dusky seaside sparrow, and California condor have joined the list in my lifetime. What species will be next—the Kirtland's warbler, buff-breasted sandpiper, black-capped vireo, or some other whose danger is currently unknown to us? If we wish to prevent calamity, we must be well informed on both the status of breeding populations here in North America and the rapidly changing patterns of land use in the tropics.

Being informed is only part of the battle, but an extremely important part. Neither the Congress nor the public is easily aroused by dire projections that are not convincingly backed up with facts. My recommendations for what can be done fall into three broad categories, one that involves improving the amount and quality of information that can be put to work for conservation, one that involves political action, and one that involves matters of individual conscience.

Suggestions for Improving the Conservation Data Base

Revive the practice of publishing breeding bird censuses in *American Birds*, but impose new guidelines:

1. Censuses should be sponsored by state or local bird clubs, not by individuals.
2. The plots selected for censuses should be large and should represent mature or stable vegetation types.
3. Censuses designed for long-term monitoring of populations should not be established without a commitment to continuity.
4. There should be an effort to achieve a balance in the coverage of distinct habitat types at both local and national levels.

Continue the Breeding Bird Survey under U.S. Fish and Wildlife Service sponsorship, but evaluate the results in the light of known changes in patterns of land use.

Encourage the participation of amateur and professional ornithologists in efforts to determine the current status of migrants on the wintering ground, especially the species listed in Table 12.2. Information is scarce or lacking on population densities, overwinter survivorship, habitat use, elevational ranges, degree of acceptance of modified vegetation, and current trends in land use within the winter range. The recent publication by Braun et al. (1986) on winter records of the golden-cheeked warbler provides an example of this kind of effort.

Establish through one of the internationally active conservation organizations a program for monitoring land-use trends in tropical countries that harbor overwintering migrants.

Issues for Political Action

Advocate increased foreign aid spending, specifically with the goals of reducing the rate of population growth, stimulating urban industrial development, improving agricultural yields on inherently suitable land, and initiating large-scale programs of mixed silviculture on lands unsuited to agriculture.

Oppose the practice of using National Forestlands as tree farms as an abuse of the multiple-use concept.

Oppose government-subsidized overgrazing of public lands in the West and below-cost timber harvest in National Forests (Wilderness Society 1986).

Oppose further government-supported drainage and channelization projects, especially in the prairie pothole region and along desert streams in the Southwest.

Promote further expansion of the National Forest System.

Promote conservation easements as agricultural policy in place of land banks based on the maximum extent of land under cultivation.

Advocate tertiary sewage treatment, cleaner rivers, soil conservation.

Urge Congress to seek ways of reducing the runoff of agricultural chemicals into the nation's waterways.

Advocate the restructuring of property tax laws to (1) favor conservation easements and (2) retard the further loss of prime agricultural land to urban sprawl.

Matters of Individual Discretion

Consider that the birdseed you put out for chickadees and cardinals also supports expanded populations of starlings, bluejays, and cowbirds, and that poorly covered garbage cans promote high densities of racoons and other terrestrial nest predators.

Reconsider the now hallowed notion that "edge" habitat is inherently good for wildlife.

Action on domestic issues is best pursued through writing to members of Congress and supporting nongovernmental lobbying organizations such as the Defenders of Wildlife, Environmental Defense Fund, Natural Resources Defense Council, Sierra Club, and Wilderness Society.

Opportunities to influence the course of events in foreign countries are less available to U.S. citizens. One can personally lobby his or her representatives in Congress, but the most straightforward action is to support conservation organizations that are working at the international level. These include Conservation International, International Council for Bird Preservation, National Resources Defense Council, The Nature Conservancy, Wildlife Conservation International, World Wildlife Fund, and others. These organizations are at the forefront of tropical conservation, and they need all the help they can get. Their combined budget would not buy a single high-tech military aircraft. When one thinks of the magnitude of the job they are trying to do, and the resources they have with which to do it, the contrast is ludicrous. If they should fail in their mission, we shall be reminded of it for the rest of our lives each time we venture into the woods in spring.

Contributing to and participating in these organizations is one step we can take on the home front. We can also make our values felt and appreciated overseas. Dozens of birdwatching and nature tours depart the United States for Latin America every year, visiting such countries as Mexico, Costa Rica, Panama, Ecuador, Venezuela, and Peru. Tourism is big business in all these countries, and their governments are responsive to tourist demands. The more visitors there are who seek wilderness experiences and who sign the registers of national parks, the more it will be appreciated that future business depends on maintaining protected wild places. Nothing could be better than to have ministers of tourism and local chambers of commerce on our side. So next time you think of taking a winter vacation—why not go to see some of "our" birds in the tropics?

Bibliography

Aldrich, J. W. 1980. Breeding bird populations from forest to suburbia after thirty-seven years. *Atlantic Naturalist* 33:8–9.

Alfaro, R. M., L. Malavassi, W. Murillo and G. Rojas. 1985. Programa de patrimonio natural de Costa Rica. *Diversidata* 2 (October):1–6.

Ambuel, B., and S. A. Temple. 1983. Area-dependent changes in the bird communities and vegetation of southern Wisconsin forests. *Ecology* 64:1057–68.

American Birds. 1986. 86th Christmas bird count. *American Birds* 40:607–1032.

Anonymous. 1947. Announcement of the Winter Bird-Population Study. *Audubon Field Notes* 1:165–66.

Anonymous. 1950. Revised instructions to the Winter Bird-Population Study. *Audubon Field Notes* 4:184–87.

Askins, R. A., M. J. Philbrick, and D. S. Sugeno. 1987. Relationship between the regional abundance of forest and the composition of forest bird communities. *Biological Conservation* 39:129–52.

Baird, J. 1980. The selection and use of fruit by birds in an eastern forest. *Wilson Bulletin* 92:63–73.

Barlow, J. C. 1980. Patterns of ecological interactions among migrant and resident vireos on the wintering grounds. In Keast and Morton 1980, pp. 79–107.

Barr, T. N. 1981. The world food situation and global grain prospects. *Science* 214:1087–95.

Beehler, B. 1980. A comparison of avian foraging at flowering trees in Panama and New Guinea. *Wilson Bulletin* 92:513–19.

Bertram, B. C. 1978. Living in groups: Predators and prey. In *Behavioral Ecology: An Evolutionary Approach*, edited by J. R. Krebs and N. B. Davies, 64–96. Sunderland, Mass.: Sinaur Associates.

Blake, E. R. 1953. *Birds of Mexico: A Guide for Field Identification.* Chicago: University of Chicago Press.

Bock, C. E., and L. W. Lepthien. 1976. Changing winter distribution and abundance of the blue jay, 1962–1971. *American Midland Naturalist* 96:232–36.

Bond, J. 1961. *Birds of the West Indies.* Cambridge, Mass.: Riverside Press.

Bosque, C., and M. Lentino. 1987. The passage of North American migratory land birds through xerophytic habitats on the western coast of Venezuela. *Biotropica* 19:267–73.

Braun, L. 1950. *Deciduous Forests of Eastern North America.* Philadelphia: Blakiston.

Braun, M. J., D. D. Braun, and S. B. Terrill. 1986. Winter records of the golden-cheeked warbler (*Dendroica chrysoparia*) from Mexico. *American Birds* 40:564–66.

Briggs, S. A., and J. H. Criswell. 1979. Gradual silencing of spring in Washington. *Atlantic Naturalist* 32:19–26.

Brittingham, M. C., and S. A. Temple. 1983. Have cowbirds caused forest songbirds to decline? *Bioscience* 33:31–35.

Brown, L. R., and J. L. Jacobson. 1986. Our demographically divided world. *Worldwatch Paper* 74. Washington, D.C.: Worldwatch Institute.

Brown, L. R., and E. C. Wolf. 1984. Soil erosion: Quiet crisis in the world economy. *Worldwatch Paper* 60. Washington, D.C.: Worldwatch Institute.

Buschbacher, R. J. 1987. Cattle productivity and nutrient fluxes on an Amazon pasture. *Biotropica* 19:200–207.

Buskirk, R. E., and W. H. Buskirk. 1976. Changes in arthropod abundance in a highland Costa Rica forest. *American Midland Naturalist* 95:288–98.

Clark, E. H. II, J. A. Haverkamp, and W. Chapman. 1985. *Eroding Soils: The Off-Farm Impacts*. Washington, D.C.: Conservation Foundation.

Clawson, M. 1979. Forests in the long sweep of American history. *Science* 204:1168–74.

Cody, M. L. 1971. Finch flocks in the Mojave desert. *Theoretical Population Biology* 2:141–58.

Cox, G. W. 1968. The role of competition in the evolution of migration. *Evolution* 22:180–92.

———. 1985. The evolution of avian migration systems between temperate and tropical regions of the new world. *American Naturalist* 126:451–74.

Curtis, J. T. 1956. The modification of mid-latitude grasslands and forests by man. In *Man's Role in Changing the Face of the Earth*, edited by W. L. Thomas, 721–36. Chicago: University of Chicago Press.

———. 1959. *The Vegetation of Wisconsin*. Madison: University of Wisconsin Press.

DesGranges, J. L. 1978. Organization of a tropical nectar-feeding bird guild in a variable environment. *Living Bird* 17:199–236.

DesGranges, J. L., and P. R. Grant. 1980. Migrant hummingbird's accommodation into tropical communities. In Keast and Morton 1980, pp. 395–410.

Dolbeer, R. A. 1982. Migration patterns for age and sex classes of blackbirds and starlings. *Journal of Field Ornithology* 53:28–46.

Drury, W. H., and I.C.T. Nisbet. 1964. Radar studies of orientation of songbird migrants in southeastern New England. *Bird Banding* 35:69–119.

Dunning, J. B., and J. H. Brown. 1982. Summer rainfall and winter sparrow densities: A test of the food limitation hypothesis. *Auk* 99:123–29.

The Economist. 1988. Feb. 13, p. 17.

Emlen, J. T. 1973. Territorial aggression in wintering warblers of Bahama agave blossoms. *Wilson Bulletin* 85:71–74.

Erickson, R. E., R. L. Linder, and K. W. Harmon. 1979. Stream channelization (p.l. 83-566) increased wetland losses in the Dakotas. *Wildlife Society Bulletin* 7:71–78.

Ehrlich, P. R. 1968. *The Population Bomb*. New York: Ballantine.

Ehrlich, P. R., and A. H. Ehrlich. 1981. *Extinction: The Causes and Consequences of the Disappearance of Species*. New York: Random House.

———. 1986. World population crisis. *Bulletin of the Atomic Scientists* 42:13–19.

Faaborg, J., and W. Arendt. Manuscript. Long-term declines in winter resident warblers within a tropical forest.

Faaborg, J., and J. W. Terborgh. 1980. Patterns of migration in the West Indies. In Keast and Morton 1980, pp. 157–63.

Farner, D. S., and R. H. Lewis. 1971. Photoperiodism and reproductive cycles in birds. In *Photophysiology*, vol. 6, edited by A. C. Giese, 325–70. New York: Academic Press.

Fawver, B. J. 1950. An analysis of the ecological distribution of breeding bird populations in eastern North America. Ph.D. dissertation, University of Illinois, Champaign.

Fearnside, P. M. 1980. The effects of cattle pasture on soil fertility in the Brazilian Amazon: Consequences for beef production sustainability. *Tropical Ecology* 21:125–37.

ffrench, R. 1973. *A Guide to the Birds of Trinidad and Tobago*. Wynewood, Pa.: Livingston Publishing.

Fitzpatrick, J. W. 1980. Wintering of North American tyrant flycatchers in the Neotropics. In Keast and Morton 1980, pp. 67–78.

———. 1982. Northern birds at home in the tropics. *Natural History* 91:40–46.

———. 1983. Tropical kingbird, *Tyrannus melancholicus*. In *The Natural History of Costa Rica*, edited by D. Janzen, 611–13. Chicago: University of Chicago Press.

Fitzpatrick, J. W., S. K. Robinson, and J. Terborgh. In press. Distribution and abundance of north temperate migrants in the Amazon basin and eastern Andes. *Biotropica*.

Forman R. T., A. E. Galli, and C. F. Leck. 1976. Forest size and avian diversity in New Jersey woodlots with some land use implications. *Oecologia* 16:1–8.

Foster, R. B. 1982. The seasonal rhythm of fruitfall on Barro Colorado Island. In *The Ecology of a Tropical Forest: Seasonal Rhythms and Long-term Changes*, edited by E. G. Leigh, Jr., A. S. Rand, and D. M. Windsor, 151–72. Washington, D.C.: Smithsonian Institution Press

Fretwell, S. 1972. *Populations in a Seasonal Environment*. Princeton: Princeton University Press.

———. 1980. Evolution of migration in relation to factors regulating bird numbers. In Keast and Morton 1980, pp. 517–29.

Galli, A. E., C. F. Leck, and R. T. Forman. 1976. Avian distribution patterns in forest islands of different sizes in central New Jersey. *Auk* 93:356–65.

Gauthreaux, S. 1982. The ecology and evolution of avian migration systems. In *Avian Biology*, vol. 6, edited by D. S. Farner and J. R. King, 93–167. New York: Academic Press.

Goldwasser, S., D. Goines, and S. R. Wilbur. 1980. The least Bell's vireo in California: A *de facto* endangered race. *American Birds* 34:742–45.

Goodland, R.J.A., and H. S. Irwin. 1975. *Amazon Jungle: Green Hell to Red Desert?* New York: Elsevier.

Gradwohl, J., and R. Greenberg. 1981. The formation of antwren flocks on Barro Colorado Island, Panama. *Auk* 97:385–95.

Greenberg, R. 1981. The abundance and seasonality of forest canopy birds on Barro Colorado Island, Panama. *Biotropica* 12:241–51.

———. 1985. The social behavior and feeding ecology of Neotropical migrants in the non-breeding season. *Acta Internat. Ornithol. Congr.* XVIII:769–75.

Greenberg, R. 1986. Competition in migrant birds in the nonbreeding season. In *Current Ornithology*, vol. 3, edited by R. J. Johnston, 281–307. Plenum.

———. 1987. Seasonal foraging specialization in the worm-eating warbler. *Condor* 89:158–68.

Greenberg, R., and J. Gradwohl. 1980. Observations of paired Canada Warblers *Wilsonia canadensis* during migration in Panama. *Ibis* 122:509–12.

———. 1986. Constant density and stable territoriality in some tropical insectivorous birds. *Oecologia* 69:618–25.

Greene, E., D. Wilcove, and M. McFarland. 1984. Observations of birds at an army ant swarm in Guerrero, Mexico. *Condor* 86:92–93.

Greenland, D. J. 1975. Bringing the green revolution to the shifting cultivator. *Science* 190:841–44.

Griffin, D. R. 1964. *Bird Migration*. Garden City, N.Y.: Natural History Press.

———. 1969. The physiology and geophysics of bird navigation. *Quarterly Review of Biology* 44:255–76.

Groom, M. 1984. Ecological constraints on development along the transamazon highway of Brazil. Undergraduate thesis, Princeton University.

Hall, G. A. 1984. Population decline of Neotropical migrants in an Appalachian forest. *American Birds* 38:14–18.

Hamel, P. B. 1986. *Bachman's Warbler: A Species in Peril*. Washington, D.C.: Smithsonian Institution Press.

Hamilton, W. D. 1971. Geometry for the selfish herd. *Journal of Theoretical Biology* 31:295–311.

Haverschmidt, F. 1968. *Birds of Surinam*. Edinburgh: Oliver and Boyd.

Hays, J. D., J. Imbrie, and N. J. Shackleton. 1976. Variations in the earth's orbit, pacemaker of the ice ages. *Science* 194:1121–32.

Hecht, S. 1983. Cattle ranching in the eastern Amazon: Environmental and social implications. In *The Dilemma of Amazonian Development*, edited by E. F. Moran, 155–88. Boulder, Colo.: Westview Press.

Hendrickson, D. A., and D. M. Kubly. 1984. Desert waters: Past, present, and future. *Nature Conservancy News* 34:6–12.

Hershkovitz, P. 1969. The evolution of mammals on southern continents. VI. The recent mammals of the Neotropical region: A zoogeographic and ecological review. *Quarterly Review of Biology* 44:1–70.

Hilditch, C.D.M., T. C. Williams, and I.C.T. Nisbet. 1973. Autumnal bird migration over Antigua. *Bird Banding* 44:171–79.

Hilty, S. L. 1980. Relative abundance of north temperate zone breeding migrants in western Colombia and their impact at fruiting trees. In Keast and Morton 1980, pp. 265–71.

Hilty, S. L., and W. L. Brown. 1986. *A Guide to the Birds of Colombia*. Princeton: Princeton University Press.

Hoffman, C. O., and J. L. Gottschang. 1977. Numbers, distribution, and movements of a raccoon population in a suburban residential community. *Journal of Mammalogy* 58:623–36.

Holden, C. 1988. The greening of the world bank. *Science* 240:160.

Holmes, R. T., and F. W. Sturges. 1975. Avian community dynamics and energetics in a northern hardwoods ecosystem. *Journal of Animal Ecology* 44:175–200.

Horton, T. 1984. The people's bay. *Amicus Journal* 6:12–19.

Hutto, R. L. 1980. Winter habitat distribution of migrant land birds in western Mexico, with specific reference to small foliage-gleaning insectivores. In Keast and Morton 1980, pp. 181–204.

———. 1986. Migratory landbirds in western Mexico: A vanishing habitat. *Western Wildlands* 11:12–16.

James, F. C., and W. J. Boecklen. 1984. Interspecific morphological relationships and the densities of birds. In *Ecological Communities: Conceptual Issues and the Evidence*, edited by D. R. Strong, Jr., D. Simberloff, L. G. Abele, and A. B. Thistle, 458–77. Princeton: Princeton University Press.

Janzen, D. H. 1967. Synchronization of of sexual reproduction of trees within the dry season in Central America. *Evolution* 21:620–37.

———. 1973. Sweep samples of tropical foliage insects: Effects of seasons, vegetation types, elevation, time of day and insularity. *Ecology* 54:687–708.

Janzen, D. H., and T. W. Schoener. 1968. Differences in insect abundance and diversity between wetter and drier sites during a tropical dry season. *Ecology* 49:96–110.

Johnston, D. W., and E. P. Odum. 1956. Breeding bird populations in relation to plant succession on the piedmont of Georgia. *Ecology* 37:50–62.

Johnston, D. W., and D. I. Winings. 1987. Natural history of Plummer's Island, Maryland. XXVII. The decline of forest breeding birds on Plummer's Island, Maryland and vicinity. *Proceedings of the Biological Society of Washington* 100:762–68.

Jordon, C. F. 1986. Local effects of tropical deforestation. In *Conservation Biology: The Science of Scarcity and Diversity*, edited by M. E. Soulé, 410–26. Sunderland, Mass.: Sinauer Associates.

Karr, J. H. 1976. On the relative abundance of migrants from the north temperate zone in tropical habitats. *Wilson Bulletin* 88:433–58.

Keast, A. 1980. Migratory parulidae: What can species co-occurrence in the north reveal about ecological plasticity and wintering patterns. In Keast and Morton 1980, pp. 457–76.

Keast, A., and E. S. Morton, eds. 1980. *Migrant Birds in the Neotropics: Ecology, Behavior, Distribution and Conservation*. Washington, D.C.: Smithsonian Institution Press.

Kendeigh, S. C. 1944. Measurement of bird populations. *Ecological Monographs* 14:67–106.

Kendeigh, S. C., and B. J. Fawver. 1981. Breeding bird populations in the Great Smoky Mountains, Tennessee and North Carolina. *Wilson Bulletin* 93:218–42.

Kent, M. M., and C. Haub, eds. 1987. 1986 world population data sheet. Washington, D.C.: Population Reference Bureau.

King, J. R., and R. Mewaldt. 1981. Variation of body weight in Gambel's white-crowned sparrows in winter and spring: Latitudinal and photoperiodic correlates. *Auk* 98:752–64.

Klinger, D. 1982. 1980 fishing and hunting survey results told. *Fish and Wildlife News* (April–May): 1–7.

Kroodsma, R. L. 1984. Effect of forest edge on breeding bird species. *Wilson Bulletin* 96:426–36.

Lack, D. 1968. Bird migration and natural selection. *Oikos* 19:1–9.

Land, H. C. 1970. *Birds of Guatemala*. Wynewood, Pa.: Livingston.

Landeau, L., and J. Terborgh. 1986. Oddity and the "confusion effect" in predation. *Animal Behaviour* 34:1372–80.

Larkin, R. P., D. R. Griffin, J. R. Torre-Bueno, and J. Teal. 1979. Radar observations of bird migration over the western North Atlantic Ocean. *Behavioral Ecology and Sociobiology* 4:225–64.

Leck, C. F. 1972. The impact of some North American migrants at fruiting trees in Panama. *Auk* 89:842–50.

Leck, C. F., and S. L. Hilty. 1968. A feeding congregation of local and migratory birds in the mountains of Panama. *Bird Banding* 39:18.

Ledec, G., and R. Goodland. 1989. Epilogue: An environmental perspective on tropical land settlement. In *The Human Ecology of Tropical Land Settlement in Latin America*, edited by D. A. Schumann and W. L. Partridge. Boulder, Colo.: Westview Press.

Lockwood, J. G. 1979. *Causes of Climate*. New York: Wiley.

Loiselle, B. A. 1987. Migrant abundance in a Costa Rican lowland forest canopy. *Journal of Tropical Ecology* 3:163–68.

Loiselle, B. A., and W. G. Hoppes. 1983. Nest predation in insular and mainland lowland rainforest in Panama. *Condor* 85:93–95.

Louma, J. R. 1985. Nursery on the northern plains. *Nature Conservancy News* 35: 8–12.

Lynch, J. F., E. S. Morton, and M. E. Van der Voort. 1985. Habitat segregation between the sexes of wintering hooded warblers (*Wilsonia citrina*). *Auk* 102: 714–721.

Lynch, J. F., and D. F. Whigham. 1984. Effects of forest fragmentation on breeding bird communities in Maryland, USA. *Biological Conservation* 28:287–324.

MacArthur, R. H. 1972. *Geographical Ecology*. New York: Harper and Row.

McClintock, C. P., T. C. Williams, and J. M. Teal. 1978. Autumnal bird migration observed from ships in the western North Atlantic Ocean. *Bird-Banding* 49:202–77.

McLellan, C. H., A. P. Dobson, D. S. Wilcove, and J. M. Lynch. 1986. Effects of forest fragmentation on new and old world bird communities: Empirical observations and theoretical implications. In *Modeling Habitat Relationships of Terrestrial Vertebrates*, edited by J. Verner, M. Morrison, and C. J. Ralph, 305–13. Madison: University of Wisconsin Press.

Marshall, J. T. 1988. Birds lost from a giant sequoia forest during fifty years. *Condor* 90:359–72.

May, R. M., and S. K. Robinson. 1985. Population dynamics of avian brood parasitism. *American Naturalist* 126:475–94.

Mayfield, H. 1965. The brown-headed cowbird, with old and new hosts. *Living Bird* 4:13–28.

———. 1977. Brown-headed cowbird: Agent of extermination? *American Birds* 31:107–113.

———. 1983. Kirtland's warbler, victim of its own rarity? *Auk* 100:974–76.

Meanley, B. 1971. Blackbirds and the southern rice crop. *U.S. Sport Fisheries and Wildlife Bureau—Special Research Publication* 100.

Melillo, J. M., C. A. Palm, R. A. Houghton, G. M. Woodwell and N. Myers. 1986. A comparison of two recent estimates of disturbance in tropical forests. *Environmental Conservation* 12:37–40.

Meyer de Schauensee, R. 1970. *A Guide to the Birds of South America.* Edinburgh: Oliver and Boyd.

Monroe, B. L., Jr. 1970. Effects of habitat changes on population levels of the avifauna in Honduras. In *The Avifauna of Latin America,* edited by H. K. Buechner and J. H. Buechner, *Smithsonian Contributions to Zoology* 26:38–41.

———. 1986. Summary of highest counts of individuals for Canada and the United States. *American Birds* 40:1084–90.

Morse, D. H. 1967. Competitive relationships between parula warblers and other species during the breeding season. *Auk* 84:490–502.

———. 1980. Population limitation: Breeding or wintering grounds? In Keast and Morton 1980, pp. 505–16.

Morton, E. S. 1971. Food and migration habits of the eastern kingbird in Panama. *Auk* 88:925–926.

———. 1973. On the evolutionary advantages and disadvantages of fruit eating in tropical birds. *American Naturalist* 107:8–22.

———. 1980. Adaptations to seasonal changes by migrant landbirds in the Panama Canal Zone. In Keast and Morton 1980, pp. 437–57.

Morton, E. S., J. F. Lynch, K. Young, and P. Mehlhop. 1987. Do male hooded warblers exclude females from nonbreeding territories in tropical forest? *Auk* 104:133–35.

Munn, C. A. 1985. Permanent canopy and understory flocks in Amazonia: Species composition and population density. In *Neotropical Ornithology,* edited by P. A. Buckley, M. S. Foster, E. S. Morton, R. S. Ridgley, and F. G. Buckley, 683–712 *Ornithological Monographs* 36:683–712.

———. 1986. Birds that "cry wolf." *Nature* 319:143–45.

Munn, C. A., and J. Terborgh. 1980. Multi-species territoriality in Neotropical foraging flocks. *Condor* 81:338–47.

Myers, J. P. 1980. The Pampas shorebird community: interactions between breeding and non-breeding members. In Keast and Morton 1980, pp. 37–50.

———. 1981a. A test of three hypotheses for latitudinal segregation of the sexes in wintering birds. *Canadian Journal of Zoology* 59:1527–34.

———. 1981b. Cross-seasonal interactions in the evolution of sandpiper social systems. *Behavioral Ecology and Sociobiology* 8:195–202.

———. 1986. Sex and gluttony on Delaware Bay. *Natural History* 95:67–77.

Myers, J. P., R.I.G. Morrison, P. Z. Antas, B. A. Harrington, T. E. Lovejoy, M. Sallaberry, S. E. Senner, and A. Tarak. 1987. Conservation strategy for migratory species. *American Scientist* 75:18–26.

Myers, J. P., and L. P. Myers. 1979. Shorebirds of coastal Buenos Aires Province, Argentina. *Ibis* 121:186–200.

Myers, N. 1980. *Conversion of Tropical Moist Forests*. Washington, D.C.: National Academy of Sciences.

———. 1984. *The Primary Source: Tropical Forests and Our Future*. New York: Norton.

———. 1986. Tropical deforestation and a mega-extinction spasm. In *Conservation Biology: The Science of Scarcity and Diversity*, edited by M. E. Soulé, 394–409. Sunderland, Mass.: Sinauer Associates.

Nisbet, I.C.T. 1970. Autumn migration of the blackpoll warbler: Evidence for a long flight provided by regional survey. *Bird-Banding* 41:207–40.

Nisbet, I.C.T., W. H. Drury, and J. Baird. 1963. Weight-loss during migration. I: Deposition and consumption of fat by the black-poll warbler *Dendroica striata*. *Bird-Banding* 34:107–59.

Nolan, V. 1978. The ecology and behavior of the prairie warbler (*Dendroica discolor*). *Ornithological Monographs* 26.

Norris, R. 1988. Data for diversity. *Nature Conservancy Magazine* 38(1):4–10.

Nottebohm, F. 1981. A brain for all seasons: Cyclical anatomical changes in song control nuclei of the canary brain. *Science* 214:1368–70.

Orth, R. J., and K. A. Moore. 1983. Chesapeake Bay: An unprecedented decline in submerged aquatic vegetation. *Science* 222:51–53.

Paddock, W., and P. Paddock. 1966. *Famine-1975! America's Decision: Who Will Survive?* Boston: Little, Brown.

Paynter, R. A. 1955. The ornithogeography of the Yucatán Peninsula. *Bulletin of the Peabody Museum of Natural History* 9:1–347.

Pearson, D. L. 1980. Bird migration in Amazonian Ecuador, Peru and Bolivia. In Keast and Morton 1980, pp. 270–84.

Perry, J., and J. G. Perry. 1980. The random guide to natural areas of the eastern United States. New York: Random House.

Phelps, W. H., and R. M. de Schauensee. 1978. *A Guide to the Birds of Venezuela*. Princeton: Princeton University Press.

Plucknett, D. L., and N.J.H. Smith. 1982. Agricultural research and Third World food production. *Science* 217:215–25.

Pond, C. M. 1978. Morphological aspects and mechanical consequences of fat deposition in wild vertebrates. *Annual Review of Ecology and Systematics* 9:519–70.

Post, W., and J. W. Wiley 1977. Reproductive interactions of the shiny cowbird and the yellow-shouldered blackbird. *Condor* 79:176–84.

Powell, G.V.N., and J. H. Rappole. 1986. The hooded warbler. *Audubon Wildlife Report 1986*, 827–53. New York: National Audubon Society.

Pulliam, H. R., and M. R. Brand. 1975. The production and utilization of seeds in plains grassland of southeastern Arizona. *Ecology* 56:1158–66.

Pulliam, H. R., T. Caraco, and S. Martindale. 1980. Avian flocking in the presence of a predator. *Nature* 285:400–401.

Rappole, J. H., and E. S. Morton. 1985. Effects of habitat alteration on a tropical avian forest community. *Ornithological Monographs* 36:1013–21.

Rappole, J. H., E. S. Morton, T. E. Lovejoy, and J. L. Ruos. 1983. *Nearctic Avian Migrants in the Neotropics*. U.S. Department of the Interior, Fish and Wildlife Service, Washington, D.C.

Rappole, J. H., and D. Warner. 1980. Ecological aspects of migrant bird behavior in Veracruz, Mexico. In Keast and Morton 1980, pp. 353–95.

Reffalt, W. C. 1985. A nationwide survey: Wetlands in extremis. *Wilderness* 49: 28–41.

Richardson, W. J. 1976. Autumn migration over Puerto Rico and the western Atlantic: A radar study. *Ibis* 118:309–32.

————. 1979. Southeastward shorebird migration over Nova Scotia and New Brunswick in autumn: A radar study. *Canadian Journal of Zoology* 57:107–24.

Ridgely, R. S. 1976. *A Guide to the Birds of Panama*. Princeton: Princeton University Press.

Robbins, C. S. 1979. Effect of forest fragmentation on bird populations. In *Workshop Proceedings: Management of North Central and Northeastern Forests for Nongame Birds*, coordinated by R. M. DeGraaf. *USDA Forest Service General Technical Report NC-51*.

————. 1980. Effect of forest fragmentation on bird populations in the piedmont of the Mid-Atlantic region. *American Naturalist* 33:31 36.

Robbins, C. S., D. Bystrak, and P. H. Geissler. 1986. The breeding bird survey: Its first fifteen years, 1965–1979. U.S. Department of the Interior, Fish and Wildlife Service, Resource Publication 157, Washington, D.C.

Robinson, M. H., and B. Robinson. 1970. Prey caught by a sample population of the spider *Argiope argentata* (Araneae: Araneidae) in Panama: A year's census data. *Zoological Journal of the Linnean Society* 4:345–57.

Robinson, S. K. 1981. Social interactions and ecological relations of Philadelphia and red-eyed vireos in a New England forest. *Condor* 83:16–26.

Rothstein, S. I., J. Verner, and E. Stevens. 1984. Radio tracking confirms a unique diurnal pattern of spatial occurrence in the parasitic brown-headed cowbird. *Ecology* 65:77–88.

Runte, A. 1979. *National Parks: The American Experience*. Lincoln: University of Nebraska Press.

Russell, S. M. 1964. A distributional study of the birds of British Honduras. *Ornithological Monographs* 1:1–195.

————. 1980. Distribution and abundance of North American migrants in lowlands of northern Colombia. In Keast and Morton 1980, 249–52.

Rybczynski, R., and D. K. Riker. 1981. A temperate species-rich assemblage of migrant frugivorous birds. *Auk* 88:176–79.

Sader, S. A., and A. T. Joyce. 1988. Deforestation rates and trends in Costa Rica, 1940 to 1983. *Biotropica* 20:11–19.

Salomonsen, F. 1955. The evolutionary significance of bird migration. *Dansk Biol. Medd.* 22:1–61.

Sanchez, P. A., D. E. Bandy, J.H. Villachica, and J.J. Nicholaides. 1982. Amazon Basin soils: Management for continuous crop production. *Science* 216:821–27.

Sanchez, P. A., and J. R. Benites. 1987. Low-input cropping for acid soils of the humid tropics. *Science* 238:1521–27.

Schemske, D. W. 1980. Floral ecology and hummingbird pollination of *Combretum farinosum* in Costa Rica. *Biotropica* 12:169–81.

Schneider, J. C. 1980. The role of parthenogenesis and female aptery in microgeographic, ecological adaptation in the fall cankerworm (*Alsophila pometaria*: Lepidoptera: Geometridae). *Ecology* 61:1082–90.

Schnell, G. R. 1965. Recording the flight speeds of birds by doppler radar. *Living Bird* 4:79–87.

Schwartz, P. 1964. The northern water-thrush in Venezuela. *Living Bird* 2:169–84.

Scott, G. 1975. Soil profile changes resulting from the conversion of forest to grassland in the montaña of Peru. *Great Plains–Rocky Mountain Geographical Journal* 4:124–30.

Seliger, H. H., J. A. Boggs, and W. H. Biggley. 1985. Catastrophic anoxia in the Chesapeake Bay in 1984. *Science* 228:70–73.

Shelton, N. 1981. Improving management of Chesapeake Bay. *Atlantic Naturalist* 34:14–18.

Smith, E. E. 1954. The forests of Cuba. *Maria Moors Cabot Foundation Publication*, no. 2.

Smith, N. G. 1980. Hawk and vulture migrations in the Neotropics. In Keast and Morton 1980, pp. 51–66.

Smith, N.J.H. 1981. Colonization lessons from a tropical forest. *Science* 214:755–61.

Smith, P. W., and A. Sprunt IV. 1987. The shiny cowbird reaches the United States. *American Birds* 41:370–71.

Smith, R. A., R. B. Alexander, and M.G. Wolman. 1987. Water-quality trends in the nation's rivers. *Science* 235:1607–15.

Smith, S. M. 1984. Flock switching in chickadees: Why be a winter floater? *American Naturalist* 123:81–98.

Snyder, D. E. 1966. *Birds of Guyana*. Salem, Mass.: Peabody Museum.

Steinhart. P. 1987. Empty the skies. *Audubon* 89:70–97.

Stiles, E. W., and D. W. White. 1986. Seed deposition patterns: Influences of season, nutrients, and vegetation structure. In *Frugivores and Seed Dispersal*, edited by A. Estrada and T. H. Fleming, 45–54. Dordrecht, Netherlands: W. Junk.

Stiles, F. G. 1983. Birds. In *Costa Rican Natural History*, edited by D. Janzen, 502–43. Chicago: University of Chicago Press.

Sullivan, K. 1984. The advantage of social foraging in downy woodpeckers. *Animal Behavior* 32:16–22.

Teale, E. W. 1951. *North with the Spring*. New York: Dodd, Mead.

Terborgh, J. W. 1980. The conservation status of Neotropical migrants: Present and future. In Keast and Morton 1980, pp. 21–30.

———. 1983. *Five New World Primates: A Study in Comparative Ecology*. Princeton: Princeton University Press.

———. 1985. Habitat selection in Amazonian birds. In *Habitat Selection in Birds*, edited by M. L. Cody, 311–38 Academic Press.

———. 1986. Community aspects of frugivory in tropical forests. In *Frugivores and Seed Dispersal*, edited by A. Estrada and T. H. Fleming, 371–84. Dordrecht, Netherlands: W. Junk.

Terborgh, J. W., and J. Faaborg. 1980. Factors affecting the distribution and abundance of North American migrants in the eastern Caribbean region. In Keast and Morton 1980, pp. 145–55.

Terborgh, J. W., C. Janson, and M. Brecht. 1986. Cocha Cashu: Su vegetacion, clima y recursos. In *Reporte Manu*, edited by M. A. Rios, 1–18. Centro de Datos para la Conservación: Lima, Peru.

Terborgh, J., and J. S. Weske. 1969. Colonization of secondary habitats by Peruvian birds. *Ecology* 50:765–82.

Terres, J. K. 1980. *The Audubon Encyclopedia of North American Birds*. New York: Knopf.

Tiner, R. W., Jr. 1984. Wetlands of the United States: Current status and recent trends. U.S. Department of the Interior, Fish and Wildlife Service.

Torre-Bueno, J. R. 1978. Evaporative cooling and water balance during flight in birds. *Journal of Experimental Biology* 75:231–36.

Torre-Bueno, J. R., and J. Larochelle. 1978. The metabolic cost of flight in unrestrained birds. *Journal of Experimental Biology* 75:223–29.

Tramer, E. J., and T. R. Kemp. 1980. Foraging ecology of migrant and resident warblers and vireos in the highlands of Costa Rica. In Keast and Morton 1980, pp. 285–96.

Tropicus 2 (Winter 1988).

Tucker, V. A., and K. Schmidt-Koenig. 1977. Flight speeds of birds in relation to energetics and wind directions. *Auk* 88:97–107.

Uhl, C., and J. Saldarriaga. 1986. Fragilidad de la pluviselva Amazónica. *Ciencia y Investigación* (Barcelona), pp. 72–81.

U.S. Fish and Wildlife Service and Canadian Wildlife Service. 1986. 1986 status of waterfowl and fall flight forecasts.

Van Velzen, W. T., and A. C. Van Velzen, eds. 1984. Forty-seventh breeding bird census. *American Birds* 38:64–68.

———. 1988. Fifty-first breeding bird census. *American Birds* 42:145–48.

Vine, I. 1971. Risk of visual detection and pursuit by a predator and the selective advantage of flocking behavior. *Journal of Theoretical Biology* 30:405–22.

Waide, R. B. 1980. Resource partitioning between migrant and resident birds: The use of irregular resources. In Keast and Morton 1980, pp. 337–52.

Walkinshaw, L. H. 1983. *The Kirtland's Warbler*. Bloomfield Hills, Mich.: Cranbrook Institute of Science.

Wallace, D. R. 1985. Wetlands in America: Labyrinth and temple. *Wilderness* 49:12–27.

Wambeke, A. van. 1978. Properties and potentials of soils in the Amazon Basin. *Interciencia* 3:233–42.

Whitcomb, R. F., C. S. Robbins, J. F. Lynch, B. L. Whitcomb, M. K. Klimkiewicz, and D. Bystrak. 1981. Effects of forest fragmentation on avifauna of eastern deciduous forests. In *Forest Island Dynamics in Man-dominated Landscapes*, edited by R. L. Burgess and D. M. Sharpe. New York: Springer Verlag.

Whitcomb, B. L, R. F. Whitcomb, and D. Bystrak. 1977. Island biogeography and ''habitat islands'' of eastern forest. III. Long-term turnover and effects of selective logging on the avifauna of forest fragments. *American Birds* 31:17–23.

Wilcove, D. S. 1985a. Forest fragmentation and the decline of migratory songbirds. Ph.D. dissertation, Princeton University.

———. 1985b. Nest predation in forest tracts and the decline of migratory songbirds. *Ecology* 66:1211–14.

———. 1988. Changes in the avifauna of the Great Smoky Mountains: 1947–1983. *Wilson Bulletin* 100:256–71.

Wilcove, D. S., and J. W. Terborgh. 1984. Patterns of population decline in birds. *American Birds* 38:10–13.

Wilcove, D. S., and R. F. Whitcomb. 1983. Gone with the trees. *Natural History* 92:82–91.

Wilderness Society. 1986. *Conserving Biological Diversity in Our National Forests*. Washington, D.C.: Wilderness Society.

Wiley, K. J. and V. Giampa. 1978. Habitat use by yellow-rumped warblers at the northern extremities of their winter range. *Wilson Bulletin* 90:566–74.

Williams, T. C. 1985. Autumnal bird migration over the windward Caribbean islands. *Auk* 102:163–67.

Williams, T. C., J. M. Williams, L. C. Ireland, and J. M. Teal. 1977. Bird migration over the western North Atlantic ocean. *American Birds* 31:251–67.

Willis, E. O. 1966. The role of migrant birds at swarms of army ants. *Living Bird* 5:187–231.

Willis, E. O., and Y. Oniki. 1978. Birds and army ants. *Annual Review of Ecology and Systematics* 9:243–63.

Wolda, H. 1978. Fluctuations in abundance of tropical insects. *American Naturalist* 112:1017–45.

Wyatt-Smith, J. 1987. Problems and prospects for natural management of tropical moist forests. In *Natural Management of Tropical Moist Forests*, edited by F. Mergen and J. R. Vincent, 5–22. New Haven, Conn.: Yale University School of Forestry and Environmental Studies.

Author Index

Subject Index

advance hypothesis, 93, 94
Agency for International Development,
171, 172, 177
agricultural chemicals, 26, 33, 185; export
commodities, 173; surplus, 180
agriculture, no-tillage, 32, 33
American Birds, 12, 14, 15, 21, 40, 43, 69,
70, 72, 75, 79, 91, 154, 184
amphibians, 27, 28–30
antshrike, 111
antvireo, 111
antwren, 111
aquatic vegetation, submerged, 24, 30–31,
33, 34, 37
artic, 86
area-sensitive species, 41, 44
area-insensitive species, 44
army ants, 101
Audubon Field Notes, 12, 43
Audubon Naturalist Society, 40, 60

bamboo, 148
bananas, 144
bass, striped, 26, 27, 28, 30
bayberries, 91
beef production, 175–76
birdwatching, 11
bison: American, 37, 85, 150, 159; forest,
10
blackbird, 102; yellow-shouldered, 53
Blue List for tropical migrants, 154–55
bluebird, eastern, 10
bobcat, 48
bobolink, 71, 81
brant, 22
Breeding Bird Census, 11, 12–16, 17, 18,
40, 43, 69, 184; Cabin John Island, Md.,
40, 42, 43; recommendations, 16; Rock
Creek Park, Md., 40, 43
Breeding Bird Survey, 11, 16–18, 66, 184;
survey method, 16–17
Brooks Bird Club, 14, 63
bufflehead, 23, 24
bunting: indigo, 65, 80, 114, 141; lark, 71;
lazuli, 72, 80, 155; painted, 126, 141;
snow, 72

canvasback, 19, 24
cardinal, 41, 42, 43, 52, 168

cash crop, 162, 173, 177
catbird, gray, 5, 19, 41, 47, 52, 85, 141,
142
cattle: pasture, 137–39, 142; ranching, 174–
77
channelization, stream, 36, 185
chaparral, California, 71
chat, yellow-breasted, 19, 80
Chesapeake Bay, 11, 19–39, 63
chestnut, American, 10, 64
chickadee, 5, 41, 59, 89, 102, 111; black-
capped, 92; boreal, 89; Carolina, 42, 43;
in winter flocks, 102–104, 106
chicken, prairie, 144, 150
Christmas Count, 11, 18, 20–25, 34, 54,
66, 79, 89, 91, 97, 146; Annapolis, Md.,
21; Back Bay, Va., 21; Chincoteague,
Va., 21; Fort Belvoir, Va., 21; Hopewell, Va., 21; Little Creek, Va., 21, 25;
Newport News, Va., 21; Ocean City,
Md., 21; Port Tobacco, Md., 21; Saint
Michael's, Md., 21; Southern Dorchester
County, Md., 21; Washington, D.C.,
21
chuck-will's-widow, 80, 90, 91
climates, tropical, 145–46
clear cutting, 182
Cocha Cashu Biological Station, 107
cock-of-the-rock, 137, 139
coffee, 162, 173
Combretum fruticosum, 100
competition, 113
competitor, 47
condor, California, 184
Congress, 186
Conservation International, 186
conservation easement, 185
contamination: non-point-source, 32; point-
source, 32; runoff of agricultural chemicals, 33
controls in ecology, 7–10
cornfield, 66, 71–72, 139, 144, 168
Corturnix, 48
cost-benefit analysis, 177
cowbird: brown-headed, 10, 42, 43, 52–58,
67; shiny, 53
crab, 26; blue, 27, 28; horseshoe, 88; soft-
shelled, 28